P9-CEL-465

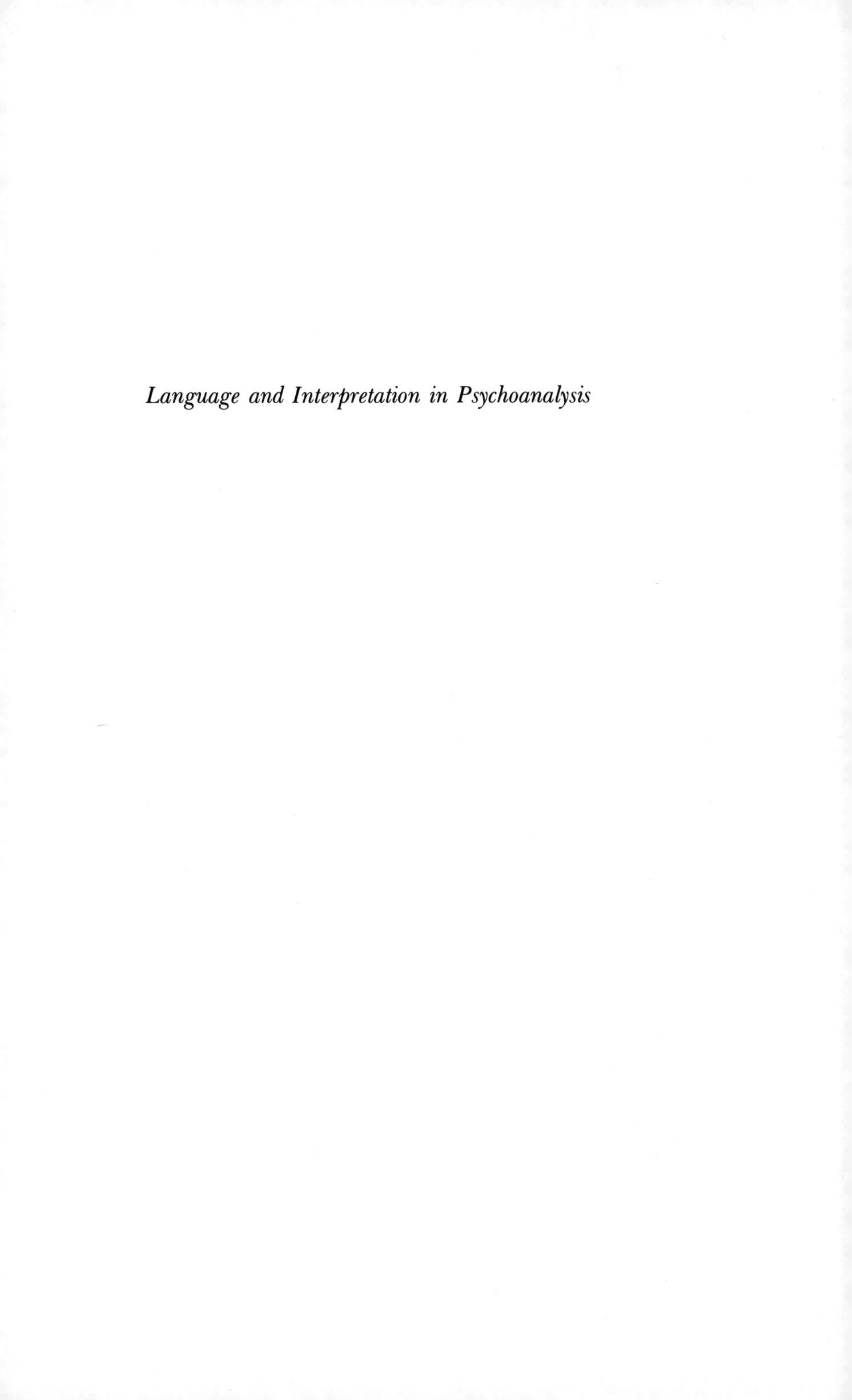

Language and Interpretation in Psychoanalysis

Books by Marshall Edelson

The Termination of Intensive Psychotherapy (1963)
Ego Psychology, Group Dynamics and the Therapeutic Community (1964)
Sociotherapy and Psychotherapy (1970)
The Practice of Sociotherapy: A Case Study (1970)
The Idea of a Mental Illness (1971)

Language and Interpretation in Psychoanalysis

MARSHALL EDELSON, M.D., Ph.D.

New Haven and London, Yale University Press, 1975

Library of Congress catalog card number: 74-29717
International standard book number: 0-300-01853-3

Designed by Sally Sullivan
and set in Baskerville type.
Printed in the United States of America by
Vail-Ballou Press, Inc., Binghamton, N.Y.

Published in Great Britain, Europe, and Africa by
Yale University Press, Ltd., London.
Distributed in Latin America by Kaiman & Polon,
Inc., New York City; in India by UBS Publishers'
Distributors Pvt., Ltd., Delhi; in Japan by John
Weatherhill, Inc., Tokyo.

Acknowledgment is extended to Alfred A. Knopf
for permission to quote from the copyrighted poetry
of Wallace Stevens.

In memory of

my father George (1901–1971)

and my niece Michal (1953–1974)

The Snow Man *

One must have a mind of winter
To regard the frost and the boughs
Of the pine-trees crusted with snow;

And have been cold a long time
To behold the junipers shagged with ice,
The spruces rough in the distant glitter

Of the January sun; and not to think
Of any misery in the sound of the wind,
In the sound of a few leaves,

Which is the sound of the land
Full of the same wind
That is blowing in the same bare place

For the listener, who listens in the snow,
And, nothing himself, beholds
Nothing that is not there and the nothing that is.

Contents

Preface

This book is a fourth step toward a theory of clinical interpretation in psychoanalysis. In the first of three previous works (Edelson, 1971a), I considered the importance of a view of man as animal symbolicum for the psychiatrist who seeks to understand and treat mental illness. I also made some tentative suggestions concerning ways in which Freud might have reformulated some of his explanations of psychological phenomena given the present-day scientific milieu he helped to create, in which the significance of psychic reality, of symbolic process, of language, of value as well as fact, and of meaning for understanding man tends at least to be accepted. In a second work (Edelson, 1971b), I examined the essential role of symbolic process in both psychoanalytic theory and Talcott Parsons' theory of action, with particular attention to Freud's discovery and conception of psychic reality. The third work (Edelson, 1972) was a rereading of Freud's *The Interpretation of Dreams* in the light of current linguistic theory, particularly the transformational-generative theory of Noam Chomsky; I emphasized the saliency of language for Freud and the close relations between linguistic and psychoanalytic science.[1]

What experiences have led to these works? In my first or second year of formal training to become a psychoanalyst, I read a paper on the wondrously various forms of derivatives of the anal instinct—from money in the bank to white pebbles on a beach (Jones, 1913). I was dazzled by the array of

1. In order to avoid unnecessary repetition and remain within the scope of this work, I shall have to assume that the reader is at least somewhat familiar with the principal arguments and terminology used in these studies or has access to them.

objects and acts whose similarities were typified by aspects of the paradigm of objects and acts governed by the anal sphincter. I thought to myself, how like metaphors in poetry this all is. The thought was vaguely disquieting. How could this exuberant proliferation of metaphors, which I thought must be generated by language, be explained by the properties and activities of a hypothetical instinct as mysterious as the phenomena which were its manifestations? [2] What if "instinct" were another name for an inveterate, peremptory process: the metaphorical construction of psychic reality? What if psychoanalytic theory is in fact primarily a theory about symbolic systems and symbolic functioning, and especially about language and the use of language?

Perhaps it is this fact that makes psychoanalytic theory seem so peculiar and unscientific to most other scientists, since they study the intrinsic characteristics of objects and their relations rather than objects and events that stand for other objects and events. Sexuality as studied in the psychoanalytic situation is clearly not so much a matter of the physicochemical processes of the body as it is a matter of words, of symbolic functioning, of particular ways of representing inner reality. Although Freud emphasized that "instinct" is a psychological construct, he was nevertheless more disturbed as a scientist by his discovery of "psychic reality" (the world created by symbolic functioning)—his discovery that nonsubstantial phantasies have powerful effects—than he was by his realization of the ubiquity of sexual motives and interests (Edelson, 1971b).

Despite these questions and contradictions, I had no interest in a quarrel with psychoanalytic theory as it was presented to me, especially before I had achieved mastery of it. I had and have a strong feeling for the community and traditions of science which maintain it against the barbarism, the chaos, the infatuation with novelty, and the wishes for an

2. Later, I would understand "generated by language" to mean: generated by the rules of language, by linguistic transformations.

easy victory over reality constantly assailing it. Science is maintained by the discipline of apprenticeship. The continuity between new and old is important to it; that which is new, no matter how well established as "fact" or argued as theory, will be rejected if it does not fit into what is known—unless and until connections between them can be demonstrated. In addition, the acceptance and rejection of ideas in a realm where skill as well as knowledge is involved (as in any science) usually imply consequences for performance. The too facile rejection of an old, perhaps somewhat inconvenient idea, the overenthusiastic espousal of another, lead inevitably to oversimplification and may lead to practices that erode the discipline that is the special characteristic of psychoanalysis not only as an endeavor requiring clinical skills but as a unique method of investigation.[3]

Therefore, I had no desire in raising questions about the concept "instinct" to dismiss carelessly what was valuable in psychoanalytic theory—its emphasis on the ubiquity of sexual interests and motives, for example—because much of the theory is related to and required by many thousands of observations by skilled clinical investigators.

Furthermore, I felt obliged to dissociate myself from certain criticisms made by others—for example, the complaints of some of my colleagues that "instinct theory" and metapsychology in general are too abstract and therefore of no use to the clinician. It seemed clear to me that if any such objection could be raised against metapsychology it was rather that its formulations were too close to those that patients made in talking about and explaining themselves. In other words, it seemed to me metapsychology was not abstract enough. (The work of such men as Claude Levi-Strauss in anthropology and Noam Chomsky in linguistics—like Freud before them—has more recently confirmed my conviction that a movement away from phenomena to a discernment of

3. Later, I found this view of science beautifully described and exhaustively documented by Polanyi (1958).

the abstract structures underlying such phenomena is the way to understanding in science.) [4]

My teachers, however, constituting an intellectual community whose members were, I think, to some extent unaware of the particular shared interest I noticed, kept me disquieted and, in a variety of ways, alert to language. Hans Loewald (1970, 1971), with his scholarly sensitivity to the nuances of language, made me wonder if I could know from an English translation what Freud had actually written or intended by what he wrote; Loewald's own beautiful writings, especially on psychoanalytic theory and the psychoanalytic process and on interpretation, are alive with suggestions for illuminating rereadings of words and their meanings. Stanley Leavy (1970) bade me as psychoanalyst to learn from, and not merely analyze, the poet; later (1973), he shared with me his sense of the importance of the philosophy of language for psychoanalysis. Henry Wexler, in one of the seminars we had together, demonstrated with skill and pleasure the contribution psychoanalysis could make to the understanding of literature we both loved. William Pious (1961) spoke and wrote not of interpretation but of translation—at the same level, if the psychoanalyst uses the same mode of symbolic representation as the analysand, and at another level, if the psychoanalyst uses a mode of symbolic representation different from that used by the analysand. Roy Schafer (1973) frequently warned against the reification of psychoanalytic concepts and raised provocative questions about the implications and consequences (e.g., "disclaimed action") of certain locutions and syntax used not only by the analysand but by the psychoanalyst in his communications to the analysand as well as in his theoretical formulations. Shortly before his tragic death, Seymour Lustman (1972) was reading Cassirer on language; he quoted Cassirer's definition of man as the "animal symbolicum" and cited

4. In this connection, see, e.g., Katz (1971).

Chomsky's criticism of the Skinnerian account of how man acquires language.

For the last three years, I have taught a seminar on psychotherapy, psychopathology, and language to medical students in the Behavioral Sciences Track at Yale University; members of the seminar have attempted, with exciting results, to use linguistics to analyze and understand samples of language from clinical interviews; their efforts have instructed me. During the last year, I participated with similar benefit in a study group on language and schizophrenia composed of Yale faculty, including Theodore Lidz (1963) and the late Victor Rosen (1961, 1966, 1967, 1968, 1969a, 1969b), both of whom brought their long-standing interests in and reflections on language, psychiatry, and psychoanalysis to the group's discussions.

During this period, I studied music theory with Paul Klein and discussed with him many thoughts about the nature of symbolic functioning and the interpretation of what is constructed by it—especially musical compositions.

And, of course, the analysands with whom I work in psychoanalysis have instructed me, however unwittingly, in language and its interpretation.

In this preface I have stated from what background this book has emerged. In the introduction which follows, I shall state where I intend this book to take us.

Introduction

I have written this book as a psychoanalyst for those concerned with psychoanalysis both as a theory of mind and a clinical discipline. I have found it necessary to discuss language, a poem by Wallace Stevens, a prelude by Bach, and the difference between explanation and interpretation, but this book does not contribute to linguistics, literary criticism, music theory, or philosophy as independent domains of knowledge. Nor is it written for linguists, literary critics, music theorists, or philosophers—all of whom, as this book implies, may have more to tell the psychoanalyst than he them—except insofar as its pages suggest to occasional readers among them a way or two in which they could be helpful to a psychoanalyst who is struggling with problems of theory and interpretation in psychoanalysis.

Nevertheless, my book does necessarily dwell on the boundary where psychoanalysis and linguistics or literary criticism or music theory or philosophy face each other. Therefore, I had a choice of two strategies. I could have organized a colloquium, in which papers by a psychoanalyst, a linguist, a literary critic, a music theorist, and a philosopher were written separately and then strung together. Such an enterprise would have profited from the confidence aroused in others when an authority in each field addresses problems that lie within his domain. A probable lack of coherence and true integration was for me an overriding disadvantage.

So, I chose instead the second strategy: to master and integrate within myself as best I could whatever in each field seemed to me to be to my purpose, risking that, lacking insight, I might mistake notational differences or similarities for substantive ones; that I might think and write out of error or ignorance; and—since every step depends upon the extent to which I am able to master alien terminologies and knowledge and achieve some inner integration of these—that I must proceed slowly, with much reworking and repetition of the same material, with digressions, and with the style that results from an uncertain image both of one's subject matter and one's audience.

I accept these disadvantages with as much patience as I can because of my hopes for the future work I shall do. I have no right, I suppose, to ask my reader to accept them—except that I do believe that if I had decided on the first strategy the disadvantages following from it, though less glaring perhaps, would in the long run have been no more acceptable.

What is my aim? I want eventually to formulate a theory of interpretation in psychoanalysis, and to test such a theory against clinical experience. I am not yet ready to do so. This book is merely a preparation for such a theoretical formulation and empirical test; understandably, it will frustrate many readers, for it is not even a partial achievement of either.

Here, I want to share a hunch with my reader. Preparing a paper on symbolic process in psychoanalysis and the theory of action (1971b), I began to read Noam Chomsky's work on transformational-generative grammar. At the same time, I became interested in understanding through theoretical analysis the construction of musical compositions I heard or attempted to play.

Gradually, a hunch with two aspects took form. First, I noticed that in many ways Chomsky thought and wrote like Freud. Chomsky's theory of language and psychoanalysis were significantly congruent because of: his interest in the implications of linguistic theory for a theory of "mind" (a word he was far from reluctant to use); his postulation of innate psychological structures; his defense of theory against radical behaviorism, on the one hand, and the taxonomic-empiricist-structuralist linguistic tradition on the other; his distinction between surface structures (accessible to empirical inspection) and deep structures (which must be inferred to reveal unexpected relations among empirical phenomena or to account for characteristics of these phenomena that must otherwise remain inexplicable); his explicit formulation of transformational operations, which change deep structures upon which cognitive meanings depend (while holding such meanings invariant) into surface structures upon which perceptible representations depend (these transformational operations thus mediate between meaning and sound in language); and his insistence on the rule-governed creative nature of mind, which is capable of generating an infinitude of linguistic forms appropriate to but not controlled by the situations in which they are used.

Chomsky has written, "One difficulty in the psychological sciences lies in the familiarity of the phenomena with which they deal. A certain intellectual effort is required to see how such phenomena can pose serious problems or call for intricate explanatory theories." He continued:

> We tend too easily to assume that explanations must be transparent and close to the surface. The greatest defect of classical philosophy of mind, both rationalist and empiricist, seems to me to be its unquestioned assumption that the properties and content of the mind are accessible to introspection; it is surprising how rarely this assumption has been challenged, insofar as the organization and function of the intellectual faculties are concerned, even with the Freudian revolution. Correspondingly, the far-reaching studies of language that were carried out under the influence of Cartesian rationalism suffered from a failure to appreciate either the abstractness of those structures that are "present to the mind" when an utterance is produced or under-

> stood, or the length and complexity of the chain of operations that relate the mental structures expressing the semantic content of the utterance to the physical realization.
>
> A similar defect mars the study of language and mind in the modern period. It seems to me that the essential weakness in the structuralist and behaviorist approaches to these topics is the faith in the shallowness of explanations, the belief that the mind must be simpler in its structure than any known physical organ and that the most primitive of assumptions must be adequate to explain whatever phenomena can be observed (1972, p. 24 ff.).

Chomsky also wrote:

> We live, after all, in the age of "behavioral science," not of "the science of the mind." I do not want to read too much into a terminological innovation, but I think that there is some significance in the ease and willingness with which modern thinking about man and society accepts the designation "behavioral science." No sane person has ever doubted that behavior provides much of the evidence for this study—all of the evidence, if we interpret "behavior" in a sufficiently loose sense. But the term "behavioral science" suggests a not-so-subtle shift of emphasis toward the evidence itself and away from the deeper underlying principles and abstract mental structures that might be illuminated by the evidence of behavior. It is as if natural science were to be designated "the science of meter readings" (1972, p. 65).

I detailed the resemblance between Freud and Chomsky, which I felt was fundamental, in my 1972 paper "Language and Dreams: *The Interpretation of Dreams* Revisited." I sought to demonstrate exhaustively the fit of transformational-generative theory and the interpretation of dreams—the sine qua non of psychoanalytic theory and practice. That paper is de facto the first chapter of this book and, if read as such, links theory to data familiar to every psychoanalyst in a way that I hope will lead the reader to want to know more about transformational-generative theory. The demonstration in that paper is especially important because I have offered little in this book in the way of clinical illustrations, which ordinarily might be expected to serve as an incentive for a reader interested primarily in psychoanalysis to expend effort in exploring the alien realm of linguistic theory. I regret burdening my psychoanalytic colleagues with an alien terminology, but I know no way around this, given my aims. There are good introductions to Chomsky's work and terminology.[5] I myself prefer to approach him through his own exposition.[6]

The linguist who strays into these pages may be disturbed by my choice of Chomsky's transformational-generative grammar rather than some other linguistic theory for my study of language and psychoanalysis. It is not ignorance of other linguistic theories or a response to a fad that results in this choice. Reading Chomsky, I was led to study other linguists; however, the scope of this work does not permit a scholarly disquisition comparing and evaluating a multitude of other approaches to linguistics. I am convinced that Chomsky like Freud is one of the great ones; he has changed entirely the study of mind. Nothing I have read has disturbed my sense that there is a significant relation between psychoanalysis and transformational-generative theory in particular among linguistic theories. My sense of this relation may be mistaken. If so, then like many before me, I will have to live with the consequences of such a mistake.

It is important for the psychoanalyst reader to keep in

5. See Jacobs and Rosenbaum (1968); Katz (1971); Lyons (1970).

6. *Syntactic Structures* (1957), while somewhat difficult on first reading, is a revolutionary classic work in social science. *Language and Mind* (1972) is a collection of essays and lectures that tells much about the scope of Chomsky's inquiry and its applications, his intellectual tradition, his values, and the style of his thought.

mind that the apparent merit or attractive simplicity of a linguistic theory as a *linguistic theory* cannot be the sole consideration in such a work as this; we must be predisposed to that theory which is built upon assumptions about and has a view of science, man, and mind congruent with psychoanalysis. I have been somewhat distressed when such colleagues as Rosen, Edelheit, or Lacan (see my 1972 paper), to name but three, have turned to linguists who work in a way and who belong to a tradition (e.g., taxonomic-empiricist-structuralist or radical-behaviorist) not consistent with psychoanalysis. This misalliance is one of the risks of interdisciplinary work.

For this reason, I am not altogether happy about my own past use of Roman Jakobson's elegant, persuasive work. His observations are keen, perceptive, and altogether impressive and cannot be ignored. Some of his conceptualizations, however, may be too general or too simple, considering the complexity of the phenomena. I exclude from this judgment his major contributions—for example, the discovery and description of a specific universal set of a fairly small number of distinctive phonemic features—which are easy to assimilate into Chomsky's work. But his emphasis on the priority as an operation of the permutation of binary terms and on metaphor and metonymy, similarity and contiguity, simultaneity and sequentiality as central classificatory concepts is suspect, considering what Chomsky has taught us about language. His ideas are also insufficient to account for the generation of musical structures (a subject I shall consider in this book), although a commonsense inspection of a musical composition beguiles one into basing the distinction between harmony and melody, mistakenly I think, upon the difference between simultaneity and sequentiality of tones. Writers in various fields, however, such as Levi-Strauss and Lacan, some literary critics, as well as some psychoanalysts, and on occasion myself, have responded to the accessibility, and thus the attractiveness and fatal allure, of these notions by adopting them to analyze phenomena of interest to them.

I digress here to indicate that I am aware that the psychoanalytic reader, and in fact these days almost any member of a university community, might well ask why in a book on language and psychoanalysis there is no use made of the work of Jacques Lacan. His writings on this subject span a longer than twenty-year period. His work and his reputation particularly in European intellectual circles (especially connected with the present furor of interest in structuralism) may seem to some readers to have established his priority and eminence in the area of my inquiry and perhaps to have preempted it. Neglect of his work justifiably arouses suspicions that the writer of this book either is too provincial to be aware of any developments outside his own country or in any language but his own, or is improperly or unfairly biased against this work by Lacan's disputes with the International Psycho-Analytical Association.

While in my 1972 paper I accorded priority in the area of language and psychoanalysis to Freud (I do not think Lacan would argue with that choice), I did discuss throughout that paper the relation of Freud's ideas and work to structuralism. "Throughout Freud's scientific life, he did his most creative work not when he tried to formulate a general psychology but in attempts to explain—by showing how constructed—relatively definite, discrete or bounded, isolatable symbolic structures: dreams, jokes, the psychopathology of everyday life, neurotic symptoms, works of art. He was . . . an ardent constructionist, the progenitor and prescient exemplar of constructive structuralism" (p. 250). I also emphasized (as has Lacan) that we ought frequently to return to the many examples and discussions of these examples in *The Interpretation of Dreams, The Psychopathology of Everyday Life,* and *Jokes and Their Relation to the Unconscious* "to remind ourselves of and to examine the semiological foundations of psychoanalysis" (p. 255). Although I had arrived at this view independent of reading Lacan, I make no claim of originality; such ideas seem to me to be in the air in which one does one's thinking (see Merton, 1973). I had been struck myself by the significance of Freud's description of the dream as a kind of rebus, was happy to find this valuation confirmed by Lacan, and wrote that Freud's passage on the dream as rebus in *The Interpretation of Dreams* was one "to which Lacan (1957) at least has drawn our attention as crucial in understanding the work of Freud as semiologist" (p. 252).

However, it is also already abundantly clear in this 1972 paper that—where Lacan has been concerned to show that Freud's terminology "can be translated into the terms and categories of modern structural linguistics," and has been led by "the correspondence between Freud's terms and system and the structures discovered by modern linguistics" to his "startling conclusion, that *the structure of the unconscious is the structure of language*" (Miel, 1966, p. 98)—I was and am, on the other hand, struck *primarily* by the relation between Freud's method and formulations about his discoveries and Chomsky's transformational-generative theory and method. (Lacan does not remind me at all in style or method of Freud.)

I do not know if Lacan knows or has considered the work of Chomsky. But I hope that a psychoanalyst studying "language and psychoanalysis" may be permitted to choose, if he wishes, between structural linguistics and transformational-generative linguistics as a theoretical model of language. Differences in the choice of intellectual schemes or conceptual strategies (even if these should have their origin in special sympathy or rapport with a particular thinker, body of work, or area of knowledge) should remain permissible in intellectual life for all of us. The value of any such choice should depend on: (1) the degree to which a conceptual strategy makes possible an *explicit* statement of *alternative* formulations, such that a decision between these may be made through examination of empirical evidence; (2) the extent to which a conceptual strategy results in theoretical formulations that are consistent with an established corpus of knowledge; and (3) the strategy's apparent implications for clinical practice. (These implications are unhappily not necessarily unequivocally derivable from theory.) Of course, one must consider not only the efficacy of, but also the values exemplified by, a clinical practice—or change in clinical practice—which is apparently, but often sophistically, justified by some theoretical formulation.

Fortunately, no one, including myself, has to be cut off by ignorance of the French language from comparing the work of Lacan (linked as it is to structuralist linguistics) and that of Chomsky. Lacan's corpus is already in good part and is or soon will be almost entirely available in English translation. As a beginning, the reader may examine "Seminar on 'The Purloined Letter' " (1956); "The Insistence of the Letter in the Unconscious" (1957); *The Language of the Self: The Function of Language in Psychonalysis* (1968); and "Of Structure as an Inmixing of an Otherness Prerequisite to Any Subject Whatever" (1970). The titles themselves, contrasted with some of Chomsky's, hint at the difference between these two.

All these points having been made, I must also admit honestly that, as I am now at least, I simply prefer Chomsky's mind to Lacan's. Chomsky, however technical, mathematical, and forbidding his writing seems, strives to be explicit, so that he can seek and state the decisive counterexample that is evidence against one or another formulation. He reveals lucidly the basis for a choice between two alternative formulations or two different strategies in the development or emendation of a theory—and the consequences of the choice. He argues logically, analytically, systematically; his arguments march. With respect to philosophical predilections, one notes that the title of one of his books is *Cartesian Linguistics: A Chapter in the History of Rationalist Thought* (1966). The range of his knowledge is impressive; his ability to detect vacuity in the formulations of others (and to root it out of his own) is exhilarating; and his awareness of the political and social implications of an inadequate, scientistic view of man is critically corrective for our time. After struggling with Chomsky, I feel the delight of coming into light.

Reading Lacan is a different experience. Almost immediately and for me almost overwhelmingly, I feel I am becoming increasingly, fatiguingly entangled in a thicket. The writing is prophetic and evangelical (I distrust charisma). "Dr. Lacan has been greatly influenced by his extensive knowledge of phenomenological and existential philosophy" (Miel, 1966, p. 100). I do not find this philosophical tradition congenial. "Dr. Lacan does not begrudge himself the advantages of a complex literary expression" (Miel, 1966, pp. 100–01). I find him arcane (I mean "obscure"), allusive, elliptical, aphoristic, and occasionally evocative. A phrase here and there excites in me my own train of thought; I value that. But his thought, while suggestive, has for me—unlike Chomsky's—little or no architecture. His writing has the rhythm of incantation rather than syllogism. "I feel," he has said, "a great personal connection with Surrealist painting" (1970, p. 97). At this time in my life, Lacan, despite what we might share and whatever in him I can appreciate, is on the whole not my cup of tea.

I also believe—this is my best guess now—that Lacan's philosophizing and his linguistics are probably wrong for psychoanalysis. Writing in a style that his translator and expositor Wilden has described as "dense" and "hermetic" (1966, pp. 253–54), Lacan does give us occasional passages that gleam, provoke, and fascinate. "And how could a psychoanalyst of today not realize that his realm of truth is in fact the word, when his whole experience must find in the word alone its instrument, its framework, its material, and even the static of its uncertainties" (1957, p. 103). Then, a passage like this is followed by what, for a person of my cast of mind, seems to be a rigmarole of philosophic preoccupations and literary allusions, without one logical tool I can use, one conceptual distinction that clarifies, or one sensible discussion of any empirical phenomenon.

Certainly, I find the content and method of the 1956 paper more interesting than the 1957 one, perhaps because of Mehlman's contribution as translator-commentator, or perhaps because as an inveterate reader of detective stories, I am familiar with the Poe tale, which is a favorite of mine. I believe I understand (more so perhaps when I read Mehlman on Lacan than when I read Lacan) that Lacan is concerned, as I am concerned, that Freud's basic insights—the unconscious, the operations of the dream-work and the joke-work, and psychic reality—are continually threatened. They are translated into physicalistic language. They are lost as each group or generation again takes the easy way of understanding man as the sociologized ego who is merely shaped by, or who responds to, social conditions, social institutions, parents as they were, and historical events as they happened—rather than understanding man as the creative constructor of the symbolic world that is the only world in which he can live. Lacan writes, "it is the symbolic order which is constitutive for the subject" (1956, p. 40). He has also said:

> if you open a book of Freud, and particularly those books which are properly about the unconscious, you can be absolutely sure—it is not a probability but a certitude—to fall on a page where it is not only a question of words—naturally in a book there are always words, many printed words—but words which are the object through which one seeks for a way to handle the unconscious. Not even the meaning of the words, but words in their flesh, in their material aspect. A great part of the speculations of Freud is about punning in a dream . . . or still the division of a word into many parts with each part taking on a new meaning after it is broken down. It is curious to note, even if in this case it is not absolutely proven, that words are the only material of the unconscious. It is not proven but it is probable (and in any case I have never said that the unconscious was an assemblage of words, but that the unconscious is precisely structured). . . . we are talking about structure and the unconscious is structured as a language (1970, pp. 187–88).

Lacan is convinced, as I am convinced, that Freud's basic insights are hard-won and must be rediscovered again and again. This book and my previous work (1971a, 1971b, 1972) testify that I share his particular anxiety about the state and future of psychoanalysis, as well as his conviction that only a steady awareness of language as the psychoanalyst's primary tool and object of study can preserve these basic insights.

But then I am brought up short by the thought that probably we do not mean the same thing by "language." For he writes: "By 'linguistics' we understand the study of existing languages in their structures and in the laws revealed therein; *this leaves out . . . any semiology more or less hypothetically generalized*" (1957, p. 105, italics mine). And I understand him to mean that what he would leave out would be abstract theory—a scientific abstract theory of language, language universals and linguistic competence, such as Chomsky is formulating.

In fact, although Lacan writes of signifiers and signifieds, of symbols and signs, of metaphor and metonymy, my sense is that he is interested primarily in what is represented by philosophical terms like "Subject" and "Object," and "Self" and "Other" (or "Otherness"), and in language only insofar as man's use of language bears upon the philosophical questions and perhaps the psychological experiences involving the meaning and relation of such terms. He is not especially interested, as Chomsky is, in language itself, in the underlying reality of language as an abstract system, in a theory of language that is designed to account for characteristics of utterances generated by such a system. Chomsky regards such a theory of language as logically prior to investigations of the use of language in performance; the acquisition of language; and the actual psychological processes involved in producing and understanding utterances. Chomsky also believes that a satisfactory theory of human language (including linguistic universals), which as an internalized capacity is essentially a definition of linguistic competence, will provide important insights into the nature and structure of mind.

My doubts about Lacan are, in their purest least trivial form, doubts about the nature of his interest in, and use of, "language" in his formulations; and also doubts about the advisability in general of using structural linguistics as an adequate account of language for the study of "language and psychoanalysis." However, my reader may after all read for himself, compare, reflect, and make up his own mind.

The first aspect of the hunch, which led ultimately to the writing of this book, was concerned with the congruence of the theories of Freud and Chomsky. A second aspect of the hunch arose from the observation that language (*as understood by Chomsky*) and music, as symbolic systems, seem to have certain fundamental similarities. For example, musical compositions contain syntactic ambiguities, disambiguated by context, and musical compositions seem to be surface realizations of deep structures. These surface realizations depend in part upon recursive transformational operations. For example, one structure such as a harmonic progression may be embedded within another harmonic progression that has the same structure. This transformational operation may be repeated over and over in modulating from one key to another.

I shall offer one illustration. A harmonic progression such as I-V-I in the key of C major (where the Roman numerals stand for triadic chords built respectively on the first, fifth, and first notes of a scale) may be the deep structure of a musical composition. That is to say, many events in the composition, whatever its multitude of details, may be understood to be governed by an overall progression from the tonic triadic I chord C-E-G (built upon the first note of the C major scale) to the dominant triadic V chord G-B-D (built upon the fifth note of the C major scale) and finally a return to the tonic triadic I chord C-E-G.

But, in the deep structure, a I-V-I progression in the key of G may be embedded in the I-V-I progression in the key of C. In the same way, the syntactic structure underlying one possible sentence may be embedded by a transformational operation in the syntactic structure underlying another possible sentence to form a surface structure underlying a complex or compound sentence. The dominant V chord in the key of C may be expanded to become a I-V-I progression—this time in the key of G. The dominant V chord G-B-D becomes a tonic I chord (built upon the first note of the G major scale), moves to the dominant V chord D-F sharp-A (built upon the fifth note of the G major scale), returns to the tonic I chord in the key of G (which is also the dominant V chord in the key of C), and ends finally on the tonic I chord in the key of C. So, we have (I in C)-(V in C)-(I in C) rewritten as (I in C)-(I in G, which is also V in C)-(V in G)-(I in G, which is also V in C)-(I in C).

Similarly, we might embed still another I-V-I progression, in the key of D, substituting it for the V in G, which is also the tonic I chord in the key of D major. Then, we would have: (I in C)-(I in G, which is also V in C)-(I in D, which is also V in G)-(V in D: A-C sharp-E)-(I in D, which is also V in G)-(I in G, which is also V in C)-(I in C).

Still, this is a I-V-I progression—much prolonged, and involving ambiguous chords. These chords have potentially different meanings or implications, depending upon the key to which they are thought at any point in the composition to belong.

As Chomsky has indicated in discussing the similar generation of complex sentences, there is no theoretical limit to this process or any limit (remember, other progressions than I-V-I might have been embedded) to the complexity of the structures resulting from such transformational operations.

Then—and this is the main idea motivating this book—language, music, and dreams as systems are significantly alike. The theories that account for linguistic utterances, musical compositions, dreams, symptoms, character traits, and transference by explicating the rules or operations that generate or construct such symbolic forms should be significantly alike. The process by which we interpret linguistic utterances, music, dreams, symptoms, character traits, and transference should also be significantly alike.

Although in my previous paper (1972), I carefully distinguished between semiotics or semiology, language, symbol, and symbolic function, and did commit myself to the priority of language over dreams (i.e., the dependence of dreams upon language), I am not now ready to commit myself about two critical issues raised by my "hunch."

First, I am not yet ready to state a hypothesis similar to the one on language and dreams concerning the relation between language and music—which might lead some readers to conclude mistakenly that I make no distinction between them or between semiotics and linguistics.

Second, I am not yet ready to choose between asserting that psychoanalysis has paid too little attention to language as its fundamental data and to the implications of this for revising the terms in which psychoanalytic theory casts its propositions and accounts for its clinical practice and asserting that exploring the implications of my hunch will eventually result in a theory of interpretation requiring a radical revision of psychoanalytic theory, clinical practice, or both. This may seem, and indeed is, evasive on my part. However, as a member of a profession and as a scientist, I regard it as cautious and responsible.

Consequently, in this book, I shall merely hint at the implications that attention to linguistic phenomena may have for psychoanalytic theory and clinical practice; developing these lines lies in the future. Taking the risk of arousing expectations in my reader I cannot yet satisfy, I shall be content to heighten the psychoanalyst's awareness of linguistic (and, to a much lesser extent, musical) objects and their structures, in order to stir up questions to be further discussed with my colleagues about the relevance such an awareness may have for a theory of interpretation in psychoanalysis. I hope to have as a result my colleagues' thoughts, in the light of their experiences, about these issues. I do not believe that in this book I can achieve much more than that. I can half-share—but only half—the feeling of the reader who believes I should have waited until I had more to transmit.

In the first chapter of this book I shall contemplate the image of the psychoanalyst as "listener" and reflect upon the importance to him of the language to which he listens.

PART ONE

PROLEGOMENA TO A THEORY OF INTERPRETATION

1: *The Psychoanalyst Listens*

Psychoanalysis is distinguished in part by the primacy of the concept of the psychoanalyst as listener and witness. The psychoanalyst makes a difference because he listens, and in his interpretations accepts and bears witness to the presence of: meaning in what for the analysand is meaningless or unspeakable; different meanings in what for the analysand is unequivocal and unambiguous; and different kinds of meanings in what the analysand has intended as a representation of one kind of meaning. Because the psychoanalyst is present to hear and to interpret, the analysand—unlike the lone tree that falls in the forest—speaks, is heard, and the speech has sound and meaning. The psychoanalyst beholds, bears witness to, and affirms the analysand's creativity, even if the analysand does not even dream that he is constructing meaningful, incredibly complex symbolic forms.

Psychoanalysis as a science [7] is essentially a study of symbolic systems, relations among them, and the use of symbolic systems in symbolic functioning. Any theory intended to account for clinical interpretation in psychoanalysis as the object of scientific study must make use of the terminologies and conceptual distinctions of semiology or semiotics (in general) and linguistics (in particular). These terminologies are essential to a metatheory of the process of clinical psychoanalysis, because this process includes the overt and covert actions of the psychoanalyst as participant. In these actions, the psychoanalyst uses language as a clinician, but he also uses language—actually, a metalanguage—to account

7. In what sense "a science," I shall discuss further in the following chapters.

for the forms and effects of his clinical language. Any attempt to explain the phenomena of psychoanalysis that utilizes *only* the language of psychoanalysis, which is an aspect of the phenomena, runs some risk of tautology. It is well known to logicians and philosophers that a language cannot be explained by itself (thus, metalanguage, metalogic, and metaethics).

It was perhaps a partial recognition of some aspect of this problem that led Freud to develop a metapsychology, which is distinct from the clinical theory used in accounting for phenomena in psychoanalysis and is certainly not the language the psychoanalyst uses in his clinical interpretations.[8] However, despite Freud's great interest in language and symbolic functioning (Edelson, 1972), he had no access to modern semiology or linguistics. He tended to use the languages of physics, chemistry, and biology in formulating metapsychological theory, even while at the same time, in developing his clinical theory, he boldly adopted a psychological terminology.[9] However, a metapsychology constructed out of languages belonging to the physical sciences is an awkward instrument to use in accounting for symbolic objects and acts. Such objects and acts are symbolically rather than intrinsically efficacious; they are efficacious by virtue of what they represent rather than what they are.[10] And these objects and events *are* the data of psychoanalysis.

Through many psychoanalytic hours, the psychoanalyst

8. See, e.g., G. Klein's provocative paper (1973) on the "two theories" of psychoanalysis, in which the author, however, in rejecting a particular metatheory, seems close to denying the necessity for metatheory.

9. Is all "explanation" translation: e.g., in clinical psychoanalysis, from the language of dreams and symptoms into that of waking life; in theoretical psychoanalysis, from the language of one frame of reference into the language of another; in the physical sciences, from the language of fact or of physical observation into the language of mathematical forms?

10. Freud's metapsychology does not seem to consist of propositions about reality, but propositions about ways of talking about reality. These propositions encourage multiple perspectives on complex phenomena, and therefore different terminologies in considering them; thus, an important function for psychoanalysis as a science is served.

permits himself—a unique way of orienting—to be twirled and shivered by the slight shifts, the sharp rise and soft drop, the sudden gusts and major blasts, the music of language. The psychoanalyst, whose skill in some measure depends upon his responsiveness to nuances in the speech of the analysand, waits to discover "where the analysand is." What symbolic world does he inhabit?

The analysand makes a casual comment at the beginning or end of the hour. A pause punctuates an utterance. A phrase recurs in dissimilar contexts throughout a session or in one session after another. An attitude is taken by the analysand toward his own speech or silence; or toward the speech or silence of the psychoanalyst. A word is used, strangely altered, or in a strained or unexpected way. A simile or metaphor gleams abruptly in a gray discourse; a flat factual proposition is set down solidly among exclamations and imperatives.

Affects are indicated by the use of linguistic resources that are not required to distinguish the sense of an utterance. For example, since in English, at the phonological level, the pitch at which a word is uttered does not change its cognitive sense or the conception it represents, pitch may be used to indicate affect. Jakobson (1955) describes a Norwegian woman who "had been struck by a bomb-fragment and had lost her ability to distinguish the two word-differentiating intonations of her mother tongue." As a consequence "her use of intonation was fully released for expressive variation" and "she was mistaken by her countrymen for a Norwegian-speaking German and often met their animosity in Nazi-occupied Oslo" (p. 69).[11]

The inverse relation between the use of linguistic resources for the *indication* of affect (what psychoanalysts are accustomed to regard as the *discharge* of affect) and the use of linguistic resources for the representation of abstractions or conceptions, the sine qua non of human language, should

11. We need to know more about the difficulties of psychoanalysis when psychoanalyst and analysand do not share the same mother tongue.

raise doubts about views, popular among psychoanalysts, of the origins of language in purely emotional, interjectional acts.

The representation of a *conception* of an internal affective state (an altogether different matter from discharging an immediately existent affect) makes use of a variety of linguistic resources. Among these are: ambiguity; deviance from the rules of language; stylistic reliance on certain usages; metaphor; other rhetorical devices; a complex interrelation of sense representation at the syntactic and semantic levels and what is often termed "sound symbolism"—to name just a few. In the psychoanalytic situation an analysand is often constructing a symbolic representation of a *conception* of an inner state (an aspect of psychic reality, an affect). Such a construction should be distinguished, as few psychoanalysts do, from "affect discharge." The difference may be made clear by a comparison of the poem as a linguistic object (indeed of any work of art) and the cries of a distressed child or animal.[12]

To understand that immediate existent affect is indicated by a particular intonation, for example, the psychoanalyst must, of course, have some internalized knowledge, however unwitting or unstatable, of the rules of language. Therefore, he knows what intonational features make a difference in a particular language in deciding the cognitive sense of an utterance, and that these features are unavailable for indicating or expressing affect and therefore cannot be interpreted under usual circumstances to be indicating or expressing affect.

So, also, conceptions of self are represented by syntactic preference (e.g., the passive construction, the nominalization of verbs of feeling). Phantasies are suggested by semantic choices (each with its many kinds of meaning), by implications, by allusions, and by that which is left unsaid.

The psychoanalyst, listening to what the analysand says,

12. See Langer (1942, 1953, 1962).

responds in his own mind with feelings, phantasies, with silent speech—internal dialogues to which he also listens. And suddenly—or gradually—he may feel he knows what the analysand means by his language. The analysand's representations are to be understood as members of a set of transforms of one basic pattern or paradigm—among many possible ones. The psychoanalyst has his own terms for these patterns: such terms, for example, as oral, anal, phallic, narcissistic, oedipal, or the names of the defenses. These terms among others are part of his theory, which is essentially a theory of interpretation, a theory about the different ways of constructing symbolic representations and the kinds of meaning these representations may have.

Symbolic representations of psychic reality are of primary interest to the psychoanalyst. These are constructed according to the canons of the primary process—which is not to say, without language (Freud, 1900, 1901, 1905; Edelson, 1971a, 1972)—and are prototypically exemplified by symptoms, parapraxes, dreams, and transference.

The process of interpretation, however, is not straightforward. The psychoanalyst must wait to discover where the analysand is. For in any utterance, any phrase, metaphor, or word, of the analysand, linguistic ambiguities, both syntactic and semantic, are likely to evoke alternative symbolic worlds and to raise questions concerning the coexistence of these symbolic orders and the relations among them. These ambiguities threaten the psychoanalyst with the possibility of partial or incorrect interpretations. Yet—a paradox Freud was the first to appreciate and exploit—such ambiguities act at one and the same time not only as obstacles to the psychoanalyst's understanding but as occasions for his interpretations (e.g., of resistance, impulse and defense, conflict).

What we call "intuition" in the psychoanalytic process may be an end-product of the psychoanalyst's disciplined preconscious decision to permit himself to hear all the possible meanings of the analysand's language, no matter what particular meaning seems dictated by an immediate context.

The psychoanalyst listens in a way that allows him to recognize out of his own knowledge of language that an utterance is intrinsically ambiguous, if separated from its immediate context or (to put it another way) even when the immediate context insists so rapidly on a disambiguation of the utterance that the ambiguity would ordinarily slip by unnoticed. This permission and this kind of listening, informed by an unusual skill in making use of knowledge of language itself, enable the psychoanalyst ultimately to interpret what the analysand means by his language. The distinction between these two senses of the word "meaning"—"the meaning of the language" or dictionary sense of language and "what the analysand means by his language" or his intention in uttering it—should be kept in mind.

The psychoanalyst must wait, sometimes for months or years, to hear revealed what can only be heard through time: the sufficient context of the analysand's utterance, which disambiguates the utterance by making it possible for the psychoanalyst to assign a particular kind of meaning or many meanings to it where before only one kind of meaning or none was apparent. In the same way, the combination of words "flying planes can be dangerous" cannot be disambiguated without some context that in this example, however, immediately follows it and is sufficient to disambiguate it: "to a careless or inexperienced pilot" or "to those who live in skyscrapers."

One way the psychoanalyst begins to interpret the seemingly meaningless is to imagine the context in which it would be meaningful. One way he begins to interpret an utterance with apparently only one obvious meaning is to imagine other contexts in which the same language would have other meanings.

The sufficient context enables the psychoanalyst to choose among the utterance's possible incompatible meanings or to integrate its various interdependent meanings. Psychoanalysis is distinguished by the extent of the context, unfolding through a long period of time, that it requires for what the psychoanalyst regards as an adequate understanding of an utterance. The psychoanalyst has hovered over possible meanings, over ambiguities and anomalies, holding off the moment of selection and rejection, warding off the seduction of premature certainties, until—as a context unfolds further and further—a synthesis occurs of a multitude of meanings, which may have previously appeared incomparable, unfathomable, and incompatible. The psychoanalyst has allowed himself to listen and wait, knowing that it is the extension through time of the context that, finally wide enough to embrace a multitude, makes synthesis possible.[13] I touch here on matters discussed in the psychoanalytic literature under the rubrics "free floating attention," "multiple determination," and "working through."

In hours when language continues relentlessly to be fixed, stripped of alternatives, when there is no deviance, no ambiguity, nothing to wonder about, the psychoanalyst responds, no matter what the subject matter, with a keen sense of the obstacles (the analysand's "defenses") to understanding what the analysand means by his language. No matter how logical such a discourse, vital connections seem to be missing. No matter how detailed and sequential, some necessary context seems to be lost.

Then there are hours of what seem to be almost pure symbolic presentations. In such presentations, acts, images, and interactions are constructed in the way a dream is constructed, and language is a material used as it is used in dreams. The psychoanalyst responds with a sense of other obstacles (the analysand's "histrionic affect," "vagueness," "impulsive acts," "silence," "disorganization")—fog instead of barricades, shifting sand instead of walls—to understanding what the analysand means by his language. Everything is possible. Everything is confusing, so much so that it is difficult to grasp something to wonder about. No word means what the psychoanalyst knows its sense to be, but apparently

13. For a discussion of ambiguity and psychoanalysis, see Kris (1952).

serves primarily as an allusion—to what?—to something absent and not yet known. The psychoanalyst is held in suspense. What can be recognized as deviant, when no norm has been established? So even deviance does not appear, to insist that it be interpreted. The psychoanalyst does not know how to take this language. He feels either too far—on a different level or at a remove—from the analysand or too close to or merged with him; either way, all language from either direction seems to have no target or, having one, to miss it, to pass it by.

In these two kinds of hours, the psychoanalyst and analysand do the arduous work of the psychoanalysis, the work that prepares for and makes possible the "breakthroughs," the "insights," and the consolidation of insights, the change from one plateau to another, from one level of symbolic functioning to another (Edelson, 1971a). It is the relatively infrequent optimal synthesis of these two modes of representation, when each supports the other, as in a good poem, to which the psychoanalyst may respond with the recognition of what Kris (1956a) has discussed in other terms as "the good hour." These are the hours, rare though they may be, that—ripped from the context of the labor that delivers them—are perhaps responsible for unduly glamorous, dramatic, popular conceptions of psychoanalysis.

Of course, I do not imply that ordinarily we are focally aware of the speech of the analysand, of the linguistic object as such, of phonology, syntax, and semantics, or of the relations among these. I have, at times, confronted analysands with their use of language, and sometimes I have been happily able to illustrate a point or open a discussion thereby. Although some self-consciousness may result and some defensive effort to alter a linguistic style may occur, these are usually short-lived. In fact, the stability of language as a system and its realization in individual performance and style enhances its value as an object of study in the realm of mind where surface phenomena, at any rate, yield so easily to influence by the investigator.

The psychoanalyst is not necessarily focally aware of the speech of the analysand as an opaque object of attention, any more than is the athlete of his muscle's actions or the musician of his fingers' movements. Language is transparent; we hear through it to what is signified by it. We are focally aware of what we understand language to represent—its meaning or what is intended by its use. We are only subsidiarily aware of the multidimensional characteristics of linguistic objects, but, usually without realizing it, we depend upon this subsidiary awareness for understanding the full import of these symbolic entities. What else but such a subsidiary awareness of language as a system, which in its fantastic complexity matches the complexity of the phenomena the psychoanalyst investigates, can account for the startling intuitions and strange knowledge he possesses? What else but linguistic competence, the internalized knowledge of language that is possessed without conscious awareness of it or even the ability to explicate it, can constitute the foundations of the psychoanalyst's skill? [14] What of self-knowledge as such a foundation? Even the psychoanalyst's own psychoanalysis, which has prepared him for this work, has been an exploration of his own symbolic functioning—his own use of language to represent and in fact to formulate his inner reality—and an opportunity to put into words the wordless or unspeakable and thereby to reshape that reality.

The crucial empirical questions are then: How much of the psychoanalyst's understanding of what the analysand says depends on linguistic competence; on knowledge of the way sounds and meanings are associated in language, of the rules by which they are associated? More generally, how much of the psychoanalyst's understanding depends on semiological competence; knowledge of the way symbolic entities and meanings are associated in any symbolic system; knowledge, for example, of the canons of primary process as

14. For a discussion of focal and subsidiary awareness, see Polanyi (1959, 1966). For discussions of linguistic competence, see references cited in footnotes 5 and 6 above.

described by Freud in discussions of the dream-work and the joke-work? [15] And how much of the psychoanalyst's understanding depends on extralinguistic and extrasemiological factors: beliefs and knowledge about nonlinguistic and nonsymbolic features of the speaker and the situation?

I have come to believe that the particular skills of the psychoanalyst owe much more to his linguistic competence (as defined by Chomsky) than is generally appreciated and that much of the understanding the psychoanalyst attributes to conscious or unconscious extralinguistic information actually derives from his own internalized linguistic competence of whose nature and existence he may be altogether unaware.

These data of psychoanalysis, the language of analysand and psychoanalyst, are susceptible to explanation in terms of symbolic forms and symbolic functioning. Perhaps only a theory of language can begin to account adequately for the complex phenomena embraced by psychoanalysis—most critically, the phenomena observed in the psychoanalytic situation itself, including the psychoanalyst's acts of interpretation.

I shall argue that this proposition is plausible by demonstrating in Part Three, through an extended analysis of a very short, ostensibly simple poem, the complexity of language; the various uses that may be made of language; and the subtlety and scope of the categories and distinctions required to describe aspects of linguistic objects and to state the relations among these.

First, however, in the following chapters and in those of Part Two, I shall explore certain implications of ideas about psychoanalysis and language for conceptions of psychoanalysis as a science and as therapy. What, for example, does a psychoanalyst do when he interprets a phenomenon? Does psychoanalysis enable us to explain human behavior, or to interpret semiotic phenomena, or to do both? If psychoanal-

15. Let us suspend for the present any decision concerning how much linguistic competence is in fact a precondition for a more general semiological competence (see Edelson, 1972).

ysis may be considered in some respects interpretation and in others explanation, to what extent, and in what ways, is it one of the other? Are interpretation and explanation related to each other in any consistent, coherent way in psychoanalysis?

2: *The Distinguishing Characteristics of Interpretation*

In *The Interpretation of Dreams,* Freud (1900) strives to approach "more closely to the unknown reality" (p. 610). Certainly, no one can doubt that in this work Freud does indeed help us to understand the unknown. *The Interpretation of Dreams* is one of those major works of insight that changes forever the reader's view of himself, others, and the world.

Science may be defined as an enterprise combining conceptual invention and empirical observation to reveal an abstract order underlying empirical reality that satisfies our yearning to approach ever more closely "the unknown reality." Then *The Interpretation of Dreams,* progenitor, model, and exemplar of psychoanalysis, is a work of science.

Yet Freud seemed to have been uneasy about "interpretation" as an instrument of scientific understanding. In the physical sciences, there are no questions of meaning and no phenomena involving symbolic functioning. Scientific explanation is defined in terms of generality. Explanation requires regularity of co-occurrence; specifies necessary and sufficient antecedents that must inevitably be followed by consequents; and formulates general laws. From these, theoretically significant, observable facts may be deduced, irrespective of contingent circumstances or context.[16] Freud de-

16. However, it is important to distinguish between the myths of science and how scientists actually work. (See Brush, 1974, and Polanyi, 1958.) The scientist is supposed to abandon willingly "a priori" beliefs (to be held only as tentative hypotheses) when these are not supported by empirical evidence, especially experimental evidence. But James Joule, for example, deduced a value for the mechanical equivalent of heat and spent thirty-eight years in repeated efforts to determine this value experimentally, because he

cided that his theory, too, must be general, must "explain as many as possible" observed characteristics of a phenomenon and at the same time define the position of the phenomenon in a "wider sphere of phenomena" (p. 75).

His brilliant chapter "The Dream-Work," concerned with the interpretation of dreams, is followed by the chapter "The Psychology of the Dream-Processes," with its startlingly different formulations. Here he attempted "to set up a number of fresh hypotheses which touch tentatively upon the structure of the apparatus of the mind and upon the play of forces operating in it" (p. 511). He did this in order to provide the missing psychological theory "under which we could subsume what the psychological examination of dreams"—presumably, the interpretation of dreams—"enables us to infer as a basis for their explanation" (p. 511). Apparently, he assumed that interpretations of dreams were less general formulations to be derived from more general ones. And that, because he could *interpret* dreams, dreams could be *explained* by a general psychological theory (ideally having the same characteristics as theory in physical science).

Since many social scientists as well as psychoanalysts are uniquely committed to the struggle to understand symbolic phenomena, it is important to distinguish "interpretation" and "explanation" as two alternate, sometimes complementary, ways to understand reality. Even if we accept, since explanation and interpretation both involve empirical investigations and conceptual systems, that they are therefore scientific (as we have defined science), it is still possible that they represent different and perhaps incommensurate modes of understanding reality.

If we assume otherwise, as Freud did, we run the risk that interpretation of semiotic phenomena will be judged by the

---

was convinced that "the grand agents of nature are, by the Creator's fiat, *indestructible;* and that whatever mechanical force is expended, an exact equivalent of heat is always obtained" (Taylor, 1943, p. 205). This conviction remained unshaken despite the variability of his experimental results and the disparity between them and the theoretically deduced value.

standards of explanation in physical science. In that case, interpretation may be wrongly rejected on incorrect grounds as "a priori" (involving standards of validity independent of observation) or "subjective" (involving a process of empathic ineffable "verstehen"). Or wrongly rejected on correct but not telling grounds as "ad hoc" (involving conclusions that are applicable for special purposes or with respect to individual objects only) or "ex post facto" (involving a retrospective understanding of events from what occurs or is done afterward).[17]

What are the distinguishing characteristics of interpretation?

The utterance "I don't understand this (event)" may call for an explanation. The speaker may mean by this utterance that he does not know the necessary and sufficient antecedent(s) of the event. A satisfactory reply to his utterance is an explanation. "This event occurred as a consequence of that previous event. You could have predicted the occurrence of this event, if you had known its antecedent(s)." The speaker may mean that he does not know what to expect to follow this event. A satisfactory reply to his utterance is an explana-

17. Discussions of explanation may be found in Borger and Cioffi (1970); Louch (1966); Winch (1958). Psychoanalysis as a science has been discussed by Hartmann (1958, 1959); Hartmann, Kris, and Loewenstein (1953); Pumpian-Mindlin (1952); Rapaport (1959).

Discussions of clinical interpretation may be found in Erikson (1958); Freud (1911–15, 1937); Hammer (1968); Paul (1963). Freud's *The Interpretation of Dreams* is, of course, the critical work for studying psychoanalytic interpretation.

With regard to paradigms of interpretation in nonclinical areas, I have found the following works especially useful: in studying interpretation in music, Cooper and Meyer (1960); Forte (1962, 1973); Meyer (1956, 1967, 1973); Salzer (1962); and in studying the interpretation of chess moves and games, e.g., Wimsatt (1968). In the study of what I would now call the interpretation of play and myth, and for a consideration of the methods of structuralism, I have, of course, drawn upon Piaget (1945, 1970); Piaget and Inhelder (1966); Levi-Strauss (1958, 1962, 1964). I shall indicate throughout Part Three the sources to which I turned in studying the interpretation of poetry.

I have largely adopted the terms Piaget (1945) and Piaget and Inhelder (1966) used in discussing the semiotic or symbolic function.

tion. "This event will inevitably and necessarily be followed by some future event. Knowing this present event, you can predict that future event." In both cases, it must be so that the inevitable co-occurrence of two (kinds of) events has been reliably verified by repeated observation.

The speaker may then say, "I don't understand why these two events always co-occur." The empirical generalization has itself become an event to be explained. A satisfactory reply to this utterance is an explanation which states a general law. "This empirical generalization is only one of many different empirical generalizations, all of which may be deduced from a still more general law."

Another request for explanation may follow this explanation. "I don't understand why this general law should be so." The information satisfying this request might be a still more general theory from which one could deduce this general law (and also still other general laws explaining empirical generalizations from very different phenomenal realms).

In every case, the lack of understanding has been met with an explanation. The explanation demonstrates that what has not been understood may be deduced from some more general proposition or set of propositions. In these cases, it is unlikely that any of the explanations would be termed an "interpretation" of the not-understood event.

When may we use the term interpretation comfortably to describe that which makes sense of what is not understood?

"I can't make *sense* of this (event)" may call for an interpretation. The reply might be, "you can't make sense of this event, because it is not a permissible event. It is not allowed. It is not acceptable." So, one might say of a collection of English words, "that is not a sentence in the English language." Or of a move in chess, "that is not a proper move." Or of a combination of pitches, "that is noise not music." Or of a series of lines, "that is not poetry." Or of an action, "that is not rational," or "that is not human." In general, then, if a system of obligatory context-independent rules is incapable of generating such an event, the event is considered not a proper member of the system or of the class of events that have been or may be generated by the rules of the system.

These replies are not explanations. They are *evaluative assessments* (although not necessarily moralistic indictments) of a particular event (Louch, 1966). That is, the "reasons" for an event are grounded in a system of normative propositions, rules, conventions, standards. Knowledge of this system underlies minimal expectations of what such an event should be like if it is to make sense at all. The interpreter who makes the evaluative assessment does not have to "believe in" these normative propositions; but he must know or discover what normative propositions might satisfy him as grounds for an event or what will make sense of it. Random events or chaos can be explained but are not susceptible to interpretation. Interpretation is only possible from the perspective of a conception of normative order. Departure from normative order is deviance, not randomness, and if severe may lead to the complaint, "that does not make any sense at all." Some position akin to this underlies Talcott Parsons' claim that a theory of action in social science can be value-free while necessarily concerned with understanding the critical role of values in human action.[18]

Even though such an event does not make sense because it violates rules or conventions, it may still occur. Occurring, then, it potentially can be explained; an event that violates all laws of nature is unthinkable in a way that an event that does not make sense is not. Also, an event that does not make sense may come to make sense without any change in it, if the rules or conventions of the system change. Clearly, rules and conventions are alterable in ways that natural law in physical science is not. A system of rules may change without any retrospective disqualification of the system, which may still be usable to understand the events once generated by it—as an example, the system of rules that generate tonal music. An event considered a member of one system may not make sense, but if considered a member of another

18. See Edelson (1971a, 1971b).

it may make sense. Generalizations, law, or general theory in physical science, however, are either invalidated, in which case they could never be or have been satisfactory explanations of any event, or are superseded by or subsumed under more general formulations, with no loss of explanatory power within the boundaries of a particular empirical realm. That is why historical classics in the humanities, and possibly in social science, have a status and validity that is quite different from historical work in physical science.

"I can't make sense of this (event)" may mean "I don't know what it signifies. I can't grasp the conception it represents (or presents)." What is lacking is an understanding of the relation between this signifier and what it signifies. What is required to interpret the event is knowledge of the particular rules capable of generating an abstract (inferred) structure, assigning a meaning to such a structure, and transforming (with meaning held invariant) this abstract structure into a structure underlying a perceptible representation. Or what is required is a knowledge of the particular criteria or canons—e.g., resemblance—relating a *presentation* to what it signifies.[19]

A knowledge of these rules makes sense of the event. An explication of one among a number of types of rules may be sufficient to achieve understanding, depending on what event is not understood. For example, in one interpretation of "The Snow Man" in Part Three, we shall appeal to rules of the syntactic component of language as grounds for an interpretation of the cognitive meaning of the poem. Rules of transformation relate deep sense-bearing structures to the poem as a perceptible object. For some events in the poem, an appeal to the rules of the semantic, phonological, or rhetorical component of language provide better grounds for understanding emotive, conative, phatic, or poetic meanings.[20]

19. The difference between "presentation" and "representation" is discussed in Chapter 5.

20. See Part Two for a discussion of the rules and components of language (Chapter 5), and of kinds of meaning (Chapter 6).

"Better" implies that an evaluative judgment must be made in the process of interpretation about what grounds are to be preferred as the grounds for making sense of a particular event, in terms of such standards as economy, coherence, and extension or range of applicability. Insofar as the grounds for an event are found in an organized system of rules—postulated or attested to—interpretation like explanation requires conceptual invention or theory.

In music, too, we may appeal to rules or conventions, for example, of harmonic practice. "This event is to be understood as part of the harmonic progression I-IV-V-I," (chords built respectively on the first, fourth, fifth, and first notes of a scale).

In language, we interpret an event by giving priority to one set of considerations or rules over another as decisive in generating it. The event is viewed as generated primarily by considerations of syntax, semantics, phonology, or rhetoric; or some combination of such considerations; or some compromise between them; or some conflict between them; or some synthesis of them. In interpreting a poem like "The Snow Man," we consider events, features of the poem, to be grounded in compromises or clashes between, or syntheses of, requirements of syntax and rhyme, of semantics and meter, yielding cognitive, conative, emotive, phatic, and poetic meanings.

In interpreting the meaning of a chord in tonal music, we may give priority to considerations or the rules or conventions of the harmonic process of chord generation (a way of understanding sixth chords, for example); the melodic process of chord generation (a way of understanding seventh chords); or the rhythmic process of chord generation (a way of understanding suspension chords) (Forte, 1962). In addition, chords may be generated by rules or conventions governing the process of modulation from one key to another, which is a recursive process similar to the one that generates a series of subordinate clauses in language, as in "The Snow Man." A chord progression (e.g., I-IV-V-I in the key of C major) may be prolonged by repeating the progression in the key of the fourth note of the scale (F major) to give the progression I in C, (I, IV, V, I in F—the IV of C), V in C, I in C. Chords may also be generated by rules governing the relation of co-occurring melodic lines. One basis for evaluating Bach's achievement is the discovery of the way in which he managed to create events that simultaneously satisfy many or all these considerations. For example, in the Prelude in C major, The Well-Tempered Clavichord, Book I, a progression of arpeggiated chords also forms a compound melodic progression.[21] In addition, the progression of arpeggiated chords form repeated upward thrusts in the upper voices which contrast with the long slow downward movement of the lower voices.

In interpreting semiotic phenomena in psychoanalysis, the psychoanalyst regards id, ego, and superego as organizations of acts each giving priority to different considerations, rules, standards, principles, or values. For example, an act maximizes adaptation to external reality and possession of means for achieving ends according to the reality principle; it maximizes immediate gratification and attainment of relation to goal-objects or states of affairs valued as ends in themselves according to the pleasure principle; or it maximizes conformity to moral values or ego-ideal. Or, from another perspective, the avoidance of realistic anxiety, instinctual anxiety, or superego anxiety provides the reason for, or warrants, or justifies an act. The psychoanalyst thus understands features of a symptom, for example, as generated primarily by one or another of these different subsystems of the personality. He evaluates events in terms of whether one set of considerations (one of these organizations) is sacrificed in favor of another, or there is some compromise between them, or some synthesis of them.

It is also possible to make sense of an event by constructing a paraphrase of it. Knowledge of a system of rules makes

21. I shall discuss "compound melody" in chapter 12.

it possible to interpret an event by paraphrasing it. That is, a sentence or poem may be interpreted by saying, "it means the same as this other (sentence or poem)." We understand it means the same because we know the deep sense-bearing structures underlying both the event and its paraphrase are the same and we know by what rules or operations this one deep sense-bearing structure can be transformed to yield different perceptible representations.

An interpretation of an event, then, may require the demonstration that it and another event can be generated, by known transformational operations or rules, from a single underlying inferred event or structure.

So, many compositions in tonal music can be shown to be different realizations of the same underlying structure I-V-I, which in each case has been submitted to a variety of different optional transformations. Similarly, Levi-Strauss is able to demonstrate that many different myths have the same meaning, in the sense that they can be shown to be the result of performing different logical operations upon a single set of binary terms. His theory is not an explanation of myth. It does not state general laws. It does not make prediction possible. It gives a set of myths an order similar to that of a "theme and variations" in music. Levi-Strauss dedicated *The Raw and the Cooked* to music and gave such titles to parts of this book (subtitled "Introduction to a Science of Mythology") as "theme and variations," "a short symphony," "fugue of the five senses," and "well-tempered astronomy." In the introduction, he wrote that "the analysis of myths was comparable with that of a major musical score" (p. 15) and that "music is a language with some meaning at least for the immense majority of mankind, although only a tiny minority of people are capable of formulating a meaning in it, and since it is the only language with the contradictory attributes of being at once intelligible and untranslatable, the musical creator is a being comparable to the gods, and music itself the supreme mystery of the science of man, a mystery that all the various disciplines come up against and which holds the key to their progress" (p.18). Levi-Strauss has no hesitation in describing the interpretation of myth as science.

The operations of the dream-work and the mechanisms of defense may be viewed as canons of transformation. So, the psychoanalyst may interpret a manifest dream by paraphrasing its meaning in verbal representations (the latent thoughts). He may interpret different dreams, or different symptoms, or even opposite-appearing acts and traits such as kindness and cruelty, miserliness and profligacy, as having the same meaning; it is possible through different transformational operations to generate different forms or events from a single underlying structure or event. A scientist may object to the logic of interpretation—considered as explanation—but no semiologist, linguist, music theorist, or literary critic should find such a mode of understanding strange.

This discussion and these examples suggest that interpretation (unlike explanation) is unavoidably *ad hoc.* A particular interpretation may result in an understanding of a single event and conceivably no other. Most sentences, all poems, all musical compositions, and possibly a whole class of human acts (even those that phenomenally appear similar) are once-only events, which cannot be predicted in advance from a knowledge of the rules used to understand them or to interpret their meaning. I shall discuss below how interpretation is bound to an examination of a particular context to discover the warrant or justification of an event; this, too, makes interpretation unavoidably *ad hoc.*

"I can't make sense of this (event)" may mean "I don't know how to translate this signifier from one sign or symbol system into a signifier I understand from another sign or symbol system." Here the signifiers are generated by the rules of different systems. Therefore, a translation rather than a paraphrase is an interpretation of the event. What is required is knowledge of the code according to which the signifiers of two systems are related. Translation is also *ad hoc.* The event translated may be a once-only event. Its translation is unique and for it alone and does not necessarily enable us to understand any other event or depend for its acceptability or utility on enabling us to understand other events.

Translation need not involve two natural languages but may involve translation from one kind of semiotic system to another, for example, from images to language.

Piaget and Inhelder (1966) have argued that images are not derived from perception or prolongations of perceptions, but "begin only at the time of the appearance of the semiotic function," are the result of internalized imitation, and—rather than *representing concepts* as language does—function as motivated symbols to represent (present) *concrete objects* as such and "the whole past perceptual experience of the subject" through schematized "resemblance to the objects symbolized" (pp. 68–70). Images symbolize objects and experience as comprehended by the subject and not as they "are"; the form of the image is determined by the capacities and interests of the subject, not by the objective properties of the experience.

The psychoanalyst, too, understands memories as symbolic reconstructions rather than copies of past experience. Psychic reality rather than external reality is decisive (Edelson, 1971b). Symbolic reconstructions like other semiotic phenomena are interpreted (rather than explained) by paraphrase or translation through knowledge of the rules or operations (akin to the dream-work and joke-work) which have constructed or generated them. Pious (1961) described the interventions of the psychoanalyst as "translations" (rather than "interpretations") from more archaic to less archaic modes of communication.

"I can't make sense of this (event)" may mean "I don't know why this event (rather than some other event) occurs at just this time (rather than some other time)," or "I don't understand why this feature occurs just at this point," or "I don't understand why this event signifies what it does in just this way rather than some other also permissible way—that is, I think I understand what is signified (the cognitive meaning) but not why it is signified in a particular way." What is required here is knowledge of the relation between a signifier and (if it is part of a larger semiotic context) its semiotic context, or the relation between a signifier and the occasion or circumstances of its occurrence.

Interpretation of the event again involves reference to the grounds that warrant or justify it, but these grounds are now to be found in an occasion, set of circumstances, or context, such that the event is understood as appropriate on such an occasion or in such circumstances or context. Since interpretation involves an appeal to a normative standard or value such as appropriateness, it is once more clear that the interpretation of an event is ineluctably an act of *evaluative* assessment or appraisal. Inasmuch as the occasion, set of circumstances, or context must be carefully studied to discover the adequate grounds for the event, interpretation like explanation involves *empirical* investigation. However, insofar as an appraisal of an event in relation to an occasion or set of circumstances or context (a conjunction more likely than not to be novel and never-repeated) is involved, interpretation is not only also *ad hoc,* but *context-bound* as well, in a way that explanation is not. The *theory* which warrants or justifies an event consists of context-dependent as well as context-independent rules or conventions.

In addition, an interpreter of an event in examining its context to determine its meaning may argue that what follows the event, in retrospect (and according to rule or convention), enables him to assign a meaning to it. Our discussion of anticipations and retrospections in the interpretation of "The Snow Man" exemplifies such arguments. For example, observing that a sequence of sounds is followed by a combination of them, we argue that the sequence is an anticipation of, a preparation for, or an implication of the ultimate combination. Syntactic progressions, semantic progressions, phonological progressions, and rhetorical progressions reach goals out of phase with each other; the end of the line in a poem, for example, may not coincide with the end of a syntactic progression. When such progressions conclude in phase, the interpretation of "*the* end" differs from the interpretation of the significance of out-of-phase endings; this is one of the ways "major goals" are differentiated from "subsidiary goals."

An event in music (or poetry) is implicative because of the body of rules that generates it. As Meyer (1973) has demonstrated, an interpreter who knows these rules may discover the grounds that warrant or justify an event in music by examining the work itself without regard to its effect upon a listener and without using psychological language (expectation, tension, etc.). This is essentially the way in which Chomsky has studied language. However, an interesting difference exists between music theory and linguistic theory. The postulated deep structure of a sentence is, in general, more complex than the surface structure of the sentence; transformations operate to abbreviate or condense. But the postulated deep structure of a musical composition (or of a myth, as studied by Levi-Strauss) is, in general less complex than its foreground events. I am not referring now to a complete analysis of a composition. Theory here seems to serve the function of summarizing a vast multitude of events. The difference may be related to the use to which a symbolic system is put. Language is used to represent and communicate concepts, in contrast to music which can be viewed as presenting inner states. More basically, in language, cognitive meaning, related especially to deep structure, is of primary importance, rather than those emotive, conative, phatic, or poetic meanings conveyed by the surface form. It is otherwise in music. Here, the meanings conveyed by the surface form have primacy.

In examining a musical composition, we may wonder about an ambiguous chord (the chord in the twelfth measure of Bach's Prelude in C major), "what does this mean?" Looking three measures ahead, we see a I chord in C major. Retrospectively, then, we see that the I chord in the key of G (measure 11) must also be understood as the V chord in the key of C, heralding the progression: V in C (measure 11); the ambiguous diminished seventh chord (measure 12) viewed as VII in the key of D major (the second note in the key of C is the first note in the scale in the key of D and so this chord is a strong preparation for the next chord in this progression); II in C (measure 13); the ambiguous diminished seventh chord (measure 14) viewed as VII in the key of C (a strong preparation for the next chord); the goal, I in C (measure 15). The pivot chord in measure 11, meaning both I in G and V in C, which makes possible the modulatory progression from G to C, is reminiscent of the "switch-words" in a chain of free associations that Freud describes in *The Interpretation of Dreams.*

Certainly, alternative interpretations adducing different grounds to warrant or justify an event are possible. Just because interpretation is an evaluative assessment, grounds that satisfy one interpreter as adequate or primary do not necessarily satisfy another. However, these interpretations are not arbitrary, capricious, or indeterminate, since they are based on a knowledge of the rules and conventions that govern such relations. But interpretation (unlike explanation) is clearly *ex post facto,* since an event is interpreted retrospectively from what occurs afterward and indeed cannot be understood (since its consequents cannot be predicted) until what (among many possibilities) may occur does occur.

In summary, then, the distinguishing characteristics of interpretation may be formulated as follows. Interpretation, which requires careful study of actual works, contexts, and occasions, is *empirical.* It requires *conceptual invention* or *theory,* but its theory does not consist of universal, inviolable, general laws, but is rather a coherent organization or system of normative principles, standards, canons of procedure or practice, or conventions, some context-independent and some context-dependent, which warrant or justify events. Interpretation is ineluctably *evaluative*—essentially, an appraisal or assessment of events or objects in relation to contexts in the light of a body of rules and standards. Interpretation is in large part *context-bound.* It is *ad hoc*—addressed legitimately to the understanding of unique works and acts. It is *ex post facto,* especially since major criteria for assessing an event are standards for judging it in relation to some goal or event occurring afterward and retrospectively giving meaning to the preceding event viewed as part of a progression to this goal.

Interpretation, which does not conform to the logic and standards of explanation in physical science, is a necessary mode of understanding man and the works of man. It is part of the science of man, with a logic, standards, and procedures of its own appropriate to the semiotic phenomena which is its proper subject matter.

3: Interpretation and Explanation in Psychoanalysis

Freud was much exercised to demonstrate in *The Interpretation of Dreams* that dreams have meaning—that dreams make sense. That he was evaluatively assessing these acts is indicated by his repeated quarrel with those who deny that dreams make sense and *therefore* depreciate them—deny that they have any value. "It seems to be no more than putting the truth into words when we express our very low opinion of mental activity in dreams and assert that in dreams the higher intellectual faculties in particular are suspended or at all events gravely impaired" (pp. 54–55). In a similar vein, Freud wrote: "Medical writers in especial tend to regard psychical activity in dreams as trivial and valueless; while philosophers and non-professional observers—amateur psychologists—whose contributions to this particular subject are not to be despised have (in closer alignment with popular feeling) retained a belief in the psychical value of dreams" (pp. 63–64).

Here a performance was being evaluated according to unstated value-standards of what the performance should be like. The ideal of rationality was taken for granted by Freud and written of as though a value-free fact were under consideration. In the same way Piaget describes intelligence as an equilibrium between accommodation and assimilation as though a general theory and objective fact rather than an evaluative assessment of performances were at issue.

Three times Freud referred to and rejected Strumpell's comparison of dreaming with "the ten fingers of a man who knows nothing of music wandering over the keys of a piano" (pp. 78,122, 222). In view of the frame of reference in this book, it is especially important that Freud used a semiotic phenomenon as a critical example, and an example involving music at that. The opposition is between a view of dreaming as motivated—i.e., the dreamer has motives or strives to achieve ends and a dream makes sense interpreted in light of these motives or ends—or explained as the outcome of a physiological stimulus. "Dreams are not to be likened to the unregulated sounds that rise from a musical instrument struck by the blow of some external force instead of by a player's hand; they are not meaningless; they are not absurd . . ." (p. 122). Certainly it is possible to *explain* random noise, but it is not possible to make sense of it. "Unregulated," then, must imply ungoverned by a normative system; "meaningless" and "absurd" imply "makes no sense when assessed according to such a normative system."

The difference between "interpretation" and "explanation" is implied by Freud's use of this example and by his emphasis that the discovery of the conditions for dreaming or sleep is to be distinguished from the discovery of the meanings of particular dreams. One may explain dreaming or sleep, but not the form or choice of images or meanings of a particular dream. The meaning of a particular dream is discovered by interpretation.

An explanatory theory may not have been Freud's achievement in *The Interpretation of Dreams,* although it was clearly what he wanted to create. That a normative system providing a basis for interpretation is at least part of his theory is suggested, for example, by his own acknowledgment that some of his propositions are self-evident or can be neither proved nor disproved. ". . . it is self-evident that dreams must be wish-fulfilments, since nothing but a wish can set our mental apparatus at work" (p. 567). That is, we assume that human action, if it is to make sense, ought to be oriented to the achievement of ends. This assumption in Freud's words, if we strain a bit, can be viewed as an axiomatic postulate of a general theory of human action. But it does not seem possible to grant the following statement the same status: ". . . the dream-wish which provides the motive power invariably originates from the unconscious—an assumption which, as I myself am ready to admit, cannot be proved to hold generally, though neither can it be disproved" (p. 598).

The seventh lecture in the *Introductory Lectures* was called "The Sense of Symptoms" (*not* "The *Cause* of Symptoms"). It was Freud's achievement to demonstrate that symptoms as well as dreams and parapraxes could be interpreted. His actual procedure was to adduce evidence, by a careful examination of data collected in a particular way, that, once a *missing context* was recovered, these acts in *that* context were not senseless. The context provided the grounds, warrant, or justification for the previously mysterious acts. They were then seen to be like other acts, that is, *appropriate* to the context as viewed and experienced by the actor. Like other acts, they could be assessed according to ordinary value-standards and priorities—avoidance of pain; gratification; satisfaction of moral requirements.

That an evaluative assessment (I might say, a moral vision, if this phrase were not so easily misunderstood) was the very essence of Freud's insight is indicated by his frequent adjuration that we accept the fact that the neurotic is not qualitatively different from—no worse than—other men. Once we understand the context, the actual grounds for their symptoms, these are seen to make sense according to the same value standards by which we make sense (not necessarily approve or disapprove) of the actions of other men.

So, also, an evaluative assessment is the very essence of Levi-Strauss's labors of interpretation. He exhorts us to realize—he reveals to us—that the savage mind is not to be judged inferior to the civilized mind. He examines and assesses the thought of the primitive, and shows it to be interpretable, to make sense, to be logical, according to the same standards by which we assess our own performance.

I believe that in one of Hartmann's latest (1959), finest,

and most complete discussions of these problems, "Psychoanalysis as a Scientific Theory," he confessed with the honesty of a great thinker his own troubled awareness that the view of psychoanalysis as a *general* theory of human behavior (explanatory in the same way other sciences are), which he did so much—perhaps more than any other—to promote, was in some way unsatisfactory. He had previously quoted without comment Flew's conclusion that the peculiarities of psychoanalysis "must give this discipline a logical status different from, though not of course for that reason either inferior or superior to, that of sciences concerned with things other than human beings, and even from that of sciences concerned with less distinctly human aspects of human beings" (1958, p. 312). In his later essay, considering one of the inherent difficulties in our field, he touched on the possibility that psychoanalysis might "be termed a systematic study of self-deception and its motivations" (1959, p. 335). A view of interpretation as an evaluative assessment of various proffered grounds, warrants, and justifications of action seems to me implied. And,in the next paragraph, discussing the interpretation of a slip of the tongue, he used the phrase "evaluating the psychological situation" (p. 336). Later, he concluded that "the distortions of psychological observation," "the involvement of the observer and the potential sources of error of his perception and judgment" are not just problems found in all science or simply "the result of imperfections of the state of psychoanalytic theory" but rather constitute "an essential feature of certain aspects of human behavior" (pp. 338–39). Somewhat wistfully, he went on to comment, "There is always something ambiguous about the meaning of 'clinical research' in general. There exists, so far as I know, no really satisfactory presentation of the subject in terms of the philosophy of science" (p. 342). (He had just reminded us of Freud's discomfort that his case histories read like novels rather than works of experimental science.) Following upon these comments, without apparent awareness of any continuity, but rather moving from topic to topic as he was wont to do, he described psychoanalysis as not only a scientific theory but a clinical method of interpretation, concerned with signals, signs, and symbols.

I believe that some of the perplexities with which Hartmann wrestled in this essay are resolvable, if we make and pursue the implications of the distinction I have drawn between explanation and interpretation; a theory of interpretation is the way to a satisfactory presentation of the meaning of clinical research that he sought.

In this connection, we may consider Erikson's discussion of interpretation and clinical evidence. On the whole, he has been less concerned than Hartmann with psychoanalysis as a scientific theory. In discussing the nature of clinical evidence (1958), Erikson considers the clinician is "methodologically closest" to the historian.

Cassirer (1944) regards history as evaluative assessment or judgment. "Historical knowledge is the answer to definite questions, an answer which must be given by the past; but the questions themselves are put and dictated by the present—by our present intellectual interests and our present moral and social needs" (p. 178). "What we seek in history is not the knowledge of an external thing but a knowledge of ourselves" (p. 203).

The psychotherapeutic encounter, according to Erikson, is "historical." The patient has "surrendered his self-regulation to a treatment procedure." The patient is encouraged "to ponder what world order (magic, scientific, ethical) was violated and must be restored before his self-regulation can be reassumed" (p. 54). The psychoanalyst listens to the patient's free associations and is gradually impressed by the strategic intersection of recurring themes, which reveal "the nature of the patient's message and its meaning" (p. 59). Erikson candidly regards interpretation as, in essence and not accidentally, an evaluative assessment of action and, in fact, asserts that any "psychotherapist who throws out his ethical sentiments with his irrational moral anger"—the distinction is important—"deprives himself of a principal tool of his clinical perception" (p. 73).

If interpretation is an evaluative assessment of an act, object, or event as semiotic phenomenon, and if interpretation depends upon the appreciation of the normative system and (especially in psychoanalysis) the discovery and careful empirical study of the unusual and extended contexts that warrant, justify, or constitute the grounds for some feature(s) of a semiotic act, object, or event, then, some revision of our ideas about clinical skill may be in order.

A reading of Erikson, for example, suggests that the psychoanalyst as clinician is not a master of "engineering" techniques based upon the general laws of a natural science. The clinician rather employs a method of interpretation that depends not only upon his intellectual powers (his ability to see the many grounds for or meanings of the same act), as important as these powers may be, but as well upon his character (as old-fashioned as that may sound), a measure of wisdom, and perhaps most importantly what I would inadequately term his acute moral perceptivity—the capacity to respond inwardly with passion and at the same time in a disciplined way to the subtlest nuance of moral implication. Erikson emphasizes the usefulness to the psychoanalyst of a capacity for indignation and it is clear from what he writes that a psychoanalyst who possesses a theory that aspires to explain human behavior would nevertheless be lost without the capacity to appreciate rationality, beauty, and virtue and to detect, confront, and endure (though not passively) irrationality, ugliness, and lies, spite, and violence in all their guises. These are, also, the capabilities (properly adjusted to subject matter) possessed by the interpreter of myth, music, or poetry—of man and the works of man.

Erikson's work suffers from his failure to meet the need (which Hartmann identified) for a systematic rationale for clinical research—a theory of interpretation. On the other hand, Rapaport's attempts to systematize psychoanalytic theory seem to me to have been blighted by aridity when he sought primarily to construct a general theory to explain human behavior. His better papers, including his insights into (1) the "relative autonomy" of ego from id and external reality (1951, 1957) and (2) the distinction between causes and motives (1960), seem to me possible to reformulate in terms of (1) the relative weight to be given in different contexts to possible grounds for an act and (2) the distinction between explanation and interpretation. Similarly, the points of view of metapsychology (1959) might be regarded as systematic proposals concerning what an interpreter should look for, and to what normative systems an interpreter should refer, in attempts to evaluate or discover in some context or occasion grounds for an act. The 1959 paper states what is *demanded* of a psychoanalytic *explanation.* The "points of view" are thus themselves prescriptive. That is an unusual characteristic for a foundation of a theory of explanation.

Is interpretation in psychoanalysis an evaluative assessment?

Ideally, an analysand comes for psychoanalysis not simply because he suffers but specifically because he is troubled about the grounds for his acts and the "reasons" for his suffering. His acts do not make sense to him. They are, as we put it, ego-alien. He does not understand why he feels, thinks, or acts as he does. He might say he does not know what "causes" him to act this way, but ordinarily he means he does not have good reasons for doing what he does. The grounds for his acts are inadequate or obscure.

The analysand's difficulties are that: (1) he is impulsive, compulsive, or does not learn from experience (his acts are assessed by the psychoanalyst or himself as deviant with respect to standards of rationality); (2) he is not happy or he is self-destructive (his acts are assessed as deviant with respect to standards of the ultimate desirability of gratification); (3) he is guilty or conflict-ridden (his acts are assessed with respect to moral standards or an ideal of integration). Similarly, he defends himself in ways that violate standards of appropriateness and rationality; for example, he does not know or deceives himself about the reasons for his acts; his affects and ideas are not appropriately related; he justifies his acts mistakenly and inflexibly.

If a prospective analysand has no interest in the grounds for his acts or is certain that his acts are justified by circumstances over which he has no control, he may be regarded as a nonsuitable candidate (inadequately motivated or not psychologically minded) or as a potentially difficult case, one who will be difficult to get "into analysis." Of course, if the psychoanalyst agrees that the prospective analysand's acts (ideas, feelings, symptoms, etc.) are entirely warranted by a situation from which he is unable to extricate himself—by material conditions such as neurophysiological impairments or external physical or social agents which thump upon him like the unregulated hand upon a piano—then it is also unlikely that he would be considered a suitable candidate for psychoanalysis.

If an analysand insists upon regarding his acts as "caused" rather than warranted or justified (or not), his insistence is likely to be regarded by the psychoanalyst as an obstacle—thus, a resistance—to the kind of inquiry appropriate in psychoanalysis. The analysand will say, "*it* keeps happening *to* me." In the course of the psychoanalysis, such formulations tend to assume the form: "I continue to act in the same apparently senseless way." The analysand says, "the feelings—the thoughts—do this or that." In the course of psychoanalysis, such formulations are likely to assume the form, "I feel—I think—I do this or that."

For psychoanalysis is essentially an inquiry into the grounds rather than the causes of acts. Such grounds are found in subsystems of often conflicting prescriptions governing choice of means, goals, and ways of ranking or integrating alternatives. The choices are regulated by different principles or normative standards. These are usually context-dependent; they generate acts on particular occasions or in particular contexts.

During the course of a psychoanalysis, an analysand is likely to exclaim in objecting to an interpretation or self-observation: "I couldn't really have done or felt that for such a flimsy reason!" Or, "that event was so trivial; it cannot account for this terrible way I feel." Or, "I cannot stand that I am so irrational; that I feel this way does not entitle me to act in such a way." These are evaluative assessments.

If the psychoanalyst, to encourage further inquiry, points out that an emotion appears to be excessive, exaggerated, or inappropriate to the idea or event which is its occasion, that is an evaluative assessment.

Here and in many similar interventions, the psychoanalyst does not use knowledge of general law. Rather he depends on the acuity of his moral perceptivity—his sensitivity to the implications of such value-standards as appropriateness—in evaluating a particular event. Knowledge of general law, as explanation of human behavior, is not a sufficient foundation for clinical skill. Can it therefore be a sufficient means for equalizing the skill of different clinicians? If it is true that another kind of knowledge is required as a foundation for clinical skill, is not its transmission in programs of training problematic? Will not clinicians inevitably differ with respect to their possession of such knowledge (regardless of the quality of their formal training), according to their feeling for value issues, their maturity, and their capacity to evaluate and assess without oversimplification their own experience and that of others—at the same time neither incautiously nor tactlessly approving or disapproving the standards that make sense of experience?

Analysands differ in their preferences for the kind of grounds that will satisfy them as adequate to warrant or justify their acts and in the grounds they eschew. We may speak of characteristic defenses or, along with Shapiro (1965), of "neurotic styles." The term "style" is especially felicitous in a semiotic frame of reference.

The obsessive-compulsive "always feels that he is reminding himself of some compelling objective necessity, some imperative or higher authority than his personal choice or wish, which he is obliged to serve." Such people "feel that propriety requires them to dress neatly, duty obliges them to visit Aunt Tilly, the boss's expectations make it necessary to finish the job early, health requires a certain amount of calisthenics every day, mental health necessitates a certain number of hobbies and a quantity of 'relaxation,' culture a certain amount of reading and music, and so on." They "are keenly aware . . . of rules, regulations, and conventions, and, perhaps, above all, a great assemblage of moral or quasi-moral principles." When the obsessive-compulsive "is confronted by the necessity for a decision," he "will typically attempt to reach a solution by invoking some rule, principle, or external requirement which might, with some degree of plausibility, provide a 'right' answer" (Shapiro, 1965, pp. 39–40, 46). This kind of analysand uses doubt to avoid conviction about any other proposed ground for his acts, since conviction might lead to feeling. A feeling is never to him an acceptable warrant for or justification of an act.

The paranoid person finds grounds for his acts in external threats. The hysterical person finds grounds for his acts in vague transient impressions; feelings, emotional storms, and bodily states felt to be visited upon him; and the idealizations of fantasy—rather than in factual information about external reality. The impulsive person finds grounds for his acts in irresistible impulses or whims, his supposed inability to control these impulses or whims, or an overwhelming provocation or irresistible opportunity.

Many aspects of the psychoanalytic situation, which are designed to promote the development of the transference neurosis, have their raison d'être in making it possible for the psychoanalyst to demonstrate, "your feelings, fantasies, wishes, and conceptions of me cannot be warranted by actions of mine. I have done nothing to provoke or entitle you to act in these ways. I have not provided any information about myself which would justify or make sense of your acts. Therefore, in order to interpret these acts of yours, we must seek other grounds for them—other contexts or occasions, your past life, earlier significant relationships, and the ways you have symbolically reconstructed these. In studying your symbolic reconstructions, we shall discover adequate, sufficient grounds for your apparently absurd, meaningless, or unjustifiable acts, your symptoms, your suffering."

One unique contribution of psychoanalysis to the interpretation of human acts is its rejection of immediate occasions or contexts—and usual norms for ways of symbolically representing these—as sufficient grounds for understanding such acts. Psychoanalysis insists instead upon more remote or distant occasions and extended contexts as these have been and are now symbolically reconstructed (according to other norms) by the actor. These grounds are therefore part of the *present* context whether or not the actor is aware of their presence or deceives himself concerning their relevance or appropriateness.

The psychoanalyst proceeds on the assumption that if he can discover how the analysand understands and sees reality in ways unknown to himself, the analysand's fantasies, the psychic reality or symbolic world the analysand has unwittingly constructed, he (the psychoanalyst) will then know the grounds for and be able to make sense of the analysand's acts.

One way that has been offered to understand the therapeutic action of psychoanalysis is to see it as making evaluative reassessment possible. The analysand comes to appreciate that the grounds for his acts are to be found in symbolizations he constructed as a child. He realizes that the form and content of these symbolizations were constrained by limitations in his capacity to understand experience, leading to misinterpretations of it, and by his conceptions of himself in relation to others at that time. He concludes, "what might have made sense then in that context when I was a child does not make sense now that I am an adult. I no longer have to fear this-or-that danger. I no longer have to be limited in my relationships to this-or-that person."

Is psychoanalysis ad hoc and context-bound?

The psychoanalyst does not explain a dream, showing that it can be deduced from an empirical generalization. He does not seek to predict a dream. No dream-book is available to him. He is skeptical and cautious about postulating any universal symbolic equations. Symbols "frequently have more than one or even several meanings, and . . . the correct interpretation can only be arrived at on each occasion from the context" (Freud, 1900, p. 353). The dreamer's associations are essential.

The psychoanalyst interprets each dream following a painstaking empirical examination of both immediate and remote unique contexts. He endeavors to account each time for a particular choice of images in the construction of a single dream, not to provide a general explanation of dreams. An interpretation of one dream does not serve as an "explanation" of other dreams. Even understanding the canons of dream-construction, he must decide upon specific interpretations (whether or not every thought is to be understood as its opposite, or whether a sequence is to be understood as *and, or,* or *but*) by examining a particular context. "We can never tell beforehand whether it stands for the one or for the other; only the context can decide" (Freud, 1900, p. 471).

No skilled psychoanalyst has much confidence in the therapeutic efficacy of general timeless explanations. His interpretations of dreams, symptoms, transference, even his genetic reconstructions, tend to specify "when" and "then." They are context-bound. If the analysand reports a state and "explains" it, attributing it to "the kind of person I am" or "my Oedipus complex" or "my problem with authority figures," the psychoanalyst wants to know "what happened yesterday?"

The psychoanalyst's theory alerts him to the kinds of

grounds he might discover in particular cases to warrant, justify, or make sense of acts. The theory properly understood does not lead to predictions of what he *must* necessarily discover.

Do not all physicians interpret signs and symptoms in this way? Why does the patient behave in this way? He has a fever. Oh, that makes it understandable. Fever justifies, warrants, is an acceptable reason for, such behavior. It does not follow that anyone who has a fever will behave under any circumstances and in every context in this way and only in this way.

Is interpretation in psychoanalysis ex post facto?

The psychoanalyst observes patterns of events. The outcome is always the same. The analysand does not notice this. He is surprised by the outcome or speaks of it as though he does not remember any similar past occurrence. Mostly, he does not see it as an "outcome." He does not connect it with any pattern or see it as the goal of any sequence.

The psychoanalyst may speak to the analysand along the following lines, but not necessarily in these words. "Since this event has occurred again and again, let's look back at the events preceding it and see if we can understand them as leading to this event. Looked at in this way, they make sense. Otherwise, it is difficult to make sense either of this event or these other events which preceded it."

This is in part what the psychoanalyst means by a motivated event—that previous events (acts by the analysand) can be understood as steps in a progression to an end or as preparations for a particular end. This kind of thinking is not different from the retrospective understanding of the meaning of a chord, once the goal which follows it is known.

The necessity for interpretation is raised by a change, a departure from a norm, a break in a pattern. The psychoanalyst waits through days of "free" (and not-so-free) "associations" until he detects a pattern—of cognitive, emotive, conative, phatic, or poetic meanings and the way in which these are represented or presented. He must wait until the pattern has been established; otherwise, there is no meaning in the idea of "change." He notices a change. There is a break in an established motif; an unexpected change of pitch, rhythm, or rate of speech; an abrupt change of topic. The psychoanalyst wonders, what does this change mean? What is its significance?

Thus, an act of interpretation is instigated—against a normative background—by deviance.[22] The interpretation of the meaning of the change usually must wait until the psychoanalyst is able to observe what eventually happens following the change, which retrospectively gives it its significance.

For example, the later irruption of an impulse directed to the psychoanalyst gives retrospective meaning to a previous change, now understood as a shift in those tendencies—or defenses—opposing expression of the impulse. Or a later assertion of a resistance to the psychoanalysis manifested in the relation to the psychoanalyst gives retrospective meaning to a previous change or deviant event, now understood to have been an expression (however disguised) of an unwelcome feeling or impulse.

This is exactly the same kind of thinking we do when confronted suddenly by the deviant word "misery" in "The Snow Man" [23] or by an ambiguous chord in the Prelude in C.

Because of the importance of the role of *ex post facto* in the interpretation of semiotic phenomena, and its disrepute in science, I shall illustrate it once more in an extended example. The example will also in conclusion remind the reader who is patient enough to follow it of the distinguishing characteristics of interpretation, as well as of the similarity of interpretations of semiotic phenomena such as music to interpretations in psychoanalysis.

In Bach's Prelude in C, the melodic line in the upper voice

22. See Chapters 7 and 8 for discussion of the interpretation of transformation and deviance.

23. See Chapter 11.

moves stepwise, in intervals of the second. This stepwise motion is the norm. Tonal melody is essentially characterized not by linear sequentiality of pitches but by intervals of the second (or the seventh, the inversion of the second), whether arranged vertically or horizontally. The stepwise motion of the scale is an ideal melody. Tonal harmony, on the other hand, is characterized not by simultaneity of pitches, but by intervals created by the first group of, and most easily heard, overtones—the intervals of the third, fifth, and octave, or their inversions the sixth, fourth, and unison.[24]

The upper voice melody, measures I through 32. (Repetitions not indicated; see text.)

In the first four measures of the melody, during which a closed harmonic progression (I, II, V, I in C major) establishes a norm—that we are in the world of the C major scale—E (the third note in the scale) moves stepwise to F. F is repeated and returns to E.

Suddenly, there is a skip up to A (interval of a fourth), an

24. See Forte (1962, p. 209).

equilibrating skip back down to D (interval of a fifth), a skip up to G (interval of a fourth), and a skip back down to C (interval of a fifth). These skips, which—given the norm of movement by seconds—are startlingly deviant, can be rationalized (made sense of) by insisting that the essential line must be the one from E to D to C. The A that actually follows E must then be considered part of another implied melodic line, which leads stepwise a second interval down to G. But, and this is the mystery, where does *this* melody continue? What is the meaning of this step from A to G, taken out of, poised above, and isolated from what we insist on hearing as the main melodic line?

In this main melodic line, C is repeated twice again, before the melody drops stepwise to B, the note a second interval below C. The melody circles around C, coming at it from different directions. So, B (a second interval *below* C natural) moves to C sharp, which leads to D (the note a second interval *above* C). B is repeated and then finally steps a second up to C, here prefigured—as it also was by the initial harmonic progression in C major—as the goal of the melodic line.

Suddenly, another startling skip, from the C down to F (interval of a fifth). F is then repeated twice, before dropping stepwise a second interval to E. This E, an octave below the E which began the melody, becomes a quasi-cadence, which marks the conclusion of the first part of the Prelude. It is also the beginning of a prolonged cadence—a melodic progression from this E in measure 19 (which is then repeated twice more) up to the final C (in the last measure, 35), the C which has already been prefigured as the goal of the entire melody.

Now the startling skip from C to F gives meaning and place within the norms of this work to the earlier A and G. This A and G are the notes missing in the stepwise motion from E to E an octave below. A and G an octave below their first appearance fill as virtual images the gap between C and F and thus form an unbroken stepwise motion in what is now an ideal melody. The drop from C to F introduces a cadence. The A and G mend the break in the ideal melody, compensating for this abrupt departure from the norms of melodic progression.

As is usual with Bach, the events he creates make sense not only in terms of one set of norms (those of melody) but in terms of another (those of harmony) as well. The melodic sequence G, C, C, C, B (which begins with an intervallic skip down a *fifth*) is coincident with a harmonic sequence I, IV, II, V, I in the key of G major. A later melodic sequence (identical with the first but transposed a fifth lower) C, F, F, F, E, which also begins with an intervallic skip down a *fifth,* is coincident with the same harmonic sequence I, IV, II, V, I in the key of C (a key a *fifth* lower than the key of G)!

This is what Hartmann meant when he referred to similarly marvelous achievements made possible by the hierarchically higher ranking synthetic function of the ego, successfully integrating, quietly and unnoticed, the requirements of different subsystems of the healthy personality.

4: Implications, Hypotheses, Questions

In this book I have suggested the possibility that linguistics may provide psychoanalysis with an appropriate metalanguage for a theory of interpretation in psychoanalysis—a metalanguage is required because the primary data for any study of the psychoanalytic situation and process are acts of speech. I have further suggested that a theory of interpretation in psychoanalysis may depend on making clear distinctions between interpretation and explanation; and between reasons, motives, and causes. Certainly, an investigation into the use of these terms in speech acts (following Wittgenstein and J. L. Austin, among others) would be apposite, but I do not think it is necessary for me to carry out such an investigation in order to make the limited comments on these matters to be found in this book. Katz (1971, especially pp. 5–17) has written well about the relation between Chomsky's transformational-generative theory and the work of Wittgenstein, Frege, and Carnap on logical forms and language, the work of Wittenstein, Moore, and Ryle on ordinary language philosophy and the way sentences are used in life, and the work of Quine.[25]

I now conclude this part of the book by simply listing the principal implications and hypotheses (really, whatever their

25. See also Fodor and Katz (1964) and Katz (1972), where a variety of philosophical and logical problems, such as the difference between so-called analytic and synthetic propositions, and reference, entailment, and meaning, are discussed. An exposition of these topics, particularly as philosophical problems, is outside the scope of this book, although this work in philosophy and the philosophy of language will indirectly at least no doubt make a contribution to clear thinking in formulating a theory of interpretation in psychoanalysis.

syntactic form, the questions) that arise out of this book to require and (I hope) to incite further investigation.

1. Psychoanalysis is essentially a science of semiotics—a study of symbolic systems, relations among them, and the use of symbolic systems in symbolic functioning.

2. A theory of psychoanalytic interpretation will specify what the psychoanalyst must know—wittingly or unwittingly—to perform acts of interpretation.

3. Linguistic competence—the internalized knowledge of language that is possessed without conscious awareness of it or even the ability to explicate it—is a significant foundation of the psychoanalyst's clinical skill.[26] The particular clinical skills of the psychoanalyst owe much more to linguistic competence in particular (and to semiological competence, knowledge of the way symbolic entities and meanings are associated in any symbolic system, in general) than is generally appreciated. Much of the understanding the psychoanalyst attributes to empathy, intuition, or conscious or unconscious extralinguistic information actually derives from his own internalized linguistic (and semiological) competence of whose nature and existence he may be altogether unaware. To make an interpretation of a symbolic object, the psychoanalyst must understand how the symbolic object has been constructed. That is, to understand the relation between a symbolic object and its meaning, the psychoanalyst must in some way be able to reconstruct how and what operations have been used—upon what linguistic materials, related in what way to each other—to make a symbolic object that evokes the meaning for which it stands.

4. The psychoanalyst in his acts of interpretation distinguishes and responds to five kinds of "meaning"—cognitive, emotive, conative, phatic, and poetic—represented and presented by the language of the analysand.[27]

5. Explanation and interpretation both involve empirical

26. See Chapter 5 for a discussion of interpretation and linguistic competence.

27. See Chapter 6 for a discussion of the meanings of "meaning."

investigations and conceptual systems. To this extent, they both belong to science, which combines conceptual invention and empirical observation to reveal an abstract order underlying observable phenomena that satisfies our yearning to approach ever more closely "the unknown reality." However, explanation and interpretation represent different and perhaps incommensurate modes of understanding reality.

5. Explanation derives particulars from general law. Interpretation, which requires careful study of actual works, contexts, and occasions, is *empirical.* Its *theory* is a coherent organization or system of normative principles, standards, canons of procedure or practice, conventions, or rules, some context-independent and some context-dependent, which warrant or justify events. Interpretation is ineluctably *evaluative,* an appraisal or assessment of events or objects in relation to contexts in the light of a body of rules and standards. Interpretation is in large part *context-bound.* It is *ad hoc*—addressed legitimately to the understanding of unique works and acts. It is *ex post facto,* since a principal way of assessing an event is judging it, according to some standard(s), in relation to some goal or event occurring after and retrospectively giving meaning to the preceding event (viewed then as part of a progression to this goal).

7. Interpretation, which does not conform to the logic and standards in physical science, is a necessary mode of understanding man and the works of man. It is part of the science of man, with a logic, standards, and procedures of its own, appropriate to the semiotic phenomena which is its proper subject matter.

8. Interpretation in psychoanalysis, which involves empirical investigation and conceptual invention, is *evaluative assessment, ad hoc, context-bound,* and *ex post facto.* The attempt to build a general theory to explain human behavior upon such interpretations results in dilemmas of purpose, difficulties of formulation, and incoherencies and inconsistencies. A highly abstract psychoanalytic theory should properly resemble in

its formulations Chomsky's linguistic theory, Forte's theory of tonal harmony or the structure of atonal music, Meyer's "explanation" of melody, Levi-Strauss's theory of myth, or some literary-linguistic theories of literary structure and style, rather than theory in physical science. Psychoanalysis is inevitably more successful in interpreting—discovering adequate but unsuspected grounds for—puzzling, deviant, or unconventional semiotic events than in explaining human behavior according to the model of physical science.

9. Given the nature of interpretation as evaluative assessment, different interpretations by different interpreters of the same semiotic phenomena (which are unavoidably ambiguous acts or events) are inevitable. Further, while the distinguishing characteristics of interpretation do not change, the normative propositions constituting a particular theory may. Therefore, semiotic phenomena (including "psychopathology" *insofar as it is such a phenomenon*) in different societies or in different epochs may have different meanings—may be interpreted according to different theories—in the same way that the theory which makes sense of events in atonal music is different from the theory which makes sense of events in tonal music.

10. We shall not lose our way in considering the problems of psychoanalysis as science, theory, method of interpretation, and therapy, if we keep before us as a model *The Interpretation of Dreams,* the progenitor and still the exemplar of psychoanalysis.

PART TWO

PSYCHOANALYSIS AND LANGUAGE

5: *Interpretation and Linguistic Competence*

In Part Three, we shall "interpret" the poem "The Snow Man" as a linguistic object in three different ways, scrutinizing in turn the details of syntactic transformations, semantic deviance and ambiguity, and patterns of sound. The reader may well ask what this cataloguing of literary effects, this syllable counting and ruminating about sounds, has to do with interpretation in psychoanalysis. Psychoanalysts are not literary critics. Patients do not speak poetry in psychoanalysis. Exactly the opposite from this artfulness and carefully wrought invention, a freedom from these and other constraints on what is said and how it is said, is what is desired for the analysand. Surely, the psychoanalyst does not count the number of syllables or note the pattern of beats in what the analysand says, much less his rather casual syntax. This purposeful concentration on minutiae is certainly not what preoccupies a psychoanalyst. Rather, the nature of his clinical skill depends in large part on the way in which he listens to broad large themes—motifs of impulse and defense, critical representative events [28]—that appear and reappear over months, emerging when the process goes well ever more clearly from the welter of distracting and disguising details.

I am concerned about these views. Especially because I know that I am one—unlike many others—for whom only the exhaustive is truly interesting. I confess I have been studying this short poem on and off for twelve years. (Can-

28. Kris (1956b) speaks of synthetic nodes formed by the intersection of many similar experiences and encapsulating the development of an entire life.

not one find in a painstaking, sympathetic examination of one leaf many of the secrets of the forest? [29]) And I do not yet feel that I have exhausted its use of linguistic resources.

However, the reader shall not be subjected to this prolonged description of a literary object for its own sake. Certainly, this object and the long, thorough contemplation of it do have value other than utility in illustrating resources of language and exemplifying processes of interpretation. Perhaps there is little in such a poem to interest a clinician. But then perhaps many psychoanalysts may have made the mistake of neglecting Freud's theoretically important *Jokes and Their Relation to the Unconscious* because jokes are cultural rather than clinical phenomena.

I decided to make use of a poem as linguistic object primarily because, as I shall have reason to state again, poetry seeks to exhaust the possibilities of language, to make the most concentrated use of all the resources of language. While no analysand may use even a small portion of these resources at any one time, there is reason to suppose that every and any one or number of them may be used by some analysand at some time in some psychoanalytic session. And it is possible that the psychoanalyst's competence, exemplified in his acts of interpretation, may be defined in part at least as a knowledge, witting or unwitting, of such linguistic resources.

It may be true that psychoanalysts in their clinical work

29. Randall Jarrell (1962), as a foreward to his wonderful contemplation of Robert Frost's "Home Burial," writes:

> "Home Burial" is a fairly long but extraordinarily concentrated poem; after you have known it long enough you feel almost as the Evangelist did, that if all the things that could be said about it were written down, "I suppose that even the world itself could not contain the books that should be written" [p.192].

Jarrell's essay is a masterful exemplification of a tactful application of psychoanalytic insights as part of both a loving and technical appreciation by a literary critic of a work of literary art—detailing especially the varied uses of language and the kinds of responses and inferences these evoke. A reading of it is more likely than any act I can imagine to make the psychoanalyst glad to claim kinship between his own acts of interpretation and those at least of as gifted a literary critic as this.

are not ordinarily focally aware of such linguistic details. Nevertheless, the formulation of a theory of interpretation, having a requisite degree of abstractness, must indeed involve careful attention to just these minutiae. The aim of such a theory of interpretation is not to prescribe what the psychoanalyst should do, but to explain what he does; not to instruct him in how to proceed in the formulation of interpretations, but to try to account for how he does proceed, for the nature of his acts of interpretation in relation to the occasions when these occur. Above all, the aim of a theory of interpretation is to specify what the psychoanalyst must know—wittingly or unwittingly—to perform such acts of interpretation. Similarly, Chomsky's transformational-generative theory is not a prescription of rules to be followed in speaking a language. It is not an account of how exactly a speaker uses rules, the mechanisms involved or steps traversed, in speaking a language. Rather it is a theory in the form of a statement of what a speaker must know—the knowledge which is the competence he must possess to do what he does—if we are to be able to account for what he does in understanding and speaking a language.

Clinicians may not focus on the thousands of details that confront them, but a scientist has no choice but to do so. In this connection, one may think of Piaget's patient examination of hundreds of samples of children's behavior and of Levi-Strauss's examination of hundreds of myths—their detailed accounts of these are very hard on the reader to be sure, but productive nevertheless. It is well to keep in mind Freud's own labors (1900) and his comment about Hildebrandt that he

> is unquestionably right in asserting that we should be able to explain the genesis of every dream-image if we devote enough time and trouble to tracing its origin. He speaks of this as "an exceedingly laborious and thankless task. For as a rule it ends in hunting out every kind of utterly worthless psychical event from the remotest corners of the chambers of one's memory, and in drag-

> ging to light once again every kind of completely indifferent moment of the past from the oblivion in which it was buried in the very hour, perhaps, after it occurred." I can only regret that this keen-sighted author allowed himself to be deterred from following the path which had this inauspicious beginning; if he had followed it, it would have led him to the very heart of the explanation of dreams [p. 19f.].

It is possible that psychoanalysis as science suffers from its relative lack of specification of detail; especially our case histories, and there are relatively few of these, tend to be writ in broad outline. Our generalizations, in their dependence on brief vignettes and illustrations and their distance from the mass of data in which the psychoanalyst is actually immersed, risk for these reasons alone rejection as banal or incredible. It may be, of course, that the unit in understanding the psychoanalyst's act of interpretation will not involve the analysand's single sentence or utterance. The symbolic form the psychoanalyst understands might better be conceived as created session by session rather than sentence by sentence; the boundaries or pauses that mark semi-cadences or cadences as occurring at the end of sessions rather than as periods or semicolons; the syntax as that of discourse rather than of sentence. Even if this were so, the symbolic form created in a session or a number of sessions must still have its structure and therefore its parts and their organization.

The objection by a practising psychoanalyst, that he does not notice these exotic linguistic minutiae, has the same status (that is, not very much) for the enterprise of formulating a theory of interpretation, as the objection of the language-speaking and language-understanding citizen, that he certainly does not know and cannot even comprehend the intricate rules of transformational-generative linguistic theory, has for the enterprise of developing a theory that will account for that citizen's fantastically creative competence in speaking and understanding language.

The Knowledge that Makes Interpretation Possible

What is the competence or knowledge that we must assume to account for the psychoanalyst's ability to interpret or understand? To what extent can it be stated as an internalized body of linguistic or semiotic classifications, operations, rules, principles? These are exactly the questions I wish to address; they should not be prejudged. In this chapter I shall merely sketch in a somewhat oversimplified way what kind of linguistic and semiological knowledge it seems probable to assume a psychoanalyst possesses.

I postulate that the psychoanalyst possesses and uses in his work knowledge that may be described in a theory of language and symbolic systems. The empirical question, which calls for further investigation, then becomes: To what extent is it this knowledge that constitutes the psychoanalyst's competence, that he uses to make interpretations, that enables him to perform acts of interpretation? In other words, can we explain in part at least (and to what extent) the kinds of interpretations the psychoanalyst makes, and even how and when he makes them, by a theory that specifies (with increasing precision and explicitness) the properties of language among all symbolic systems—and of other symbolic systems especially to the extent it can be demonstrated that these are dependent upon or related to language?

To make an interpretation of a symbolic object, the psychoanalyst must understand how the symbolic object has been constructed. That is, to understand the relation between a symbolic object and its meaning, the psychoanalyst must in some way be able to reconstruct how and what operations have been used upon what linguistic materials related in what way to each other to make a symbolic object that evokes the meaning for which it stands. Freud (1900) knew this and based his major work upon this kind of formulation.[30]

30. See Edelson (1972).

The question of the relation between a symbolic object and its meaning is logically prior to the one the psychoanalyst as clinician is focally aware of asking: Toward what end, to create what effect, to bring about what consequence, has the symbolic object been constructed and used? There are two very different meanings of "meaning" here, although the psychoanalyst is likely to consider either (1) the reconstruction of the relation between the symbolic object and that for which it stands or (2) the answer to questions concerning the suasive effects of the symbolic object (the uses to which it is put) as *the* discovery of the meaning of the symbolic object. At the same time, he is often relatively unaware of passing from one sense of "meaning" to the other.

Synonymous, Anomalous, and Ambiguous Sentences

A proposition is a conception or thought, which has a minimum of two elements (both abstractions): a subject, which is what the proposition is about, and a predicate, which relates at least one other idea or concept to the idea or concept of the subject.

A sentence is a linguistic object, which satisfies certain linguistic rules for its organization. (An utterance may or may not be a sentence.) There are different types of sentences: assertions, questions, commands, etc.; however, the sense of a sentence is a proposition or, if it has more than one sense, its senses are propositions.

The same proposition may be represented by more than one sentence. (There is more than one way to say something. The same thought may be realized in different forms.) Such sentences are synonymous. The degree of synonymity of two sentences, each of which represents more than one proposition, is the number of propositions represented by one that are also represented by the other.

One sentence may represent a combination of a number of propositions, as we shall observe in the analysis of "The Snow Man." Also, a sentence may represent no proposition;

such a sentence has no sense or is anomalous. A sentence may represent more than one proposition (it has alternative senses). Such a sentence is the number of ways ambiguous as the number of propositions it can represent.[31]

Sentences are linguistic objects that have some intrinsic properties not depending on their utterance and remaining invariant no matter how the sentence is uttered or performed. For the present, let us slide over a number of difficulties and say that any proposition represented by a sentence (the *sense* of the sentence) is such a property.[32]

Linguistic Competence

For the reader who is interested, this section contains a somewhat technical discussion of the nature of linguistic theory and competence, according to Chomsky, and a definition of symbolic *representation* based on this theory. Following this discussion, in the next section, the important difference between *representation* and *presentation* is explicated.

The relation of sound and meaning in a symbolic representation is arbitrary. One set of rules governs the combination of phonemes. (Each phoneme is defined by a cluster of distinctive phonological features.) Another set of rules, independent of the set governing the combination of phonemes, governs the combination of semantic elements (morphemes or words) which constitute the propositions represented by sentences. (Each word is defined by a cluster of semantic features or semantic markers.) But the *relation between sound and meaning* is mediated by the rule-governed

31. For a more detailed and somewhat different discussion of types of propositions, types of sentences, and the relation between propositions and sentences, see Katz, 1972, especially pp. 120–27.

32. Psychoanalyst and analysand are often confronted by a fascinating problem: What intervenes or what happens to change—and in what way—a sentence that has been constructed by the analysand between his realization of the sentence (even his preconscious realization of it) and his actual performance or utterance of it. Something like this problem is what Balkanyi (1964, 1968) discussed under the rubric "verbalization."

transformation of syntactic forms. (The structure of a sentence is its syntactic pattern or organization as this is revealed by syntactic analysis, using syntactic categories each of whose members is ultimately defined by a cluster of syntactic features.)

The surface structure of an observable sentence as a concatenation or string of sounds or phonemes does not directly reflect the meaning of the sentence. This structure is not the same that the sentence as a concatenation of semantic elements would have if it were unambiguously to represent the proposition (or in their entirety the combination of propositions) that constitutes its sense. This second structure is the deep structure of the sentence.

An ambiguous sentence has one surface structure but as many different deep structures as it has senses. Similarly, the surface structures of fully synonymous sentences may be different but these sentences share the same deep structure.

Interpretation of the meaning of a concatenation of sounds or phonemes is made possible by knowledge of those rule-governed operations that have transformed the syntactic deep structure underlying the concatenation of words into the syntactic structure underlying the concatenation of phonemes while holding invariant the sense of the sentence. Transformational rules operate not on single syntactic categories (as do the rules that generate deep structures) but on concatenations of syntactic categories.

In fact, the possibility of interpretation also depends on knowledge of the rule-governed operations that generate deep structures. A deep structure is generated by a rule-governed combination of syntactic categories, related to each other both sequentially and hierarchically. The syntactic category "sentence" is formed by the operation of substitution. By rule, two syntactic categories "noun phrase" and "verb phrase" are combined and "sentence" may be substituted for this combination. "Noun phrase," similarly, is formed by the operation of substitution. The two syntactic categories "determiner" and "noun" are combined by a rule, which indicates that this combination and "noun phrase" may substitute for each other. "Noun phrase" and "verb phrase" and also "determiner" and "noun" are related sequentially; but "sentence," "noun phrase," and "noun" are related hierarchically.

After a series of such operations, a final string of categories is formed. Each such category, through still other kinds of operations, is transformed into a particular cluster of syntactic features. These features govern which members of categories in final strings can be combined with each other.

Only certain of such operations as deletion, substitution, expansion, condensation, addition, and permutation can be used to form such final strings. Others can be used to transform deep structures into surface structures.

The entire hierarchy formed by these operations is a necessary and sufficient structure for a sentence which unambiguously represents a proposition. That is, at another level of analysis, a word can be substituted for each one of these clusters of syntactic features in the final string. The words combined in just this order constitute the sense of the sentence, the proposition it represents. These hierarchical structures are the deep structure of language. They are forms governed entirely by the requirement to represent the sense of a sentence, whose syntactic analysis therefore involves an order of syntactic categories exactly paralleled by just that order of words which combined concept by concept in that sequence compose the proposition represented by the sentence.

The surface structures of representational language, on the other hand, are governed by requirements for representability, usually (but not necessarily) in sound. Syntactic strings are generated so that substituting clusters of phonological features for clusters of syntactic features to construct a concatenation of phonemes results in a sentence that may be comprehensibly uttered.

All this has been described elsewhere in greater detail and

more precisely by Chomsky and his colleagues.[33] The important point is that to understand symbolic representation requires a knowledge of the rule-governed operations that have transformed sense-bearing forms into sound-bearing forms, sense and sound having no other and no intrinsic relation.

The psychoanalyst's skill in interpreting a symbolic representation includes the knowledge of the way one form, serving one kind of function (the direct representation of meaning), is transformed into another form, serving another function (fulfillment of requirements for representability in a concrete objectified medium), in such a way that the sense of the symbolic object remains invariant. This skill makes it possible for him to recognize, for example, the degree to which a symbolic representation is ambiguous and the degree to which two or more symbolic representations are synonymous.

The sine qua non of an act of interpretation of symbolic representations (when meanings are combined by rules that are independent of the rules that combine the elements of a concrete medium) is to be able to reconstruct the transformations or operations by which the forms that bear meaning have been transformed (in ways that conserve meaning) into forms that can be objectified or incarnated in a concrete medium. Clearly, for example, a psychoanalyst makes use of this aspect of linguistic competence in interpreting dreams (see Edelson, 1972), as we shall make use of it in interpreting "The Snow Man."

Representation and Presentation

Linguistic materials may be used to construct two kinds of symbolic objects: representations and presentations. A representation is related to its meaning by "rules." A presentation is related to its meaning by "resemblance."

33. See references cited in footnotes 5 and 6, above.

A representation symbolizes meanings according to the rules that constitute language. A representation is "transparent." It calls no attention to itself. We see or hear through it to the meaning it represents.

A presentation (Langer, 1953) symbolizes meanings by calling attention to and exploiting the attributes and relational properties of symbolic entities as objects in themselves. Such objects include linguistic entities (phonemes, syntactic structures, words and sentences) belonging to any one of the subsystems or components of language (phonological, syntactic, semantic). Each of these components is defined by a different level of analysis of language.

In presentation, the attributes and relational properties of the entities of one realm (symbolic objects belonging to the realm constituted by a symbolic system) analogically or metaphorically reflect the attributes and relational properties of the entities of another realm (e.g., physical or psychic, external or inner, reality). In other words, the entities of one realm belong to the *same class* of attributes or relations as the entities of another realm. They may, therefore, evoke (rather than represent according to rule) these attributes or relational properties. Presentation is metaphor; to present a conception of reality, one may make use of resemblances between some aspect of that reality and aspects of symbolic objects and the systems to which these belong.[34]

34. Peirce (1893–1910) saw that the use of mathematics in science—ordinarily thought of as at an opposite pole from metaphorical presentation—is just such a process.

> This capacity of revealing unexpected truth is precisely that wherein the utility of algebrical formulae consists, so that the iconic character is the prevailing one [p. 106]. The reasoning of mathematicians will be found to turn chiefly upon the use of likenesses, which are the very hinges of the gates of their science. The utility of likenesses to mathematicians consists in their suggesting in a very precise way, new aspects of supposed states of things. . . . When, in algebra, we write equations under one another in a regular array, especially when we put resembling letters for corresponding coefficients, the array is an icon. . . . This [example] is an icon, in that it makes quantities look alike which are in analogous relations to the problem. In fact, every algebraical

"Presentation" should be distinguished from the process—characteristic of an early phase in the development of the symbolic function—in which there is a failure to differentiate a symbol from its meaning. An example of this kind of failure is the treatment of the word "dog" as if it were the physical object "dog" or itself possessed the attributes of such a physical object, or as if it were one of the intrinsic properties of the physical object. I think that what I have called "presentation" is a specialized mode of symbolic functioning in its own right, not simply a regression to an earlier or debased form of mature symbolic functioning. It is this mode of symbolic functioning (presentation) that should be connoted by the terms "primary process," as "representation" should be connoted by the terms "secondary process." [35]

Examples of presentation are to be found throughout Freud's writings. Any manifest dream is a presentation (not a representation, as he termed it) of latent thoughts. The presentation in a dream of the idea "it is absurd" by an absurd arrangement of symbolic entities (we know it is an absurd arrangement because we know the rules for constructing an arrangement that would make sense) is one example (Freud, 1900). The omission of two numbers from a sequence of numbers to present the meaning "a wish to remove or get rid of" is another (Freud, 1901); we recognize the omission because we know the rules for constructing a sequence in this symbolic system. We know the system of rules. Further, we know that these rules are capable of generating symbolic forms that are ambiguous, deviant, and anomalous. Our knowledge enables us to recognize these

---

> equation is an icon, in so far as it *exhibits,* by means of the algebraical signs (which are not themselves icons), the relations of the quantities concerned (p. 106 f.).

See also the discussion by Buchanan (1929) of poetry and mathematics, and the discussion by Black (1962) of models and metaphors.

35. For a somewhat different and the more traditional view, see Freud (1915) and Werner (1955).

characteristics. It is important to note that it is only because these symbolic entities are generated by such symbolic systems that they can be used in the ways illustrated by the examples to *present* as well as to *represent* meanings.

It should be clear that presentational symbolic objects signify what they stand for by virtue of what they are. A symbolic object is a physical object as well as a symbolic object. As a whole, it (and also any part of it) has observable characteristics that may be described or named. When the name of such a characteristic is also part of the symbolic significance of the object—what it signifies or stands for—then the symbolic object is to that extent a presentation.

It follows then that presentation cannot simply be the same as failure to differentiate signifier from signified. Resemblance between a symbolic object and its significance or what it evokes is not the same as identity or even partial identify of signifier and signified. Presentations are susceptible to analysis at different levels. The observable presentation by some property or properties of the *manifest* form can be differentiated from presentation that depends upon the deep sense-bearing form.[36]

The deep sense-bearing form may be the kind that underlies linguistic representations. One can state then in some cases—when sense is the kind of meaning or significance at issue—that the *name* of the property presented may be found as a word or a number of words in the deep sense-bearing form. And also the name of the property itself may be related (hierarchically, sequentially or as part of a rule-governed context, or by shared class membership) to another name and that name to still another name before one reaches through a reconstruction of such a chain the name that is found in the deep sense-bearing form. Freud (1900)

36. For example, the manifest dream and latent dream-thoughts. Freud (1900) discussed the means of representation in dreams (I would speak of presentation) and repeatedly (pp. 49, 574, 617) equated thoughts or ideas—and therefore of course latent thoughts—with verbal forms (again, he refers to "verbal presentations," where I would speak of "verbal representations").

has described this in considerable detail, especially in connection with the rebus model for the interpretation of dreams (Edelson, 1972).

Our "interpretations" of "The Snow Man" will demonstrate that a symbolic object may be both representational and presentational. Perhaps most symbolic objects are. In any event, in a symbolic object, these two aspects may support or complement each other. That suggests there could be symbolic objects in which representational and presentational aspects conflict with (or even are unrelated to) each other.

Music is probably the best example of a symbolic object that is pure presentation. Music makes use of all the operations of language—deletion, substitution, expansion, condensation, addition, permutation—and its entities are related hierarchically, sequentially, and by similarity just as are the entities of language. However, its distinctiveness is in its use of just those materials of language—for example, pitch and ordered sequences of pitch and rhythm—that are not required to represent propositions. Musical events resemble, have the same properties as, or are metaphorically related to the inner states they signify or evoke (Langer, 1953; Meyer, 1956).

The characteristics of a symbolic object may result from the exploitation of any linguistic resource. Such characteristics may arise from the nature of the medium used, or from the choices made in the construction of the symbolic object whenever these choices are optional—that is, when a particular operation, arrangement, or selection is one of a number of possibilities any one of which could have been used to represent a particular sense. Whenever an operation is used that is not obligatory with respect to the representation of sense, and especially when this operation results in an ordered or patterned event, the probability is high that the operation serves the construction of a presentation rather than a representation.

For example, as we shall observe in our study of "The Snow Man," an operation may generate a pattern of similar or contrasting phonemes, words, or syntactic categories which might then signify connection or opposition. Or an identifiable sequence of alterations in the arrangement of phonemes, words, or syntactic categories might signify intensity, excitement, tension, or relaxation. Either the operation or its effects may be named or described. Such a name or description may constitute the significance or meaning—or be part of the significance—of a symbolic object.

Other linguistic resources that may be exploited to construct a presentation include deviance (both qualitative and quantitative), anomaly, ambiguity, and semantic density.[37]

Qualitative deviance is a deviance from the rules that govern the construction of a sentence as symbolic representation. Such deviance—depending on its degree (Chomsky, 1961, 1965)—may result in a semi-sentence (Katz, 1964) or an anomalous sentence (Katz, 1972). An absurd utterance may signify absurdity just as "an absurd dream" may signify that "absurd" is part of the latent thought-content signified by the dream.[38]

Quantitative deviance implies a normative or statistical basis for comparison. It is an unusual degree of recursion or repetition—an unusually frequent or infrequent usage of a particular syntactic transformation, phoneme or class of phonemes, word or class of words; for example, as we shall see, in "The Snow Man," the selection of monosyllabic words and the lack of evaluative adjectives signify bareness and reality as it is. Recursiveness itself, as we shall see when we examine "The Snow Man," may signify length or distance.

Neither qualitative nor quantitative deviance necessarily

37. See, e.g., Chatman, 1971; Chatman and Levin, 1967; Freeman, 1970; Greenberg, 1966; and Sebeok, 1960.

38. For a treasure of examples of presentational devices, see Freud (1900) especially the section "The Means of Representation in Dreams," pp. 310–38 (where he, of course, is using "representation" as I am using "presentation").

imply by their presence anything about the degree of comprehensibility of a linguistic object. If sentences were embedded by the recursive application of a syntactic transformation over and over again (a quantitative deviance), the resulting linguistic object might well be incomprehensible, even though no qualitative deviance is involved and no rule of language has been violated. Similarly, comprehensible metaphors may involve sentences with some degree of qualitative deviance.

Ambiguity may signify an unresolved process, complexity, duality, confusion, or suspense. If the number of propositions represented by a single sentence or the number of propositions represented by a given number of sentences is high, then density, depth, difficulty, or tortuosity may be signified; if low, shallowness, directness, simplicity, or emptiness may be signified.

The psychoanalyst's skill in interpreting a presentation depends upon his sensitivity to the possibilities of metaphor, his responsiveness to resemblance and particularly his readiness to perceive the unexpected similarity, and his capacity to detect patterns, arrangements, and significant form. If these are the characteristics of a poet, then at least to this extent the psychoanalyst must be a poet.

The psychoanalyst's act of interpretation of a symbolic presentation requires that he be able to shift from a focal awareness of the sense represented by a linguistic object to a focal awareness of the linguistic object itself, to the symbolic object now become opaque rather than transparent. Also, that he then be able to describe the symbolic object aptly with at least an adequate apprehension of nuance and to discover just those characteristics of the symbolic object that constitute its significance or meaning. Since in these acts he is not guided by rules, it might be stated that he imposes an interpretation upon a presentation, whereas he understands a representation.

His skill then in interpreting a presentation must include a knowledge of the criteria of economy, plausibility, and coherence with regard to the relation of his interpretation of a symbolic presentation to the context of that presentation, both immediate and extended, and also with regard to the relation of the meanings his interpretation imposes upon the *presentation* to those meanings *represented* perhaps by the same symbolic object.

6: *The Meanings of "Meaning"*

As we shall observe, language in "The Snow Man" has many kinds of meaning. So does language in the psychoanalytic hour. At the level of deep structure, we are given the syntactic information required to interpret the semantic sense of language—its *cognitive* or propositional aspect, which remains invariant under transformational operations that generate surface structures. Propositions may be "about" any aspect of reality, including imaginary realities (a proposition may have no observable referent) and also language itself. (Language about language may be difficult to recognize as such; it often comes masquerading in other guises.)

Because of his linguistic competence, the psychoanalyst is able to reconstruct this level of language. Therefore, he knows—although he may not know how or even that he knows—what propositions are presupposed and what propositions are entailed or implied by any utterance on linguistic grounds alone. Investigation of this competence and what it contributes to clinical skill is logically prior to concern with empathy and intuition.

Some of the embedded kernel sentences belonging to the deep structure of "The Snow Man" (for example, those resulting in adjectives or adjectival phrases in the surface structure), can be regarded as presuppositions (that "the time is long," that "the pine-trees have boughs," that "the glitter is distant," that "the sun causes the glitter," and that "the leaves are few") of the principal assertions of the poem (the matrix sentences).[39] A psychoanalyst's act of interpreta-

39. See Chapter 10.

tion is often preceded by a sudden shift of focus from an assertion by the analysand to something odd, questionable, or not actually known by the psychoanalyst prior to this utterance, which is given as presupposition in the assertion. Analysand: "My mother's first husband used to visit us." Psychoanalyst (to himself): "What's that he said? I didn't know his mother was married more than once." In less obvious examples, the psychoanalyst may ask himself: "What does he mean by that? But can that be so?" In other words, the psychoanalyst does not take for granted information that is presupposed, as the analysand's "slipping in" this information as presupposition in an assertion might ordinarily in other situations lead an interpreter of the utterance to do.

Katz (1972) distinguishes between *presupposition,* which is part of the deep structure of a sentence, and *presumption,* which is "something the hearer is entitled to take the speaker to believe by virtue of the manner in which the speaker has chosen to express what he or she wants to say" (p. 428). In other words, presumptions are conveyed by surface form. In Katz's example, "Will you pass the dessert?" and "Won't you pass the dessert?" both have the same deep structure. However, the second, unlike the first, "conveys the speaker's presumption that the person to whom his request is addressed has some reason for wanting to withhold the dessert from him" (p. 428). Many interpretations the psychoanalyst makes concerning the analysand's images and conceptions of the psychoanalyst follow from the psychoanalyst's understanding of the presumptions the analysand conveys by the way he chooses to say what he wants to say. Here, we are in the realm of what Katz terms *rhetoric.* The province of rhetoric is that meaning—which is other than the cognitive sense represented by deep structure—conveyed by the choice of a particular surface structure.

At the level of surface structure, we are given the syntactic information required to construct a phonological representation or presentation. The exact form of this representation or presentation (compared to some paraphrase of it, whose cognitive sense is similar or identical)—ultimately, the particular arrangement of phonemes, which may also be analyzed as an arrangement of syntactic and semantic units—is a result of choices. These choices are (a) from among syntactic transformations and (b) from among words each one belonging to a set of words with similar senses, sharing distinctive semantic features or semantic markers. These choices may be used to evoke, convey, or objectify other kinds of meaning, and to support cognitive meaning.[40]

When we speak of the *emotive* or evaluative meaning of language, we allude to those linguistic features and their deployment that evoke a *conception of an attitude* toward a proposition—the cognitive sense that a linguistic form represents or presents.

The idea or conception of this attitude is represented or presented solely because particular linguistic choices have been made in constructing a linguistic form that is only one way among many to represent or present the proposition or cognitive sense. However, the attitude, while intrinsic in the language itself, is attributed to the maker or user of the linguistic form. The decision whether or not this is the "real" attitude of the maker or user of a linguistic form may depend on inferences from paralinguistic or nonlinguistic data which, as actual aspects of an immediate, existent affective state, are indices rather than symbols of an attitude.

The recognition of attitudes conveyed by nuances of linguistic choice is one kind of clinical skill the psychoanalyst should possess. Decisions concerning the authenticity of such attitudes, logically secondary to their recognition, are based on criteria of congruity with attitudes inferred from indices to which the psychoanalyst is responsive. His sensitivity to these indices may involve a somewhat different kind of clinical skill.

The language chosen conveys an evaluation of the proposition or cognitive sense, an estimation of its significance, a

40. However, see footnote 42, below.

conception of what dispositions to act are implied supposing that action were to be governed by such a proposition and the intensity of this evaluation or disposition—all from the point of view of the maker or user of the linguistic form. Another way to state what we mean by the emotive meaning of particular language would be: a conception of the putative state of the maker or user of such language.

Since value is not only a question of cathexis but of the relative degree of cathexis, then a deployment of linguistic features that foregrounds, focuses upon, or emphasizes one element or relation of elements among others makes some aspect of the sense more important than another or, in other words, distributes value. The psychoanalyst's response to and use of strategies of syntax should therefore be as critical to his act of interpretation as his response to and use of semantic strategies. (A discussion of displacement in these terms would be fruitful.)

Knowledge of how deployment of particular linguistic resources evokes emotive meaning is essential to the psychoanalyst's interpretation of an analysand's affects (including anxiety) and value attitudes (including moral value attitudes).

When we speak of the *conative,* suasive, or incitive meaning of language, we allude to those linguistic features and their deployment that evoke a *conception of intentions* toward some other, who is the one addressed.

The idea or conception of this intention is represented or presented solely because particular linguistic choices have been made in constructing a linguistic form that is only one way among many to represent or present a proposition or cognitive sense. However, the intention, while intrinsic in the language itself, is attributed to the maker or user of the linguistic form.

Decisions about the actuality, authenticity, or success of such intentions have the same status as decisions about the actuality of attitudes just discussed. Whether or not a putative intention to maintain a state or to bring about a change of state in another is in actuality realized is contingent upon many factors in a situation including nonsymbolic conditions. The question of outcome does not bear upon the status of a conative meaning intrinsic in such linguistic forms as commands, for example.

The language chosen conveys an attitude toward and an idea of the other, a conception of the relation of the maker or user of a particular linguistic form to the recipient of it (for example, formal or informal, superior and inferior), and a conception of some contingent act by, or state of, the other for which the linguistic form may serve as occasion by virtue of its symbolic rather than intrinsic efficacy.[41]

An appreciation of the linguistic resources for evoking conative meaning is essential to the psychoanalyst's interpretation of the analysand's motives, especially as these are directed to the psychoanalyst.

We may also speak of the phatic and poetic meanings of language.[42] When we speak of the *phatic* meaning of language, we allude to those linguistic features and their deployment that evoke a conception of a system of social interaction and of the process of, and the obstacles to, transmission of a linguistic form within such a system. These features and their deployment are designed to control the

41. Loewenstein (1956) has described the aim of psychoanalytic interpretation as the translation of conative meanings of language (what he calls the appeal function) into cognitive and emotive meanings (what he calls cognitive-expressive functions).

42. The extent to which emotive and conative meanings are an aspect of the deep structure level of language (e.g., questions, commands) and to what extent an aspect of the surface structure level (e.g., that aspect Katz [1972] distinguishes from phonology, semantics, and syntax as the rhetorical component of language) is a matter for investigation. While phatic and poetic meanings may be primarily determined by the generation of surface structures, the poetic function especially—involving as it does integration and synthesis of all levels and components of language—could be more complicated. See Jakobson (1960) for a discussion of what he calls six functions of verbal communication (referential, metalingual, emotive, conative, phatic, and poetic) with special emphasis on consideration of the poetic function. His definitions of these terms differ in some critical respects from mine.

effectiveness of transmission within an interactional system according to that conception. Examples are: redundancy in language; constraints upon the use of certain transformations and especially the recursive use of such transformations to avoid strains upon memory or other capacities; constraints upon selection of words that may offend or result in disruption of contact; language that establishes, checks on or monitors, and maintains the contact between the members of an interacting system; language that mobilizes and maintains attention, that is designed to create anticipation, suspense, and surprise, or to arouse, to frustrate, and ultimately to satisfy expectations.

Interpretation of resistance and defense depends especially upon the psychoanalyst's witting or unwitting awareness of the way language is used to convey phatic meaning.

When we speak of the *poetic* meaning of language, we allude to those linguistic features and their deployment that evoke a conception of, and that are designed to control according to that conception, the relation between a linguistic form and its interpreter. Such selections and combinations of linguistic resources enhance the value of, and direct the attention of the interpreter to, the linguistic object itself, to its various characteristics, to the signifier rather than the signified. These linguistic enhancements of the symbolic object enable the interpreter to recognize presentational as well as representational aspects of a linguistic form, and also to recognize the set of occasions or events to which a particular linguistic object belongs and therefore to realize what modes of attending he should appropriately bring to it.

The modes of attending to or processing language used by the psychoanalyst, the peruser of newspaper headlines, the student of theoretical physics, the devout participant in litany, the auditor of orally transmitted myth, and the reader of poetry are, as we know, different in some important ways and also alike in some important ways. However, such differences and likenesses among modes of attending await careful definition.

Poetic meaning involves synthetic functioning. The greater degree of integration, concentration, and coherence of many kinds of meaning, of representational and presentational aspects, of relations among phonological, syntactic, and semantic levels, tends to remove the linguistic object from the realm of casual utterance and to make it memorable—to endow it with some degree of permanence. Poetic meaning essentially represents and (perhaps primarily) presents a conception of organization or of form itself (including complexly interarticulated hierarchical structures), which is exemplified by particular linguistic forms resulting from strategies of selection and combination of linguistic resources.

Awareness of the analysand's capacity to organize language poetically (in the sense I have given to the word) and the occasions upon which the analysand does so organize it enters importantly into the interpretation of dreams and symptoms and other phenomena involving primary process as well as synthetic ego-functioning, and enters also into the evaluation of the modes and qualities of, and changes in, symbolic functioning.

The interpretation of transference depends upon the psychoanalyst's ability to understand and integrate cognitive, emotive, conative, phatic, and poetic meanings of language.

7: *The Interpretation of Transformation*

"Transformation," which has a key role in Chomsky's transformational-generative theory, is a basic idea in both science and art. This idea is that one or more aspects of an identifiable hypothetical or observable entity may change, while one or more aspects remain invariant through such change. The changes result from discoverable, specifiable operations. Knowledge of these operations is necessary for a comprehension of the entity resulting from transformation. Such knowledge makes possible the recovery of the entity as it was prior to change and the detection of what has remained invariant through change.

In science, invariance through change is essentially what is meant by lawfulness. In the study of man, invariance through change is the idea underlying "motive" (as when we say the motive remains the same through a thousand variations in behavior) as well as "rule-governed action" (as when we say role-performance remains essentially the same despite endless variation in personality as many different persons succeed each other in occupying the same role).

In music, "theme and variations" is an important principle in constructing a composition or part of a composition. As quintessential examples, one may study Bach's Goldberg Variations (in which a bass line or harmonic structure remains relatively invariant), Beethoven's Diabelli Variations, and Brahms' Variations and Fugue on a Theme by Handel or Variations on a Theme by Paganini. Looking at Bach's Prelude I in C from The Well-Tempered Clavichord, Book I, one may study what remains invariant and what changes, if Chopin's Etude No. 1, Opus 10, is regarded as a transformation of the same musical "idea." Similarly, a set of at least forty-eight transformational operations is available to a composer writing serial music in the twentieth century; the sequential arrangement of a set of twelve tones remains invariant through all such transformations. A composer may choose from among a number of dimensions—harmony, melody, rhythm, timbre, dynamics—what he will vary and what hold constant. He may even vary continuously but in such a sequence of carefully minimal alterations that the change from one step to another is easily reconstructed, although the final entity seems to bear little if any resemblance to the first. Freud describes such "chains" in the construction of dreams.

In linguistics, hypothetical deep syntactic structures, which order the relations of elements in a sentence in such a way that its cognitive meaning is determinate and unambiguous, are transformed into surface structures. Cognitive meaning remains invariant. Surface structures order the relation of elements in a sentence as it is to be or may be performed or given a phonological representation.

Similarly, the psychoanalyst, using linguistic tools, may study transformations through a series of utterances in the psychoanalytic situation to make explicit how he knows that: (1) the analysand represents or presents the same conception when he talks about his relation with his father, mother, brother, sister, teacher, boss, or psychoanalyst; (2) the analysand represents or presents conflicts around oral, anal, or phallic wishes, no matter how distant the subject matter appears from such wishes (defenses, like the operations of the dream-work and joke-work, are clearly transformational operations); (3) the analysand represents or presents the same phantasy or parts of the same phantasy in a variety of ways (reports of actions, thoughts, or feelings in or out of the psychoanalytic session; descriptions of physical or other symptoms; or accounts of dreams); or (4) the analysand has changed in some ways and remained the same in other ways, when the outcome of psychoanalysis is evaluated.

The psychoanalyst should study linguistic data in order to be able to make the following knowledge, which he possesses, explicit.

First, the psychoanalyst may respond to the ambiguity of an utterance, which is repeated either in the same immediate linguistic context or in many different contexts.

> Case I. (1) Transformations leading to surface-structure and phonological representation and (2) the immediate linguistic context of an utterance remain invariant as (3) deep syntactic-structure and cognitive meaning vary. (One utterance that is ambiguous—that has more than one cognitive meaning—occurs over and over in the same context.)
>
> Case II. (1) Transformations leading to surface-structure and phonological representation remain invariant as (2) deep syntactic-structure and cognitive meaning and (3) the immediate linguistic context vary. (The same ambiguous utterance occurs in different contexts.)

In Case I, the psychoanalyst may not realize for some time that the utterance is ambiguous. However, since he possesses linguistic competence, he may eventually—as the utterance is repeated over and over—become aware of its ambiguity. Even if it has only one possible meaning in the context in which it is repeated, in other contexts it would have other meanings. The psychoanalyst may imagine these other contexts and wonder if the analysand opposes placing the utterance in them. The psychoanalyst may speculate about resistance and repression.

In Case II, the psychoanalyst may realize more quickly with the changes in context that the utterance is ambiguous. The significance of the different meanings of the utterance is reason, warrant, or justification for its repetition, which also emphasizes its importance, in different contexts. Even if the contexts do not suffice to disambiguate the utterance, the repetition is warranted by the weight of meanings—the "multiple determination"—of the utterance; the psychoanalyst may be moved to offer one or more of the meanings of the utterance in an "interpretation."

Second, the psychoanalyst may respond to what I shall loosely call expressive variations, what the analysand emphasizes or focuses upon or what may be presumed about him (his beliefs, attitudes, feelings, and intentions) from the *way* he says what he says (rather than *what* he says), in utterances made either in the same immediate linguistic context over and over or in many different contexts. These variations convey possible conative and emotive meanings, and may evoke in the psychoanalyst, for example, a sense of the analysand's ambivalence or the vicissitudes of the transference.

> Case III. (1) Deep syntactic-structure and cognitive meaning and (2) the immediate linguistic context remain invariant as (3) transformations leading to surface-structure and phonological representation vary. (Different ways of saying the same thing, probably conveying, for example, different conative and emotive meanings, occur in the same context.)
>
> Case IV. (1) Deep syntactic-structure and cognitive meaning remain invariant as (2) transformations leading to surface-structure and phonological representation and (3) the immediate linguistic context vary. (Different ways of saying the same thing, probably conveying, for example, different conative and emotive meanings, occur in different contexts.)

In Case III, the psychoanalyst's attention may be focused upon the context. What is it about this context that is the reason for, warrants, or justifies such expressive variation in utterances whose cognitive meaning is the same—that (in other words) arouses such different attitudes toward the same conception?

In Case IV, the weight, significance, or value of the conative and emotive meanings conveyed—the emphasis upon these—is reason, warrant, or justification for the repetition in many contexts of utterances having the same cognitive meaning. The psychoanalyst may make inferences concerning the strength or intensity of the differences or conflicts among attitudes, beliefs, feelings, or intentions mobilized by the same conception.

Third, the psychoanalyst may hear, as in Case V, different utterances in the same context (e.g., all the different utterances that may occur in the immediate linguistic context "mother," or "angry," or "five-years-old"), which he may conceptualize under the rubric "working through." Or he may hear, as in Case VI, an insistently repeated utterance appearing in a variety of contexts. Such an utterance may have peremptory, periodic qualities which evoke in the psychoanalyst such notions as "impulse," "drive-derivative," or "unconscious."

> Case V. (1) The context remains invariant as (2) deep syntactic-structure and cognitive meaning and (3) transformations leading to surface-structure and phonological representation vary. (Different utterances occur in a repeated context.)
>
> Case VI. (1) Deep syntactic-structure and cognitive meaning and (2) transformations leading to surface-structure and phonological representation remain invariant as (3) the immediate linguistic context varies. (The same thing is said in the same way in a variety of contexts.)

8: The Interpretation of Deviance

"Rule," which like "transformation" also has a key role in Chomsky's transformational-generative linguistic theory, is similarly a basic idea in the study of art, man, and society.[43]

The idea of rule implies choice and therefore the possibility of deviance. It also may imply the possibility of *degrees* of deviance. Degrees of deviance may be defined if a theory (as in music or Chomsky's linguistics) is complex enough to include different levels of analysis, which are independent of each other; or hierarchically related categories, propositions, levels of analysis, or sets of propositions.

Freud never was able, as far as I know, to reconcile "choice"—a word he used, but mostly in passive or nominalized locutions like "the choice of a dream image" or "the image was chosen in constructing the dream," throughout *The Interpretation of Dreams*—with his ideal of a scientific, which meant to him a "deterministic," psychology. I believe one may find a way out of this difficulty by studying Talcott Parsons' voluntaristic theory of action, especially the account of it in his 1937 work *The Structure of Social Action.*

In one striking passage (1900, p. 571 f.) Freud does abandon temporarily the passive construction and describes the dreamer as an *active* agent, who, dissatisfied with the way a dream is going, is able to stop it without waking and start it again in another direction, just as a playwright may choose to give his play one ending rather than another.

The requirement for, and definition of, interpretation in relation to deviance follows from the very nature of language.

43. See, for example, Black (1962, pp. 95–139); Borger and Cioffi (1970); Louch (1966); and Winch (1958).

Language is effable. It is a device for conveying by finite means any possible meaning—an indefinite, infinite number of meanings. It is a device that, using limited resources, is capable of generating an infinite number and variety of representations of meaning.

What makes it possible to generate an infinite number of meaningful representations by finite means?

First, language consists of sets of rules. The number of such sets is limited. Each set consists of a definite, limited number of rules. There are syntactic rules, semantic rules, and phonological rules. In addition, there is a lexicon or dictionary, a compendium of meaningful elements, which over a relatively brief period of time at least may be regarded as finite in size. For any language, the range of sounds and combination of sounds from which words may be constructed, and the rules governing such construction, are also limited.

Second, the rules include recursive devices, so that the same operations (for example, those generating syntactic structures) may be repeated without limit, that is, limits that are intrinsic to the system, although, of course, limits may be imposed practically in performance by the limited extralinguistic capacities of the language user.

Third, the members of the vocabulary, finite in number, tend to have multiple potential meanings, rather than each member having a single unequivocal meaning and every possible meaning therefore having its own unique representative in the lexicon. Actual or realized meaning is the result of composition according to rules of the language, which combine the same members of the vocabulary in different ways to yield a variety of meanings. Possible meanings are excluded by context (a particular combination). Combinatory or selectional restrictions (which essentially indicate the choices that must be made among various options) are therefore critical in generating representations of unequivocal meaning.

Various uses of language also add to the capacity of language to convey an infinite number of different kinds of meanings. These uses may result in a change in language itself, in its rules or lexicon.

A user of language may violate, substitute, add or subtract rules; extend or limit the degree of recursiveness; or fail to some degree to provide contexts that exclude some number of possible meanings. Such uses yield opaque language. Opaque language requires interpretation.

In ordinary uses of language, language is transparent. Focal attention is given to the meaning of a linguistic object and only subsidiary attention to the linguistic object itself. In deviant uses, opaque language focuses attention on the linguistic object itself (whose properties, as I shall demonstrate in Part Three, may be important in *presenting* meanings).

Assume an "ideal" use of the language, in which the recursive use of operations does not result in representations exceeding in any degree the extralinguistic capacities (attention, memory, etc.) of the language user. No representation involves any degree of deviance from the rules of the language. Every context excludes all but one unique unequivocal meaning: disambiguation is complete; ambiguity or multiple meanings do not occur.

To the extent the use of language departs from this standard, interpretation is required.

The language user may choose to employ recursiveness to some degree that exceeds the extralinguistic capacities of an interpreter. An example is Henry James in his great late work.

The language user may choose to deviate from the rules of language in generating meaningful representations. He may do this in three ways, which I shall describe shortly in greater detail. One, he may extend his options beyond those permitted by the rules of the language. Two, he may impose constraints in excess of those imposed by the rules of language upon his options. These two ways of looking at linguistic deviance in poetry are employed in an interesting way by Leech in his book *A Linguistic Guide to English Poetry*. Three, he may abnegate making a choice among options (this being one way to regard ambiguous constructions); that is, he may refuse to select a context that excludes all but one cognitive meaning.

There may then be degrees of strain (the relation is between a use of language and the capacities of its interpreter); and degrees of deviance (the relation is between a use of language and the rules of language).

Modes of interpretation are used to discover reason, warrant, or justification for uses of language that involve strain or deviance. Occasionally reasons, warrants, or justifications are statements about extralinguistic conditions (physical or social) impinging coercively or quasi-coercively upon the language user. Ordinarily reasons, warrants, or justifications are statements of the way in which strain or deviance contributes to achieving an aim: that of conveying—through representation or presentation—cognitive, emotive, conative, phatic, or poetic meanings, or some combination of such meanings.

Deviance is then the critical occasion for interpretation. Deviance is implicative. It implies something about the past or future, about the significance of what has gone before or about what is to come. Since deviance is by its nature unexpected—it has no warrant in the rules of language—it instigates inquiry, retrospective and anticipatory, into the grounds for deviance. The past may be examined and re-evaluated to see if some utterance or utterances, for example, in the past may now be understood (as not understood before) to have been part of a preparation for this deviance. Some future goal may be imagined; deviance (an utterance or pattern of utterances) may be interpreted in terms of the way in which it leads to this goal. (The goal is the presentation or representation—or both—of some meaning or combination of meanings.)

A deviant utterance, which is implicative, by its nature, since it has no warrant in the rules of language, calls for resolution. Resolution occurs when deviance is interpreted, that is, when the grounds for deviance are discovered. The interpretation is the realization of an implication.

In its effect, with respect to the achievement of such a resolution, deviance may be progressive or regressive; may hold back or propel forward; delay or hasten—in part depending upon the degree of deviance and in part upon its effectiveness in instigating retrospection or anticipation or both.

It is understandable then that an act of interpretation in psychoanalysis is most likely to occur in the neighborhood of, or in relation to, linguistic deviance in the utterances of the analysand. This is a hypothesis.

Deviance may be defined with respect to four different systems of rules.

One, there is the system of rules that generates the infinite set, and all and only the members of this set, of acceptable (grammatical) sentences in a language. I shall term this system LANGUAGE.

Two, there are systems of rules that generate all the members of a finite set, and all and only members of this set, of the sentences uttered or written by one person or a particular group of persons, on one occasion or in one work, or on a specified number of occasions or in a specified number of works. For example, there are the rules generating all and only the utterances of an analysand during one session or one period of, or throughout, a psychoanalysis; or the rules generating the poem "The Snow Man," the poems in the book in which that poem appeared, the entire corpus of Wallace Stevens, the corpus of all poets sharing some significant uses of language with Stevens, or the corpus of all twentieth-century American or French or Western World poetry or prose. I shall term such a system a REALIZED LANGUAGE.

Three, there is the system of rules that governs the relation of utterances or sentences to each other. An example might be the rules concerning the permissibility of using a particular pronoun, such as "he," as the subject of one sentence that follows a sentence in which the subject is "the woman" and it is clear that both represent the same conception (the same member of the same class). Another example might concern the appropriate syntactic surface structure of the answer to a question: "Who did throw that ball?" followed by "(It was) the ball (that) was thrown by John," rather than "(It was) John (who) threw the ball"—or "What was it that John threw?" followed by "(It was) John (who) threw the ball," rather than "(It was) the ball (that) was thrown by John." I shall term such a system RULES OF DISCOURSE.

It is not clear to me at this time whether these rules are already encompassed by the system LANGUAGE. Any series of sentences may be transformed by recursive operations into one sentence using "and," "or," and "but." Rules concerning the choice of what shall be "topic" and what "comment," for example, may belong to a subset of LANGUAGE, following the suggestion of Katz (1972) who distinguishes from syntax, phonology, and semantics the subset of rules of "rhetoric."

Four, there is the system of rules or conventions that governs the relation of the use of language and some situation in which it is used. For example, the rule that is violated by a sentence or utterance "The king of France is bald," because the sentence presupposes that a king of France exists and this presupposition is not valid, or by an utterance linguistically warranting certain presumptions about the beliefs or attitudes of the speaker when these beliefs or attitudes in fact do not exist. When there is a limited, definable, practically knowable situation, with specifiable, determinable characteristics, to which a use of language may be said to be according to rule or convention acceptable or appropriate, I shall term the system of rules or conventions LANGUAGE OF SITUATION X. Obviously, the situation cannot, for practical reasons, be co-equal to "reality," for then to decide upon the acceptability or appropriateness of a sentence, one would have to have infinite knowledge.

Here we face some of the same difficulties we faced in considering whether RULES OF DISCOURSE are within, or outside of, the system LANGUAGE. One must have linguistic competence to know what a sentence or utterance presupposes or presumes or entails, or more generally what cognitive meaning a sentence has, before one can even arrive at the point of judging on the basis of a knowledge of reality or situation that there is something "wrong" with the presupposition, presumption, or cognitive meaning. The evaluation of a sentence or part of a sentence as deviant, when, for example, it is contradicted by other parts of a sentence or other sentences, also requires linguistic competence. In both cases, one must have knowledge of the rules of the semantic subset of LANGUAGE (Katz, 1972). Since the primary data of the psychoanalyst are linguistic, this competence enables him to recognize, and decide that there may be something wrong with, a presupposition or presumption.

Nor is it just a matter of deciding that there is something "wrong" about presupposition or presumption. Leech (1969, Chap. 11) describes how a poet constructs a situation, especially using words having a "pointing to" or deictic function, such as pronouns, demonstratives, and adverbs of time, place, and manner. The poet creates context—the world within the poem. It is because utterances possess *implications of context* that the analysand is able with language to construct the transference, which the psychoanalyst using linguistic competence and knowledge of the psychoanalytic situation is then able to interpret.

There are some rules or conventions, such as those governing how to talk to certain persons with certain statuses in certain places on certain occasions or what conditions must prevail to warrant the performatives discussed by Austin (1962), "I promise," "I bet," or "I marry," that do not seem to involve knowledge of all of reality, on the one hand, or knowledge only of the rules governing the construction of sentences, on the other. Regarding these, I believe one may make explicit a system of rules or conventions—LANGUAGE OF SITUATION X.

Certainly, it is important to the psychoanalyst, although he is especially interested in the nature and efficacy of psychic reality (the created context), that he be able to assess the deviance of presuppositions and presumptions particularly in relation to LANGUAGE AND THE PSYCHOANALYTIC SITUATION. However, if an individual's use of language is markedly deviant and deviant in certain ways with respect to this system, much more with respect to LANGUAGE AND REALITY, the individual is not likely to become or remain an analysand. In addition, the psychoanalyst is not likely to be able to acquire while remaining in the psychoanalytic situation the knowledge needed to assess such deviance. These considerations bear on the assessment of analyzability.

Since evaluating utterances generated by this system of rules involves other knowledge than linguistic competence, it is especially problematic; I shall do no more than note the problem here for future investigation. In general, LANGUAGE and REALIZED LANGUAGE seem to me, given the state of linguistics now, to be, as systems of rules with respect to which deviance can be defined, most promising starting points for present investigations of language and psychoanalysis.

In the case of each kind of system, one must possess or have internalized the rules of the kind of system involved to determine whether an utterance is deviant in a particular way with respect to the rules of that system. It is important to realize that an utterance which is deviant with respect to the rules of one kind of system may not be deviant with respect to another and that an utterance which is deviant in one way with respect to one system may be deviant in another way with respect to another.

I shall define three types of deviance with respect to the rules of any one of these four kinds of systems.

One, systematic or consistent, or nonsystematic or occasional violations of the rules extend the options available to a user of the language. Possibilities, alternatives, and selections are made available, transcending the constraints on these imposed by a system of rules. Here a system rules out a choice, but deviance allows it. In books on style, this is frequently called qualitative deviance. It is often typified by Dylan Thomas's "a grief ago," which according to Chomsky's theory involves a relatively small degree of deviance (violating a rule of selectional restriction that is low on the hierarchy of rules). I shall term it SYSTEMATIC (or NONSYSTEMATIC) OPTION-EXTENDING DEVIANCE.

A systematic option-extending deviance may result in a "creative" change in a language, e.g., substituting a new rule for an existing one. This kind of creativity should be distinguished not only from disorder but also—as Chomsky has—from the creativity inherent in linguistic competence: the capacity to generate an infinte number and variety of appropriate, acceptable sentences with finite means (the rules of the language). Obviously not all violations of rules are "pathological," although representations involving deviance may be assessed as "archaic" or "artistic" depending on the difficulty in comprehending their meaning and the grounds adduced to justify the deviance. Many violations are expressive; that is, they are warranted by the contribution they make to representing or presenting and conveying one or another kind of meaning. In music and poetry, different kinds of meanings are conveyed by departing unexpectedly from normative patterns. So, also, in psychoanalysis.

Two, rules are added to a system that restrict or exclude—or, from another point of view, that give special weight to some—options (operations or elements) ordinarily available to a user of the language. Deviance imposes constraints on possibilities, alternatives, or selections that are more stringent than those imposed by a system of rules. Here a system of rules allows a choice, but deviance does not permit it.

For example, syntactic transformational operations may be restricted or excluded so that only or primarily kernel sentences, or only or primarily certain kinds of syntactic structures, such as passive, genitive, or nominalizing constructions, occurring perhaps only or primarily in certain sequences or contexts, can be generated by the system. Word-formation may be restricted in such a way that only or primarily monosyllabic (or some other forms of) words are available. Vocabulary may be restricted in such a way that only or primarily a relatively small sub-set of the words available in a lexicon can be used. The selection of sounds, sound-combinations, or word-combinations may be restricted in such a way that only certain patterns of sound or accent may result. Such restrictions are apparent in the canons or rules generating any work of art, the poem "The Snow Man," the poems in the book in which that poem appeared, the entire corpus of Wallace Stevens, the corpus of all poets sharing some significant uses of language with Stevens, the corpus of another group of poets, and also the "utterances" produced by a machine. Obviously such deviance is important in any consideration of music, prose, poetry, and style, whether of an era, a group, or an individual, and especially important in considering the utterances of an analysand during one session or during one or more periods of, or throughout, a psychoanalysis.

In studies of style, this type of deviance has often been called quantitative deviance, because it results in a set of sentences or utterances generated by a REALIZED LANGUAGE that are non-deviant with respect to LANGUAGE but have features or arrangements statistically different (more or less frequent) from some hypothetical "typical" set of sentences or utterances generated by LANGUAGE or from some set of sentences or utterances generated by some other REALIZED LANGUAGE. The recognition of such deviance clearly requires comparative methodology, as used in the comparison of the work of one period with that of another, one man's style with another, or the style of a man's productions at one time in his life with those of another time. Such linguistic comparisons are strictly homologous to, if they do not indeed provide much of the data for, comparisons of the character or personality of different individuals, or the value systems of—and what is regarded as deviant in—different social systems. I shall term this type of deviance OPTION-CONTRACTING DEVIANCE.

Three, the user of a language may refuse to select among alternatives, to make certain choices. He may avoid or abnegate choice among options. The absence of a context necessary to disambiguate an ambiguous construction or a choice of a word that is capable of rendering determinate an indeterminate meaning are examples. I shall term this deviance OPTION-ABNEGATING DEVIANCE.

Leech (1969) writes of "degrees of linguistic audacity" in poetry. In discussing what I have termed OPTION-EXTENDING DEVIANCE with respect to LANGUAGE, which he calls "linguistic irregularity," he distinguishes between lexical deviation (e.g., the violation of restrictions on the operation of a rule of word-formation); syntactic deviation; phonological deviation; semantic deviation (e.g., semantic absurdities, such as may occur in metaphor); and also dialectical deviation (deviation from the standard language system of a dominant group), which one might want to consider either creative SYSTEMATIC DEVIANCE with respect to a LANGUAGE, or another LANGUAGE. He includes in this list deviation of register, the use of language in one situation that is ordinarily deemed appropriate to another particular social or communicative context or situation, or the mixing of registers, what I would term OPTION-EXTENDING DEVIANCE with respect to LANGUAGE OF SITUATION X.

For Leech, the trope in poetry is the prototype of OPTION-EXTENDING DEVIANCE with respect to LANGUAGE. Tropes include metaphor, irony, synecdoche, and also redundancy, tautology, contradiction, and other semantic oddities, absurdities, and inanities (see also Katz, 1972, for a discussion of these). According to him, tropes affect primarily deep syntactic structure and semantics, and therefore alter cognitive meaning.

The scheme in poetry, on the other hand, he describes as the prototype of OPTION-CONTRACTING DEVIANCE. Schemes include formal patterns of sound (rhyme, meter, and rhythm); figures such as alliteration, anaphora (repetition, especially initial repetition), and chiasmus (a reversal in the order of words in two otherwise parallel phrases); and, in fact, parallelism of any kind, including identical repetition, which is the limiting extreme of parallelism. Warrants for parallelism include how and what parallelism joins together in similarity or contrast, and the expectation created of a sequence and of an impending end to it. Schemes tend to affect primarily surface syntactic structure and phonology and therefore do not change cognitive meaning.

I wonder if all OPTION-EXTENDING DEVIANCE (now considered with respect to any one of the four kinds of systems of rules) affects primarily deep structure, semantics, and cognitive meaning; and if all OPTION-CONTRACTING DEVIANCE (now considered with respect to any one of the four kinds of systems of rules) affects primarily surface structure and phonology, without altering cognitive meaning. That is something to be worked out in the future.

Psychoanalysts might well eschew, temporarily at least, certain locutions in psychoanalytic theory to study and describe instead utterances in the psychoanalytic situation in terms of the type and degree of linguistic deviance manifested, and the stability or viscissitudes of such deviance. What, if any, kinds of meaning is a particular type and degree of linguistic deviance capable of conveying to the psychoanalyst? What inferences about the analysand does a particular type and degree of linguistic deviance in various contexts evoke in the psychoanalyst?

Both the psychoanalyst and the literary critic make important evaluative assessments concerning: (1) the adequacy or appropriateness of the apparent warrant, reason, or justification for deviance, and (2) the achieved balance between unusual extensions and unusual limitations of options in a particular use of language.

If the psychoanalyst automatically connects "linguistic deviance" with cognitive disorder or understands "linguistic deviance" to mean a high degree of OPTION-EXTENDING DEVIANCE with respect to LANGUAGE, he may well wonder where he is to find examples of linguistic deviance among the utterances of his analysand. For this reason, I was careful to distinguish four kinds of systems of rules and three types of deviance. Theoretically, twelve possibilities are describable.

For example, it is true that if an analysand speaks primarily in passive syntax or avoids using the pronoun "I," he may still be speaking "correct" English. These preferences may be considered features of his "style." There is no option-extending deviance, but clearly there is an option-*contracting* deviance with respect to LANGUAGE (one way of conceptualizing "style"), about which the psychoanalyst may speculate. If in a particular session, the analysand suddenly uses an active syntactic structure and the pronoun "I," he is still speaking "correct" English, but now there is an option-*extending* deviance with respect to the REALIZED LANGUAGE generating his previous utterances. Although the sentence may be "correct" English, the psychoanalyst will hear it with the little shudder of shock that accompanies an encounter with unexpected deviance.

As I suggested in Part One, interpretation in psychoanalysis as well as in the study of poetry and music could be considered the act of adducing warrants, reasons, or justifications for deviance. These, then, become the basis for "understanding" deviance.

The psychoanalyst is familiar with at least some of the functions or consequences of deviance. It focuses upon, emphasizes, and, therefore, imparts (or displaces) value or cathexis. Its novelty attracts attention and its relative opacity and complexity challenge when, arousing confusion or disorientation, they do not also repel. The economy with which deviance may connect, synthesize, and condense a multitude of meanings may be the means by which a linguistic object becomes memorable, if the meanings be grasped. Deviance is able to support a *represented* meaning by also *presenting* that meaning, but it may also mislead and deceive. A deviant utterance can provoke the listener—who may be a psychoanalyst—to try to discover through an act of imaginative reconstruction meaning he might not otherwise have sought or come to. A deviant utterance can convey to the listener—who may be a psychoanalyst—a connection or relation that might otherwise have gone unsuspected.

I postulate for future work an "interpretative competence." Two of its components at least are witting or unwitting knowledge of linguistic systems of rules and therefore the ability to recognize many kinds of linguistic deviance, and witting or unwitting knowledge of, and therefore the ability to discover, warrants, reasons, or justifications for linguistic deviance. Should I also add, as a component of interpretative competence, witting or unwitting knowledge of transformational processes, and perhaps an unusual ability to detect what is invariant through such a process of transformation?

In future work, I shall try to specify more explicitly the modes of operation or the exact operations that define this interpretative competence, and the nature of the language that calls it into action. "The nature of the language" means the relation of a use of language to one or more of the four kinds of systems of rules I have discussed. I hope also to specify obstacles that interfere with the development or the exercise of interpretative competence, as well as possible means for circumventing these obstacles.

If these goals were to be even partially achieved, we should have, if not a "theory of interpretation in psychoanalysis," at least a foundation for such a theory.

Any reader may draw upon his own experience to test the extent to which the phenomena with which the psychoanalyst is confronted can be adequately encompassed by the ideas we have so far considered and to decide upon their relevance to a consideration of acts of interpretation, both literary and psychoanalytic.

I shall end this chapter and Part Two by reminding the reader of the many times the language of poetry and the language of music have been linked in these pages. Both poetry and music are symbolic systems. We may confidently expect that we are working toward a theory of interpretation based not only upon a theory of language but upon—to use Jakobson's terminology (1960, p. 351)—a general semiotics.

We shall therefore hope eventually to discover those "pan-semiotic features" or properties (to which Jakobson alludes) that natural language shares with other symbolic systems. For such discovery, psychoanalysis is a strategic science, and the study of interpretation in psychoanalysis a critical investigation.

PART THREE

THREE INTERPRETATIONS OF A POEM AS A LINGUISTIC OBJECT

9: Psychoanalysis and Literature

An analogy exists between the reader's interpretation of a poem and the interpretation a psychoanalyst makes in the psychoanalytic situation, despite the apparent and real differences between the forms interpreted. Starting with the analogy and the differences, one may arrive at criteria for distinguishing an investigation that belongs to applied psychoanalysis, for example, the contribution psychoanalysis makes to the literary critic's attempt to interpret a poem, from an investigation that belongs to psychoanalysis proper, when the psychoanalyst is able to make a direct contribution to psychoanalytic theory or practice from the study of a work or works of art. The latter is a rare event; that it has occurred at all might be disputed, although psychoanalysts have studied: (1) the work of art as object and (2) the process by which a reader comes to understand the meaning of a work of art.[44] Such investigations may contribute to a solution of problems which are the concern of psychoanalysis proper: an adequate "theory of interpretation"; [45] and within that theory, for example, an account of metaphor.

44. For the first kind of investigation, Freud's study of the technique of joke construction (1905) is a model. In connection with the second kind of investigation, see Kris (1952) and Holland (1968a).

45. A phrase used by I. A. Richards (1925, 1929, 1936, 1955) to describe his own aims as literary critic. No psychoanalyst should fail to read Richards' empirical investigation (1929) of the obstacles that prevent readers from understanding a poem. Richards has written:

> It is an old dream that in time psychology might be able to tell us so much about our minds that we would at last become able to discover with some certainty what we mean by our words and how we mean it. An opposite or complementary dream is that . . . we may in time learn so much about words that they will tell us how our minds work (1936, p. 136).

I have been wondering, for example, whether metaphor is primarily a thing or an act—a linguistic object with unique features or immediate linguistic context, or a unique way of regarding a linguistic object. Leech (1969, pp. 1953–56) makes explicit a strategy for analyzing a metaphor. Can such a strategy be applied to any linguistic object, no matter what its intrinsic features or immediate linguistic context? Is a metaphor a recognizable entity whose characteristics or context clearly call for such a strategy of interpretation (it seems obvious that it is)—or may any linguistic object be so regarded and interpreted, so that the same linguistic object may be at one time a metaphor and at another time not, depending on the attitude of the interpreter toward it? Is "the light went out" intrinsically a metaphor or at least definitely so in certain contexts? Even in an extended context, as in the utterances of an entire psychoanalytic session, which may seem to insist on a literal hearing of it—what *does* stop the psychoanalyst, if anything, from regarding it as a metaphor if he wishes to do so? If the answers to such questions are obvious to a literary critic or scholar, I think that the psychoanalyst's own answer might play an important role in constructing a theory of interpretation in psychoanalysis.[46]

That a contribution to psychoanalysis proper may also issue from the psychoanalysis of an artist is obvious. However, I am as skeptical as Holland (1966) of the pseudo-analysis of the artist in absentia with all its probable faults of reductionistic oversimplification and nonverifiability (especially grievous for and likely to discredit psychoanalysis). With him I am also skeptical of the pseudo-analysis of a character in a work of art as though that character had a childhood prior to or a mental life outside the confines of the work of art itself. In any event, such interpretations,

46. For some discussions of metaphor and many references to other discussions, see Black (1962), Buchanan (1929), Chatman (1971), Chatman and Levin (1967), Chomsky (1961, 1965), Edelson (1972, pp. 218, 257–60), Freeman (1970), Jones (1916), Levi-Strauss (1958), Levin (1967), Richards (1936), Rubinstein (1972), Sebeok (1960), Sharpe (1940), and Voth (1970).

which can involve inspired or plausible guesses by a psychoanalyst, belong to applied psychoanalysis and may be made as well—perhaps on the whole with greater expertise and tact—by the informed literary critic or biographer.

The psychoanalyst may turn his attention to applied psychoanalysis in the realm of art as a consequence of the obstacles he faces (because he is a physician) in carrying out his activities as a clinical scientist. He may feel and in fact in many circumstances may actually be barred by considerations of confidentiality from writing about his patients. If he uses nonspecific generalities or disguises details in response to such constraints, he may conceal—especially when language itself is the object of interest—the individuality, the idiosyncrasy, the twist of phrase or nuance of expression that convinces. Even if he could surmount these difficulties, he faces those of recording, selecting from, and organizing millions of utterances. His data indeed are so incredibly multitudinous they may defeat altogether his power to discover an order underlying them. Rather, he may often simply impose an already possessed formula upon them.

So, when the psychoanalyst does make a genuine discovery or invents an apt, heuristic, conceptual scheme, he may feel forced by these difficulties to cast about for some way to communicate indirectly or conveniently what he has learned. He may write a theoretical essay, with the expectation that his colleagues will sympathetically re-create the myriad clinical data to which his abstract generalizations allude. It is possible that a psychoanalyst, seeking to follow Freud's brave example, might make use of data from his own psychoanalysis or self-analysis; however, feeling a need for the use of even greater discretion than Freud, he might disguise this data by incorporating it into an analysis of a literary work or character. Finally, the psychoanalyst may also write a study of an artist or a character in a literary work, finding in information about the artist's life, or characteristics of his work, or qualities of the fictional character, enough to provide a scaffold for what the psychoanalyst wants to say about his own work. Then, he may offer the results of his study as indirect evidence supporting hypotheses that actually have their roots in clinical practice.

Such suppositions concerning the origin of some of these essays and studies in the psychoanalytic literature, of course, do not provide us with a basis for evaluating them as contributions to applied psychoanalysis. However, all these devices are more successful (with respect to psychoanalysis as science) in delineating broad trends than they are in creating novel, adequately abstract, conceptual schemes whose evaluation depends on the availability of a multitude of critical details. That the psychoanalyst may feel forced to report the results of his clinical work in such a form does help us to appreciate some of the obstacles that prevent the development of an adequate theory of psychoanalytic interpretation as well as of psychoanalysis as a semiological science.

The following study of "The Snow Man," an exceptionally fine short poem by Wallace Stevens (1954, p. 9f.), is an exploration of what may be involved in the interpretation of a linguistic object. Following Freud's example of the study of the dream or joke, this exploration assumes that to understand a symbolic entity is to understand how it is constructed and that to reveal the techniques, canons, or rules that govern its construction is to understand the nature of the mind capable of functioning according to these to construct and use such a symbolic entity.

I chose a short poem (a tour de force five stanzas but only one sentence long) to demonstrate to any reader who might doubt it the complexity that even a short linguistic utterance might possess. After such a demonstration, my attribution of a large portion of the psychoanalyst's skill in understanding the analysand to linguistic competence—to a grasp, however unwitting, of all that is possible to language—should not seem too far-fetched.

It might well be asked why I did not make use in this book of a sample of language from the psychoanalytic situation. At this stage of my investigation, the poem as a linguistic object has certain advantages beside its intrinsic value and its completedness. First, the obstacles to understanding the language of poetry are similar in many respects to the obstacles to understanding the language of the analysand. Second, poetry is par excellence the exemplification of a skilled effort to exhaust the possibilities of language and to concentrate the realization of these possibilities in a minimal utterance that will suffice. Wallace Stevens, on poetry, writes of "the mind in the act of finding what will suffice" (1954, p. 239).

As a practical matter, to present the many samples from the psychoanalytic situation (which lacks the compression and constraints of poetry) that would be required to illustrate various linguistic resources, their interrelations, and their many uses would entail a vastly greater number of pages than are needed to demonstrate the same variety from one poem. The final task, of course—in this work, a matter of mere suggestions and allusions—is to extend our findings, when and in a way this seems fruitful, to the psychoanalytic situation as we know it.

However, having decided to examine a poem as a linguistic object, I can easily imagine a colleague, not a psychoanalyst but a scholar and critic of literature, reading the "three interpretations" and being puzzled, horrified, feeling he finds a poem bleeding in these pages, and feeling the "interpretations" as a brutal, perhaps ignorant, assault upon a work of art. For this reason, before proceeding with an examination of the poem, I want to emphasize that the interpretation of "The Snow Man" is an interpretation of a poem as a linguistic object not a poem as a work of art. I did not choose a poem as an object of analysis to give myself an opportunity to perpetrate an act of literary criticism. I shall repeat that I make use of a poem because poetry seeks to exhaust the possibilities of language, to make the most concentrated use of all the resources of language, and I wish to make the reader aware of all the linguistic features to which a psychoanalyst can conceivably respond, however unwittingly, and all the linguistic resources available in the psychoanalytic situation to the psychoanalyst and analysand for them to construct in many ways with varying degrees of awareness many kinds of representations of many kinds of meaning. Language samples from the clinical situation, if each such sample made so concentrated and yet varied use of language that their description and interpretation did not require a hundred times fifty pages, would have served as well.

Yet, of course, the critic may still cry out, "but your interpretation of the poem is completely incorrect! It is wrongheaded! Stevens did not mean that at all!" I well know that Stevens is a particularly dangerous poet for a non-literary critic to have chosen for such a venture into "interpretation." In footnote 51, I refer the reader to something close to sixty-five commentaries (including those in collections of essays) on the poetry of Stevens; if he wishes to look through these (and I have deliberately avoided the presumption of assigning them different degrees of merit), he will soon find out that there is not much agreement among literary critics themselves about the meaning of almost any poem or even any part of a poem that Stevens wrote. (One may feel that in this babel, one more reading may not do much damage; the poems are strong enough to resist and survive any comment.) I believe there is an instructive reason for these differences. It does not have to do primarily with any supposed obscurity in Stevens' use of language itself. It has to do rather with the character of Stevens' mind.

In footnote 50, I suggest to the reader that no interpretation of any single poem could be sufficient for the fullest understanding of it, if that interpretation did not involve a reading of the poem in the light of all of Stevens' poems, "in the same way that the psychoanalyst requires an unbelievably extended context (compared to that required by those engaged in other kinds of communicative enterprises) to interpret an utterance or set of utterances." Stevens struggled all his life with the relation between "imagination" and "reality." I identify deeply with the way he conducted this struggle. He did not allow himself to be forced to a final statement, to a premature conclusion. His work is a prolonged dialectic. He sides with imagination. He sides with reality. He writes the poem that celebrates imagination. He deplores the pressure of reality, a reality so oppressive it does not permit any imaginative perception of it. He writes the poem that celebrates reality, the reality of things as they are. He deplores the fancies, the fictions, the outworn symbols, and traditional expressions, that come between man and reality. He explores each "position" fully, identifying with it, giving it powerful expression—and then in another poem or part of a poem he equally holds and proclaims its opposite. Any reading of such a poem or part of a poem can never conclude, "this is what Stevens means. This is what Stevens believes."

It is one of the great experiences to read through the body of his work, to follow him to the resolution of this antithesis in the beautiful poems of his old age. At age sixty-five, he wrote,

> The greatest poverty is not to live
> In a physical world . . . (Stevens, 1954, p. 325).

He also wrote,

> From this the poem springs: That we live in a place
> That is not our own and, much more, not ourselves
> And hard it is in spite of blazoned days (1954, p. 383).

In "Credences of Summer," when he was about sixty-seven, he wrote of the self that

> having possessed
> The object, grips it in savage scrutiny,
> Once to make captive, once to subjugate
> Or yield to subjugation, once to proclaim
> The meaning of the capture, this hard prize,
> Fully made, fully apparent, fully found (1954, p. 376)

When he was seventy-three, he wrote, in "The Plain Sense of Things," that even

> the absence of the imagination had
> Itself to be imagined (1954, p. 503).

At age seventy-five, he concluded *The Collected Poems* with "Not Ideas about the Thing but the Thing Itself." Its last line is

> It was like
> A new knowledge of reality (1954, p. 534);

its last word "reality."

Rightly, the critic may refuse to be silenced. Not only the work of Stevens, but the poets, writers, and thinkers who influenced him and at the same time *against* whose influence, ideas, figures of speech, and words he had to write, must be considered. If the reader pursues the references I have given, he will read of Shakespeare, Marvell, Keats, and Shelley, of Emerson and Whitman, of the French symbolists, and of many, many others. In this connection, read Bloom's arcane (I mean "mysterious"), evocative, exciting *The Anxiety of Influence,* with its psychoanalytically enriched insights into the nature of anxiety about priority and the ways of mastering it in poetry—a book which, by the way, can usefully be read together with Merton's thoughts on the subject of "priority" in *The Sociology of Science* and *On the Shoulders of Giants.*

I hope it is clear why I cannot in this book give this kind of complete "interpretation" of "The Snow Man." Even if I had the knowledge and the will, it is not my task. However—and I am not being sophistic—my book is not fatally wounded if my interpretation of "The Snow Man" is rejected by a particular literary critic as incorrect; rather, the hunch that informs the book is confirmed. For that literary critic in so rejecting it and perhaps in rejecting it on the grounds that I interpret "without knowing enough" only declares, as I do throughout the book, that what the literary critic does in understanding a poem and what the psychoanalyst does in understanding the analysand *through his language* have a fundamental resemblance. For to understand a single utterance fully, must not the psychoanalyst understand not only the whole body of work constructed by the analysand—his life as he conceives it, his achievements, his symptoms, his image of himself and of the psychoanalyst—but also his identifications with those in his past, with which he is rarely at peace, which he has disclaimed or against which he has struggled in various other ways, and whose discovery is a major part of the process of psychoanalysis, paving the way in each psychoanalysis to at least a partial, a unique, and often what seems to be a masterful, creative resolution? But is it not also so, that throughout a psychoanalysis, the psychoanalyst, in his attempts to understand an utterance or series of utterances, must be willing to accept the fact that (given always a relatively insufficient context) for the most part at any particular time he makes *partial* interpretations, which may or may not be correct but which are almost always certainly incomplete? If the psychoanalyst cannot accept this limitation, he can make no interpretation, and there can then be no process of correction, addition, extension of context—in short, no psychoanalysis. The literary critic who raises questions about the correctness of the interpretation of "The Snow Man" in this book cannot help but inform us concerning the obstacles to, and the process of, interpreting utterances in the psychoanalytic situation; if this book provokes such questions, it begins the exchange of ideas that is one of its aims.

Finally, there are two quarrels in which the literary critic in his own discipline may be engaged. One concerns the extent and the limitations of the contribution linguistics may make to literary criticism (see, e.g., Chatman, 1971; Freeman, 1970; and Sebeok, 1960). The other concerns whether interpretation of a literary work may focus primarily upon or even be confined to a careful examination and formal analysis of the text alone, or must include for full understanding examination of the relation of the work to other works by the author, the cultural tradition (including its ideas and other arts) in which he writes or to which he reacts, the society in which he lives, and his own biography and psychology (see, e.g., Wellek and Warren, 1962). I hope it is clear that the way I have approached interpreting "The Snow Man" has to do with my own theoretical aims and is not meant and cannot be read to imply that I have been presumptuous enough to take any position in these quarrels which must be settled by members of another discipline than my own.

This is the poem by Wallace Stevens:

THE SNOW MAN

One must have a mind of winter
To regard the frost and the boughs
Of the pine-trees crusted with snow;

And have been cold a long time
To behold the junipers shagged with ice,
The spruces rough in the distant glitter

Of the January sun; and not to think
Of any misery in the sound of the wind,
In the sound of a few leaves,

Which is the sound of the land
Full of the same wind
That is blowing in the same bare place

For the listener, who listens in the snow,
And, nothing himself, beholds
Nothing that is not there and the nothing that is.

10: The Syntax of "The Snow Man": Reconstructing Deep from Surface Structures

Wallace Stevens' poem, as I have noted, is one sentence. The syntactic intricacy of this one sentence is used to *move* the reader—in one sense, affectively; in another sense, from one point in an argument to another. The syntactic ordering of the language of the poem metaphorically *presents*—it resembles—the order of thoughts in an act of meditation and also the order in a meditated-upon reality. The language of the poem also *represents*—is "about"—the substance of this meditation (concepts and the particulars these may denote).[47]

The sentence is divided into five stanzas of three lines each. The following description of the poem is designed to demonstrate that this formal serial construction—using stanzas and lines, and therefore a pattern of pauses—divides time in a way that is coordinated with the syntactic-semantic structure of the poem; it is thus comprehensibly related to its meaning.

The syntactic structure, described in transformational-generative terms, can be revealed by analyzing this one sentence into an underlying set of hypothetical basic or kernel matrix and embedded sentences. Matrix sentences are destined to become by transformation principal clauses, and embedded sentences modifiers, phrases, and subordinate

47. For excellent discussions of Stevens' exploitation of syntax as a linguistic resource, see Vendler (1965, 1969); also, e.g., Doggett (1958) and Jumper (1961). For the relation of "meditation" to Stevens' poetry, see, e.g., Doggett (1966) and Martz (1958).

clauses in the observed sentence. The syntactic structures of these simple kernel sentences (the so-called deep syntactic structures) have been altered and combined according to various hypothetical rule-governed transformational operations. These transformations generate the surface syntactic structure of the single complex-compound sentence that is the poem.[48]

Transformations are rule-governed operations of *deletion* of one or more entities, *substitution* of one entity for another, *expansion* of one entity into multiple other entities, *condensation* of more than one entity into a single other entity, *addition* of one entity to another entity, *permutation* or change of order of entities, or any combination of these.

There can be no question that the operations of the dream-work or joke-work signified by such terms as "displacement" and "condensation" are the same operations employed in the syntactic rules of natural languages. Freud (1900, 1905) has made that quite clear in his examples of dream-work and in his discussion of the techniques of the joke-work. Some of the operations at least are the same in constructing symbolic forms by primary or secondary pro-

48. For discussions of transformational-generative linguistic theory, see, e.g., Chomsky (1957, 1965, 1972); Fodor and Katz (1964); Katz (1971, 1972); Katz and Postal (1964); and Lyons (1970). Transformational-generative linguistic theory has been applied to poetry by Levin (1967) and Thorne (1965); to style by Jacobs and Rosenbaum (1971); and to prose by Holland (1968b) and Ohmann (1964, 1966).

Revisions of transformational-generative theory (e.g., Chomsky, 1965) make mine a somewhat oversimplified and in some ways misleading discussion—for example, in the emphasis on kernel sentences in discussing deep structure. See Chomsky (1971, 1972), Jacobs (1973), and Jacobs and Rosenbaum (1968, 1970) for some discussions of the continuous and still ongoing revisions of transformational-generative theory by Chomsky and his colleagues, as well as samples of the work of the neo-Chomskyans who have questioned apparently some of his most basic ideas. (Chomsky himself suspects these are quarrels about notation rather than substance.) But I am not writing a book on linguistics, but rather for colleagues concerned with psychoanalytic theory and practice. I have had to eschew what for that audience would have been impenetrable technical discussions, which would not have yielded a compensating gain with respect to achieving the purpose of this book.

cess, although the rules governing the use of these operations, the way in which these rules are applied, the order in which they are applied, and the nature and extent of the constraints upon their operations are different.

There are two matrix sentences. The first appears in the first stanza, the second in the second stanza. The first matrix sentence is:

I. *One must have a mind.*

The second matrix sentence is:

II. *One must have been cold for a time.*

These have undergone a conjunction transformation combining them into the compound sentence: One must have a mind . . . and have been cold for a time.

A kernel sentence is embedded in or combined with matrix sentence I by a transformation that yields a prepositional phrase "of winter" which functions as an adjective modifying "mind":

1. *Mind ? winter.*
   Winter ? mind.

The relationship between "mind" and "winter" is not clear at the beginning of the poem. This relationship must be interpreted to understand the poem. The preposition "of" is an operator, here relating two nouns. The phrase "mind of winter" is ambiguous at the level of surface structure, because more than one reading of such a construction is possible at the level of deep structure, i.e., the syntactic structure of more than one kernel sentence may have been transformed to yield such a construction. Extension of the context is one way to disambiguate the phrase and interpret the poem.

Some of the conditions in which "of" may relate two nouns are listed below. Since both "mind" and "winter" are abstract nouns, many of the readings of "mind of winter" derived from this list are figurative, involving the analogy:

"mind" is to "winter" as "X" is to "Y," where X and Y are so-called concrete nouns. Since nouns are symbols and represent concepts or classes, and are all in this sense abstract, the distinction between concrete and abstract nouns is a distinction between nouns representing concepts that may be used to denote observable referents and those nouns representing concepts that cannot be used to denote observable referents.

a. The relation is origin or source (e.g., a kernel sentence, *Wilson writes the missives,* may undergo transformation to become: Wilson's missives; the missives of Wilson), giving the reading: (The state of) winter creates or has created (a state of) mind—in this sense, winter's mind or mind of winter.

b. The relation is composition (*someone makes a mitten* and *someone uses wool* become: a mitten is made of wool; a woolen mitten; a mitten of wool), giving the reading: A mind is made of winter or someone thinks or feels thoughts or feelings of winter—in this sense, a wintry mind or mind of winter.

c. The relation is contents (*someone fills a mug with wine* becomes: a mug contains wine; a mug of wine), giving the reading: Mind contains winter or someone fills his mind with emotions evoked by winter or thoughts about winter, i.e., feels much or thinks a great deal about winter.

Readings *a, b,* and *c* are the same proposition, realized in the sentence (an approximation) "someone experiences winter" but stated in three different ways, i.e., undergoing three different transformations. At a surface level the emphasis, topic, or subject of reading *a*—what it is about, what it will make a comment about—is winter, that which evokes thoughts or feelings or is the occasion for such thoughts or feelings. The emphasis, topic, or subject of reading *b* is the activity of thinking or feeling (or perceiving, etc.) by an agent. The emphasis, topic, or subject of reading *c* is the content of the mental act, i.e., the thoughts and feelings about (or perceptions of, etc.) winter.

d. The relation is identity or apposition (*the wash is a mess* becomes: the wash, a mess; a messy wash, a mess of wash), giving the reading: Winter is (nothing but?) (a state of?) mind.

This reading may be an assertion of a radically solipsistic view of reality—"winter" does not exist except as a mental experience, so that mind and winter are identical. If this reading is interpreted, however, so that it concerns an imaginary or hallucinated winter, an agent who imagines or hallucinates what might have in reality an independent existence has been introduced. Such an agent is no part of the sense of an identity or appositional relation.

e. The relation specifies an item within a category (*someone remembers his wife* becomes: his wife is a memory; the memory of his wife), giving the reading: Winter is one of many states of mind or is one of many subjects about which someone may be thinking or feeling.

Reading *e* is essentially a variant of the proposition underlying readings *a, b,* and *c,* but it emphasizes that winter is one of a set of contents about which someone may think or feel.

f. The relation is possession, connection, or association (*a monarch rules Wisconsin* becomes: Wisconsin has a monarch; Wisconsin's monarch; the monarch of Wisconsin; *William owns marbles* becomes: William's marbles; the marbles of William), giving the alternative readings: Someone through mental activity rules over or conquers or overcomes the difficulties of or rises above the difficulties of winter; or thoughts and feelings about winter possess or dominate someone. This relation also gives the reading: A certain state of mind is connected with, belongs to, or is characteristic of winter.

g. The relation is quality or attribute (*a man suffers woe* becomes: a man is woeful; a woeful man; a man of woe), giving the reading: Mind is wintry, wintry mind, a mind of winter—i.e., a state of mind has qualities, which are those same qualities that define the state of winter.

This reading could be a variant or transformation of the proposition "someone experiences winter," or perhaps more accurately a transformational combination of the propositions "someone acts mentally in this way," "someone experiences winter," "the experience is then of this kind," emphasizing the qualities which, the poet asserts (as we shall discover), are necessary to perceive accurately the qualities of winter.

Of all the possibilities for kernel sentence 1, the most likely seem to be:

1*a*(1). *(A state of) mind has qualities,* or
1*a*(2). *Winter has qualities,* or (assuming the "qualities" to be the same)
1*a*(3). *(A state of) mind has the qualities of winter.*

Less likely but possible are:

1*b*. *Someone through mental activity overcomes or rises above the difficulties of winter.*
1*c*. *Thoughts and feelings about winter dominate somone's state of mind.*

The syntax, joining matrix sentences I and II by a coordinating conjunction transformation, strongly suggests the possibility that matrix sentence II is primarily a restatement of matrix sentence I, supporting an interpretation of the ambiguous "mind of winter" in terms of 1*a*(1, 2, 3). To contribute to this disambiguation may be, in fact, the raison d'être of matrix sentence II.

Another kernel sentence is embedded in matrix sentence II to yield an adjective:

2. *The time is long.*

Other kernel sentences have been altered and combined by transformations that turn them into a very long (in comparison to the time occupied by the matrix sentences in the observable sentence that is the poem) compound-complex adverbial modifier of the conjoined matrix sentences:

3. *One can regard the frost.*
4. *One can regard the boughs.*

These two embedded sentences are themselves joined by a conjunction transformation to yield: One can regard the frost and the boughs.

5. *One can behold the junipers.*
6. *One can behold the spruces.*

The conjunction "and" that joins by transformation these two sentences has been deleted and replaced by a comma.

7. *One thinks of misery in the sound plus* NEGATIVE *plus Indefinite Quantifier.*

The thought so far represented by the language may be paraphrased: One must have a mind that is like winter and have been cold a long time, in order to regard the frost and the boughs, in order to behold the junipers and the spruces, and *not* think of any misery in the sound. The negative "not" is the climax of this part of the argument.

The poem may be divided into two groups of seven lines each (lines 1–7, 9–15) connected by line 8, which is composed of twelve syllables, more than any other line except the last line of the poem, which is also composed of twelve syllables. "Not" occurs toward the end of the last line in the first group of seven lines, leading into line 8. The seventh and eighth lines form a half-cadence to the first half of the poem, the eighth line also functioning as a bridge to the second half of the poem.

Kernel sentences 8–13 are embedded in or combined with kernel sentences 3–6 by transformations that yield adjectives or adjectival phrases, including a phrase ("glitter of sun") at the end of the first half of the poem in which, as in "mind of winter" at the beginning of the poem, the preposition "of" relates two nouns. This construction will be repeated three times in the second half of the poem.

8. *The pine-trees have boughs.*
9. *The boughs are crusted with snow.*
10. *The junipers are shagged with ice.*
11. *The spruces look rough in the glitter.*
12. *The glitter is distant.*
13. *The sun in January causes the glitter.*

The following kernel sentences (14–29) are embedded in or combined with kernel sentence 7, in which the first negative of the poem appears. (The poem concludes with a climactic crescendo of four negatives.) The transformations involved operate to turn these embedded sentences into adjectives, adjectival phrases, and most importantly a hierarchy of subordinate clauses, each clause subordinate to the one preceding. This recursive, repeated use of the same transformation (also, a climactic crescendo) yields a long sequence of right-branching constructions which stretch ahead into the time in which the poem exists. Such a syntactic structure may be chosen in part because it resembles or is metaphorically equivalent to, and may therefore directly present, an aspect of spatial order—the distances of glitter, wind, and snow the poem is about or represents.

The sentences are:

14. *The wind causes the sound* (yields on transformation an adjectival phrase modifying "sound").

15. *Leaves cause the sound* (yields an adjectival phrase modifying "sound").

16. *The leaves are few* (yields an adjective modifying "leaves").

17. *The sound belongs to the land* (yields a subordinate clause modifying "sound").

18. *The land is full of the wind* (yields a subordinate clause modifying "land").

19. *The wind is the same* (yields an adjective modifying "wind").

20. *The wind is blowing in the place for the listener* (yields a subordinate clause modifying "wind").

21. *The place is the same* (yields an adjective modifying "place").

22. *The place is bare* (yields an adjective modifying "place").

23. *The listener listens in the snow* (yields with sentence 24 a subordinate clause modifying "listener").

24. *The listener beholds* $nothing_1$ (is combined with sentence 23 by conjunction transformation to yield a subordinate clause modifying "listener").

25. *The listener beholds the* $nothing_2$ (is combined with sentence 23 by conjunction transformation).

26. *The listener is himself* (yields an apposition modifying "listener").

27. *The listener is nothing* (yields an apposition modifying "listener").

28. $Nothing_1$ *is not there* (yields a subordinate clause modifying "$nothing_1$").

29. *The* $nothing_2$ *is there* (yields a subordinate clause modifying "$nothing_2$").

The thought represented by the language of the poem, which is the product of an extensive condensation by transformational operations, may be paraphrased: One must become like winter in order to perceive objects and events of winter as they are, without attributing to these objects and events human feelings or motives. One must discipline oneself not to see and hear from the point of view of one's own human feelings and motives. Paradoxically, one must in this sense become nothing, and therefore like nature, immersed in nature, which has no feelings or motives; at the same time, in the same disciplined act of perception, one must maintain the separation between the human and nonhuman, between oneself and the other. Only through such disciplined perception is one able to see and hear what is out there to be seen and heard (even if nonhuman and therefore from a human perspective "nothing"). Only through such disciplined perception is one able to see and hear nothing that is not actually there, nothing that is only the result of the projection of feelings and motives from inside oneself into objects and events outside oneself. Such disciplined perception is necessary if one is to see and hear simply and only what is there and independent of one's own existence.

This paraphrase reads like a celebration of the "reality principle"—notwithstanding Stevens' scornful comments on Freud's supposed recommendations to surrender to reality in *Future of an Illusion* (Stevens, 1951, p. 14f.)—and by implication perhaps a deprecation of psychic reality.[49] Yet it would be a mistake to attribute to Stevens an oversimplified conception. After all, Stevens (1954) wrote thirty-one years later in a beautiful poem ("The Plain Sense of Things") utilizing similar materials,

> "Yet the absence of the imagination had
> Itself to be imagined" (p. 503).[50]

A careless reading might have yielded, for example, the following paraphrase: One would have to be a cold person

49. See, however, Edelson (1971b).

50. The reader may wish to look at still another fine poem, "The Course of a Particular" (Stevens, 1957, p. 96f.), written twenty-nine years after "The Snow Man," and like the latter also five stanzas long, each stanza also three lines long, the first stanza also ending with the word "snow." Evidence suggests that Stevens himself saw his collected poems as one unified grand poem (see, e.g., Blessing, 1970, p. 2f.), and thereby tends to support the position that a reading of the three poems (and perhaps all the rest) is necessary for the fullest understanding of any one of them, in the same way that the psychoanalyst requires an unbelievably extended context (compared to that required by those engaged in other kinds of communicative enterprises) to interpret an utterance or set of utterances. ("The Snow Man" is dated 1921; Stevens was 42 years old; "The Course of a Particular," 1950, and Stevens 71; "The Plain Sense of Things," 1952, and Stevens 73 [H. Stevens, 1966, 1971].)

indeed to view this wintry scene and not to feel the misery, loneliness, and emptiness in it. In the light of a detailed syntactic analysis, this reading would have to be rejected. It would be a mistake to exploit the poet's intentional use of ambiguity, multiple meanings, and different levels of meaning—carefully, artfully, and coherently related to one another (Brooks, 1947; Empson, 1930, 1967)—to justify the assumption, held self-indulgently by some, that a poem has no preferred, "correct" meaning, that it means something different to every reader, and that there is no way to select one interpretation of it over another. The phrases "the meaning of the poem" (its intrinsic characteristics as linguistic object and symbolic form) and "what the poem means to each reader of it" (its effect upon various readers, depending to some extent at least on extralinguistic and extrasymbolic characteristics of each one) involve two different senses of the word "meaning."

Similarly, the psychoanalyst cannot claim that ambiguity or multiple meanings, multiple levels of meaning, and different perspectives on the same material (connoted by such phrases as "multiple determination," "the various perspectives of metapsychology," "working through," "free association," "primary process") mean that "almost any interpretation has some truth in it" and relieve him of the obligation to explicate precisely the criteria according to which one interpretation is to be preferred to another. Criteria for preference may include: the interpretation that has greater therapeutic efficacy (i.e., the analysand is ready to hear, understand, and make use of it); and the interpretation that integrates multiple meanings in coherent relation to one another by embracing a larger context and making use of a greater number of perspectives in viewing the material.

In interpreting a poem, we must use syntactic, semantic, and phonological levels of analysis, as well as consider the relation of these to each other, to understand it (including, when necessary, to disambiguate it). Similarly, the following criteria may determine which among many possible interpretations is the preferred and most "correct" interpretation—the best understanding—of the constructions of the analysand: that interpretation involving a consideration of ego, superego, and id functions in their relation to each other; or that interpretation involving a consideration of the material from a maximum number of metapsychological (economic, dynamic, topographic, structural, genetic, adaptive) perspectives. Such criteria may eventually require a more precise explication in the theoretical language of linguistics and semiotics.

Considering the theoretical apparatus I am bringing to bear upon "The Snow Man," an apparently slight object, the reader may enjoy Stevens's own brief, casual paraphrase in a letter written to Hi Simons (H. Stevens, 1966): "I shall explain The Snow Man as an example of the necessity of identifying oneself with reality in order to understand it and enjoy it" (p. 464).

Of course, the poet is under no obligation to reveal the complexity of his conception or the intricate means he has used to represent and present it, even when he is aware of them, and he may not always be, although—to judge from the notebooks and revisions of countless writers as well as the stated intention of many of these to veil their work in mystery—he probably is more often and to a much greater extent aware than we imagine or he lets on.[51]

51. Morse (1970) deplores the "astonishing—and appallingly detailed—analysis to which some of these 'preliminary minutiae' have been subjected."

> [Such analysis] would certainly have perplexed the man who said of poetry that "it must give pleasure." One thinks, for example, of "The Snow Man," which has suffered almost as much as "The Emperor of Ice-Cream" and "Anecdote of the Jar" from the devotions of its exegetes. For such readers, the poem becomes the occasion for an essay on phenomenology, in which Valéry, Heidegger, Georges Poulet, Merleau-Ponty, Ramon Fernandez, Santayana, and Bergson, as well as the total canon of the poetry, are rifled to "prove" its "viability" and "dimensions," as if anything less would not do the poem justice. An appreciation of the wittiness of Stevens's characterization of the snow man as "nothing himself," or of the vividness and accuracy with which the winter landscape is described, is for them superficial and of very little

> significance; yet the poet himself said, "To give a sense of the freshness and vividness of life is a valid purpose for poetry," and also, "Accuracy of observation is the equivalent of accuracy of thinking." For the truly "close" reader, any analogy between Stevens's poem and Marvell's would appear to be equally trivial—as the echo in "the sound of the wind . . . the sound of a few leaves" of Shakespeare's "When yellow leaves, or none, or few" would seem a mere matter of coincidence (p. 118f.)

For other discussions of "The Snow Man," some merely emphasizing Stevens' skill in painting a landscape and other Stevens' supposed depiction of the chaos of reality untransformed by human imagination, "static nothingness," or man's "spiritual death" and surrender to the "annihilating element," see e.g., Borroff (1963, p. 14); Burney (1968, p. 31f.); Macksey (1965, especially pp. 195–200); and Sukenick (1967, p. 9f. and p. 222).

The reader interested in the work of Wallace Stevens should consult, e.g., Benamou (1972); Blackmur (1952); Blessing (1970); Borroff (1963); Brown and Haller (1962); Brown (1970); Burney (1968); Deutsch (1952); Doggett (1958, 1966); Frankenberg (1949); Jarrell (1955); Jumper (1961); Kermode (1960); Martz (1966); Morse (1970); Pearce and Miller (1965); Pinkerton (1971); Riddell (1965); Scott (1965); Stevens (1951, 1954, 1957); H. Stevens (1966, 1971); Sukenick (1967); Vendler (1965, 1969); and Winters (1943).

Frye (1973), most suggestively for our concerns, discusses how examples of the poetry of Stevens remind us "of the variation form in music" (p. 395).

11: The Sense of "The Snow Man": Deviance and Ambiguity

I have perhaps not emphasized enough the extent to which the psychoanalyst understands the analysand's presentations through his own largely silent and skillfully regulated participation in them and his reflections upon that participation. In the transference, the psychoanalyst is assigned parts to play. As an image in his own mind and in that of the analysand, he is transformed. The analysand evokes phantasies in the psychoanalyst, including phantasied responses to the analysand. The psychoanalyst hears within himself various dialogues. He is deeply stirred by impulses he does not recognize as his own. He feels like a figure in a dream of the analysand, there as an allusion to others and other occasions (Edelson, 1971a, p. 132f.). Reflecting, the psychoanalyst asks himself, "what is the meaning of this symbolic form that I call the 'transference neurosis,' in the construction of which the analysand has used me as material?" It is from this use the analysand makes of him that the psychoanalyst may be able to infer the meaning of the analysand's symbolic presentation, the transference neurosis, and so be able to make an interpretation.

The psychoanalyst's act of interpretation arises from a subtle interaction between anticipations and retrospections. Anticipations are aroused by linguistic events—phonemes, words, phrases—which occur as the surface form unfolds through time. To a larger extent than he supposes, on the basis of his linguistic competence, his knowledge of the rules of phonology, syntax, semantic, and rhetoric, the psychoanalyst imaginatively creates in his mind at each moment what is to follow. In each moment of a present language event, the psychoanalyst is both remembering a past language event and anticipating a future language event. In music also, at each moment the listener is both remembering a past event and anticipating a future event.[52] So, imagined future events may be implied by what has preceded a particular event, which in part shapes the psychoanalyst's apprehension of it. The event confirms or rejects some previously aroused anticipation.

These imagined future events may be implied by what the psychoanalyst understands to be the syntactic-semantic meaning of a particular event. To the extent a knowledge of syntactic-semantic rules is not the basis for understanding meaning—if, for example, a sequence of phonemes is heard *only* as a sequence of sound-qualities—the implications of an event become its meaning. Its implications flow from the qualities and organization it possesses. The expectations it is capable of evoking *are* its possible meanings.

These anticipations are corrected by retrospections. "I thought such-and-such would follow event X, but it did not. Instead, the sequence of events that followed was so-and-so. What I thought was the meaning of event X was not its meaning. Instead, since it led to so-and-so, its meaning must have been. . . ." An anticipation may also be confirmed in retrospect. "What I thought would follow did follow. I was right about the meaning of event X."

In psychoanalysis, a long time may pass before an anticipation can be corrected or confirmed—before "the other shoe drops." Similarly, in a poem, many phrases and clauses may precede a subject noun or separate a subject noun from a predicate verb. In music, many repetitions, variations, prolongations, and excursions into other keys, may separate the sound of a dominant seventh chord from the sound of the cadential tonic chord which—by virtue of the rules or conventions of the system of tonality—it anticipates.

52. Personal communication from the composer Paul Klein.

Surprise is an especially important experience in music, poetry, and psychoanalysis. Surprise as well as the experience "it doesn't make sense" often instigate acts of interpretation. Surprise encompasses the disappointment of expectations and the necessity for the revision of expectations. Suddenly all that has gone before now makes sense in a way it could not before. Previous events are understandable because an extended context has made meaning or an altered meaning possible. Meanings are revised *ex post facto* and *ad hoc,* so that they imply or entail the events which have unexpectedly transpired.

In a feeble suggestion of the process of psychoanalytic interpretation, and using the expository device Freud employed in his analysis of the Irma dream, I shall imitate in what follows a stream of anticipations and retrospections, which might occur while one listens to the poem, word by word, phrase by phrase, line by line ("listening," because a psychoanalyst listens to the analysand and is often unwittingly affected by similar kinds of reactions to and observations of various features of the language of the analysand).

As I have previously stated, I do not assume consciousness or awareness of all these anticipations and retrospections. Neither do I assume focal awareness of the linguistic features evoking such anticipations and retrospections. Indeed, a focal awareness of the features of language might interfere with an understanding of its meaning, in the same way that the proverbial centipede was rendered unable to walk or the continuous monotonous repetition of a word may render it meaningless.

I do not prejudge, however, to what extent language remains transparent when the psychoanalyst is listening to the analysand's utterances or the reader is responding to a poem. It may be that in both these cases language must become to some extent opaque and an object of focal attention for understanding to occur.

I do not intend the stylistic device I am going to use to imply that understanding an utterance occurs through serial reactions to one physical signal or entity after another. I simply wish to suggest that, often and perhaps usually unwittingly and at a preconscious level, the psychoanalyst is affected by reactions to and observations of the features of the language of the analysand (as he might be by the language of the poem); and that in whatever way, organization, or pattern these features are perceived by him, they determine much of his interpretation of the analysand's symbolic constructions—sometimes constituting obstacles to, and sometimes bases for, understanding analysand (or poem).

The Snow Man

I expect a title to inform me of the topic upon which there shall be a comment. "The," a definite article, used in discourse suggests that the noun phrase that follows it refers to a topic already familiar. But this title performs its function by puzzling me, by raising questions in my mind about what in fact the poet is talking about or going to talk about. "The"? What particular or unique "Snow Man" is that? Should I know to whom or what he is referring?

Did he say "snowman" (accent on the first syllable) or "snow man" (two accented words, with heavier accent on the second word)? Is he talking about an artifact (made of snow to look like a man), or about a man (who does something with, to, or in snow, as an iceman is a man who does something with ice)? But I have no idea to what "snow man," in this latter sense, might refer? Is a "snow man" a man formed in such a way—what way?—that he resembles snow? Grim possibilities suggest themselves. Or is a "snow man" snow formed by roistering children in such a way that it resembles a man? Is not that a trivial subject?

Color and heat are absent from snow. I hear a "no" in "snow." How frequently the sound "n" is used to form words signifying the negative: un-, no, not, nothing, nobody, none, never, neither, null!

This need not imply that there is some intrinsic similarity

between the sound "n" and the concept of the negative. Only that, considering its occurrence in words representing an aspect of that concept, "n" as a sound becomes a linguistic resource which may be used appropriately through repetition, for example, in connection with syntactic and semantic resources to support a maximally integrated—with respect to the three components of language—effort to evoke that conception.[53]

The "n" in "snow" precedes the vowel. The "n" in "man" follows the vowel. What idle observations! Yet—there is resemblance here, but also difference. Is this phonological pattern of resemblance and opposition a way of signifying a difference, a separation, as well as a resemblance, between "man" and "snow?"

Why should he emphasize "snow" by placing it in the title? Is this emphasis excessive? inappropriate? Surely, he must be talking about something more or other than "snow." What if "snow" stands for "winter" and "winter" stands for "nature"? A figure of speech? A displacement—from whole to part, from superordinate to subordinate class, from one word to another whose semantic features are defined in terms of usage in propositions in which they stand in superordinate-subordinate relation to one another? A provisional hypothesis: the poet is going to say something about—or present some aspects of—the relation between man and nature. A familiar theme—for a moment, anyway, I feel I know where I am.

Do I depend here on my knowledge of that reality to which language refers—or on my knowledge of language, in which words like "snow," "winter," and "nature," are related by rules, both syntactic and semantic, to each other? Is it possible that an understanding of levels of meaning, indicated by displacements such as these, involves a translation from one word at one level (in a hierarchically organized set of semantic relationships) to another word at another level

53. See Chapter 12 for a further discussion of this point.

(or in another realm of discourse), on the basis of a knowledge of the rules of language according to which they are endowed with certain features and related to each other? In addition to knowledge of the sense of a word, which makes it possible to use the word to represent a conception of reality, knowledge of language includes also the knowledge that the word, like the name of the image in a rebus, may signify a class of linguistic entities to which it belongs by virtue of any one of a number of linguistic properties (Edelson, 1972; Freud, 1900, 1905).

There is more here than the content of the questions and their possible answers. These questions are not just questions which I must answer to understand the meaning of the poem or some part of it. Rather, the questions evoked *present* some part of the "meaning" of the poem—that meaning which is a *conception* of the *act of questioning*.

"The Snow Man," the title of this poem, seems to function then like a musical chord that at least suggests, if it does not immediately establish, a key.[54] The key in music is a normative system, a set of rules, which ultimately governs the construction and meaning of representations made from the ordered materials belonging to that system. It decides the sequences, the serial or simultaneous combinations, the substitutions, the resemblances, the contrasts and oppositions, in short all the relations we expect to occur and recur. It establishes what we experience variously as tension; deviance; violations of our expectations; unusual; tenuous or impermanent; interruption or departure. It prepares us for the return we shall await and accept with satisfaction as a resolution of these disturbances.

This formulation is reminiscent of Freud's conception of the nature of a wish in *The Interpretation of Dreams*. Surely, such a combination of normative standards, expectations, tension, and relief suggests that it is unwarranted to oppose absolutely cognitive and conative processes, to reify the con-

54. This function of the title is considered again in Chapter 12, specifically with respect to the sounds in the title.

ceptual difference between ego and id or the separation of wish and intellect, to subsume "wish" under "impulse" and "instinct" with the implication that one has entered the realm of physiological rather than mental events.

A chord in music, standing alone, is ambiguous. It belongs to more than one key. The same chord may be tonic in one key and subdominant in another. A particular chord may therefore function to switch one key to another just as a "switch word" may function to link disparate trains of thought in the construction of a dream. The discovery of the meaning of a chord—its symbolic order (key) and particular role, function, relational properties, or the "meaning" its membership in that order gives it—must await the sequence of events (context) that on a particular occasion identifies the symbolic world to which it belongs (Forte, 1962; Meyer, 1956). So, linguistic ambiguities in the title and throughout the poem, while leading us astray and impeding our understanding, yet invoke our imagination, present us with alternatives from among which we may choose, and offer us opportunities for acts of interpretation and synthesis.

Similarly, in a psychoanalytic hour, a word, a phrase, or a comment (often uttered quite casually and in the interstices of the hour, at the moment of arrival or departure) may arouse expectations of what is to follow—which may not be satisfied for many hours. Such an utterance may establish a frame of reference for understanding allusions or provide elements that serve to link disparate strands in much of what follows.

One

Who? Not "I," "he," "we," or "you." Indefinite, impersonal, formal "one." Is he talking to me? I feel I'm not present for him at all. Perhaps for him I am one of many in a large lecture hall; he does not address me in particular. Perhaps it does not matter to him whether or not I hear what he says. Then again, he may be talking to himself. Is he musing, meditating? Am I a mere, or a privileged, eavesdropper? I feel a great distance. Does he imagine or do I imagine a great distance between us—or is this linguistically evoked distance between speaker and audience a way of presenting the concept of distance itself, and thus of alluding to distance in nature or between man and nature?

There is another "n" sound in "one," following a vowel, as in "man" in the title. I hear in "one" the sounds of "snow." Is this reminiscence a symbolic presentation of the identity of "one" and "snow"—"the snow man"—and at the same time (in the reversal of sounds) an individuation of "one" and "snow?" Snow man . . . no man . . . one: "no man" is indeed more appropriately followed by "one" than "you," for example. Language is appropriate to an occasion, not determined by it.

must have

What does he mean "must"?! Is there some coercion intended, disguised by indefiniteness and lofty impersonality? Does he wish to force me to do or feel something I don't want to do or feel? Or does he, in his meditation, declare or recognize a necessity for man, which to emphasize he puts in the form of a law of nature? Must it be? It must be. He conveys his conviction. He compels my belief.

"Have" is not much of a verb. It's not like "run." It's not like "hate." It's more like "is." Being rather than doing, passivity rather than activity. "Have" is a quiet, rather neutral verb, somewhat anticlimactic after that emphatic "must." Does he intend to cancel, to exclude all feeling from his language? I picture him empty, cold, colorless—like the snow.

a mind of winter

What kind of mind is that?! Why must one have it? "Winter" and "mind" are a syntactically linked pair like "snow" and "man," and allude again to the relationship between man and nature. Only this time "snow" is replaced by "winter" to which it stands in subordinate relation and "man" is replaced by "mind" to which it stands in superordinate relation. The inversion, a musical operation, presents again the distinctness and separateness of man and nature, even as these are coupled.

"Mind of winter" is deviant syntactically and semantically. This phrase violates selectional restrictions in the rules of language. It is also ambiguous, since a number of deep structures are capable of underlying it. If I understand that "mind" is being characterized by "winter," it is an unusual, although not unheard-of, metaphor. The metaphor, instead of—as is traditional—attributing the characteristic of "animate" to inanimate "winter" or "nature," or personifying "winter" or "nature," attributes rather characteristics of what is inanimate and nonhuman to "man" and "mind." This particular departure from the usual strikes me as critical for understanding the meanings represented and presented by this linguistic object.

More "n" sounds—in fact, a crescendo of similar sounds in such a short time: "man," "min-" and "one," "win-." From that first "snow," I have been expecting the repetition of an "n" sound that will *precede* a vowel, followed by—as in "man"—or at least in the neighborhood of, an "n" sound that will *follow* a vowel. This exact arrangement, which was so striking, does not yet reappear. I'm waiting for it. But something like this integration of opposition and similarity reappears. In "one must," the "n" sound follows a w-vowel sound and precedes an "m" sound. In "min-" and "win-," the first "n" sound follows the "m" sound and precedes the w-vowel sound. Is it possible that again he presents an idea about the relation between "man" and "nature" (here, too, the two similar "n" sounds are reversed in position) by exemplifying it in the relation between linguistic entities? [55]

55. Chapter 12 focuses on the sounds in this poem and on the problem of sounds in language. A somewhat more technical and a systematic discussion is provided in that chapter, in order to make available a set of categories as well as a set of operations to the reader who wants a conceptual framework for his own study of the sounds of language.

I have a new sense at the end of this first line, of a rhythmic beat, but I am not quite certain of it. "Snow Man": two nouns, two strong accents. "Mind," "winter": two nouns, two very strong accents, but "one" which joins "mind" and "winter" phonologically has an accent, too, although not as strong as theirs. But does its accent (reinforced by its initial position) borrow some strength from theirs as well? Does the first line have two beats or three beats? I am left in uncertainty about what the norm for this linguistic object will be.[56]

At the same time, I am aware that four nouns and one pronoun receive all the emphasis. There are no real adjectives; only a noun "snow" has been pressed into service as a modifier. There are no adverbs and no real verbs. A world of nouns: of being and beings, not events; of things, not acts; of being and beings without qualities. I am imagining an expanse of snow. There is no human figure struggling or playing there. Even a tiny human figure in the distance would be a relief: someone with whom to identify, whose feelings I could share. He does not permit me to imagine such a figure. His language denies me feeling. His language exemplifies "a mind of winter."

To regard

I experience a certain relief. Apparently, I am about to hear an answer to my question: "Why must one have a mind of winter?" I realize that he evokes questions in me as a way of holding my attention, keeping me in suspense, impelling me forward into the future of what he shall say (as does the beat—I expect to re-experience it at the same time I wait for it to change).

The verb is an infinitive form, inactive, timeless. It is a neutral verb, whose sense entails no passion, feeling or evaluation.

56. For a brief, sensitive discussion of meter in this poem, see Winters (1937, p. 126f.). My reading of the meter in this chapter differs somewhat from his, but I cannot claim any special competence in metrical discernment.

the frost and the boughs

Again, two nouns are syntactically linked.

The beat is reasserted: an accent on the second syllable of "regard," which is somewhat lighter than the two strong accents on the two nouns. The accents and the distribution of sounds appear to be resources he uses to emphasize and draw my attention to certain words and kinds of words and meanings, as well as to evoke a feeling of motion in me, of moving through time from what he has said forward into what he is going to say.

Of the pine-trees crusted with snow;

"Pine" and "snow" at the end of this first stanza present again the reversal of the position in relation to the vowel sound of the "n" sound, which joins the pause of the semicolon and the completed clause-structure to make a moment of semi-cadence or quasi-closure.

A melodic overlapping or bridging device helps to move me through the third line: the combination of the "n" and "t" sounds in "pine-trees" is followed by the combination of the "s" and "t" sounds of "crusted" (the "n" sound has been dropped, the "t" sound retained), which in turn is followed by the "s" and "n" sounds of "snow" (the "t" sound has been dropped, the "s" sound has been retained, and the "n" sound has returned). The pivotal role of "crusted" has been anticipated; the similarities of sound in "must," "frosted," and "crusted" prepare for it.

The beat this time is a definite three: strong accents falling on "pine," the first syllable of "crusted," and "snow." Varying the association of the accents with syntactic categories prevents monotony: in the first line, the three accents are pronoun, noun, noun; in the second line, verb, noun, noun; in the third line, noun, adjective, noun.

Each of the first three lines has eight syllables, such a norm again awaking in me an expectation of both continuation and change. I have a feeling of listening to music, which seems to lie just below the surface of the language.

"Boughs of the pine-trees" links another pair of nouns across the second and third lines.

"Crusted" might be an adjectival transformation of a verb ("snow crusts the pine-trees"), the verb appearing here in a nonactive participial form, but the use of "with" rather than "by" seems to exclude any sense of snow as an active agent. Both adjective and verb probably derive primarily from the noun "crust" (a hard surface).

I notice again the preference for nouns in this language. When a quality like "hard" is implied by the use of a noun like "crust," or "cold" by "frost," it is the attribute of a physical object that is implied. He does not use emotive or evaluative adjectives.

A statement has been made. What will follow it? What connects the meaning of the first line with the meaning of the second two lines is not yet clear. This uncertainty prevents the conclusion of the three lines from conveying an ending. I am during this pause still expectant.

And have been cold a long time
To behold the junipers shagged with ice
The spruces rough in the distant glitter

Of the January sun;

I recognize the second stanza to be a reprise of the first, with variations to hold my attention. The meaning from stanza to stanza remains relatively invariant, while variations, departing slightly from the norms established in the first stanza, occur in the rhythm and length of the lines.

There are seven syllables in the first short line and three accents, on "cold," "long," and "time," close together at the end of the line; ten syllables in the second line and four accents, on the second syllable of "behold," on the first syllable of "junipers," on "shagged" and "ice"); ten syllables in the third line and four accents, on the first syllable of "spruces," on "rough," on the first syllable of "distant" and the first syllable of "glitter." The longer lines, their length emphasized by the contrast with the first short one, and the increased number of accents, like a change in dynamics or tempo in music, intensify the repeated meaning of the first stanza.

He does not talk about feelings. He does not represent feelings semantically through adjectives or figures of speech. He evokes feeling without naming it by organizing the formal properties of his language.

glitter
Of the January sun

Two nouns are syntactically paired across the last line of this stanza and the first line of the next, moving me along into the third stanza, just as "boughs/Of the pine-trees" connected the second and third lines of the first stanza. The opposition between the syntactic connections across boundaries and the end-of-the-line or end-of-the-stanza boundaries, which call for a pause even when there is no pause, evoke in me another cycle of alternating tension and resolution, like the "to be continued" interruptions at the end of each episode in the Saturday afternoon movie serial.

One must have a mind of winter
. . . .
And have been cold a long time

"And have been cold a long time" is connected—across the two stanzas—by the conjunction "and" with "One must have a mind of winter." The occurrence of the second half of the conjoined phrases after an interruption by two intervening lines confuses me; momentarily disoriented, I have to gather my wits together at the beginning of the second stanza, which adds weight to what follows.

I realize that "mind of winter," which has sense but does not refer to any observable entity, has been transformed, translated, or displaced downward—the hierarchy is a linguistic one. "Have been cold a long time" represents a conception of a particular physical state in time, which at this level of meaning seems to be a sensory exemplification of the "mind of winter." The presence of "mind of winter," however, makes it impossible to hear "have been cold a long time" as merely "someone was cold a long time." "Cold" is a quality of winter. One must "have been cold a long time" is translated or displaced upward: one must have shared intensely and identified with (one of the) qualities of winter—or nature.

And have been cold a long time
To behold

"Cold" and "behold" are rhymed. There is reason in the rhyme, which connects "cold" with "behold," since to "have been cold a long time" is held to be a precondition for being able "to behold" in a certain way. The rhyme presents this relation directly at the level of sound.

To regard the frost
. . . .
To behold the junipers

"To behold" like "to regard" is an infinitive; the active aspect of the verb is minimized. Although both verbs appear to be relatively neutral synonyms of "observe" or "see," the sense of "behold" seems slightly different to me. "Regard" has many noun senses; "behold" has none. "Behold" has a longer sound and, in this context, therefore is somewhat more intense. "Behold" has an imperative interjectional sense, which implies to me a slightly different, perhaps slightly less neutral, attitude, an attitude of awe, both a more intense and a more dignified state of observing.

And have been cold a long time
To behold the junipers shagged with ice
The spruces rough in the distant glitter

This second stanza has more adjectives than the first: "cold," "long," "shagged," "rough," "distant." These adjectives all represent attributes of physical objects. "Long" was once metaphorical, used like this to modify "time"; it derives from a representation of spatial extension. "Shagged" has characteristics similar to "crusted"; it is an adjective in the participial form of a verb ultimately derived from a noun (rough, matted surface). "Junipers shagged with ice" is also syntactically parallel to "pine-trees crusted with snow." The adjectives do not entail an emotive or evaluative attitude other than neutrality, the perception of reality as is, irrespective of human intentions, motives, or feelings.

Although "to regard" and "to behold" imply the act of seeing, the emphasis has been primarily on objects, surfaces, and temperature. "A long time" ushers in a new note, of extension and distance, repeated in "the distant glitter." "Glitter" is the first representation of a visual sensation of light, although its sense of "light reflected from a surface" includes also an emphasis on physical surface. I now appreciate how characteristic it is that "glitter" is not a verb in the language of this poem, but a noun.

The "n" sounds continue into the second stanza. The "g" sound of "regard" in the first stanza is echoed in similar sounds in each line of the second stanza: in "long," "shagged," and "glitter." The "g" sounds, deep in the throat, slow the speaking of the lines, and are an additional device to alter the tempo for the purpose of intensification. The "s" sound, occurring so prominently in "snow" at the end of the first stanza, is repeated in similar sounds in the second and third lines of the second stanza: in "junipers," "ice," "spruces," and "distant."

Of the January sun;

In the first line of the third stanza, there is a second semicadence—to which the "n" and "s" sounds have been directing me—at the semicolon following "January sun." "Sun," here in the same position as "snow" at the end of the first stanza, repeats the "sn" sound of "snow," but with greater intensity. The sound is prolonged by inserting a vowel between the "s" and "n" sounds, as in music a ritard may prolong a sound, or intermediate related chords between two chords may prolong one or the other chord or the transition from one to the other. "Sun" is thus formally tied to "snow"; and thereby, and not simply by the use of a modifier like "January," I am kept from being distracted by thoughts of attributes such as "hot" and "fiery."

"Junipers" and "January" have similar sounds, another link between the second and third stanzas. In addition, in both words, the "n" sound is both preceded and followed by vowel sounds, as in the multicoupled "snow" and "sun" the vowel sound first follows and then precedes the "n" sound. "Sun" is thereby coupled with "man" as well as "snow" at the sound level.

There is also a subtle pattern of alternation of long and short vowels, of sounds from the throat and sounds of tongue and teeth, of sounds with the mouth open and sounds with the mouth near-closed: speak aloud "To behold" through "January sun."

These twining similarities and oppositions in the relation of linguistic entities continue to present directly the mixture of identification and separateness that characterizes the relation between man and nature which is also being described. The cognitive meaning of the description is paraphrasable. The direct presentation of different kinds of meaning is not.

I feel tense, in suspense, struck by the contrast between the variety and motion in the language, on the one hand, and the norms established by the language, the repetitions, parallelisms, and similarities, on the other; between the variety in the scene (rough crusted surfaces, glittering light), on the one hand, and the motionlessness and invariance of surfaces covered with ice and snow in distances of time and space, on the other. The interaction of such contrasts, of cycles of tension and resolution in phase and out of phase at different levels of language, control my response, the quality and intensity of my attention, my apprehension and re-creation of meanings, what I comprehend and what feelings and attitudes are evoked in me by it.

and not to think
Of any misery in the sound of the wind,
In the sound of a few leaves,

The tentative anticipation of a negative set up by the sound "no" in "snow" and the wait for an answer to the question, "Why must one have a mind of winter?" reach a moment of resolution—five and a half lines following the first line, just preceding the exact center, but in fact creating the center, of the poem—with an emphatic "not."

One must have a mind of winter
To regard (beginning the middle line of the first stanza)
. . . .
To behold (beginning the middle line of the second stanza)
. . . .
and not to think (the middle of the first line of the third stanza).

The variation in position adds to the emphasis on "and not to think," as does the fact that the infinitives "to regard" and "to behold" are approximate synonyms, while "to think," like the former an infinitive on the syntactic level, not only contrasts with them semantically but suddenly and sharply both semantically and (slightly) in sound recalls "mind."

The objects of "regard" and "behold" represent aspects of nonhuman physical reality—"frost," "boughs," "junipers," "spruces"—words connected with "winter" in "mind of winter." A very different kind of word is the object of "think": "misery," which—as the whole argument goes—does not represent anything in nonhuman physical reality. "Misery" is the only word in the poem that represents a conception of human feeling, and it is preceded by an emphatic "not" which negates the verb of which "misery" is the object.

"Misery" occurs in the eighth line of the poem, at the exact center, and is the longest line of the poem (nine words, twelve syllables) except for the last line (ten words, twelve syllables). Along with the maximum deviation in the length of the eighth line, there is at the same time a return to the norm of three accents per line established in the first stanza: on the first syllable of "misery," on "sound" and "wind."

The first three lines of the poem have eight syllables each. Stanzas one and two have together fifty-one syllables, stanzas three and four together fifty-one syllables, stanzas four and five together fifty-one syllables. The average line length for the total of 132 syllables is 8.8 syllables; the median line length for the total fifteen lines is eight syllables.

There are 108 words in the poem, an average of 7.2 words in each line. The first two stanzas have seven words in each line, establishing this norm. The length of the line "Of any misery in the sound of the wind" is enhanced because it occurs in a stanza which contains slightly more words than any other (twenty-four words) and is composed of nine words (only the last climactic line is longer, with ten words).

The object of "think" is the prepositional phrase "of any misery." "Misery" is modified by the prepositional phrase "in the sound." "Sound" is modified by the prepositional phrase "of the wind." Intensity of meaning is created by the condensation of three propositions in little over a line ("one thinks of misery *plus* NEGATIVE," "misery is in the sound *plus* NEGATIVE," "the wind causes the sound").

The three parallel prepositional phrases in sequence reinforce the normative three accents and provide a steady, unchanging background against which the bisyllabic "any" and trisyllabic "misery" are foregrounded. I am also aware of "any" and "misery" because of the steady background presence of monosyllables.

The language of this poem is overwhelmingly monosyllabic. Of the 108 words, eighty-nine are monosyllabic, fifteen are bisyllabic, three are trisyllabic, and one has four syllables. Only the penultimate line of the poem of all the lines has more multisyllabic words (three) than monosyllabic (one). The average number of monosyllabic words in each line (with an average of 7.2 words) is 5.9 words; four of the fifteen lines each have six monosyllabic words, six lines each have seven, one line (the last line) has eight.

This monosyllabic language—bare, minimized—is appropriate to the semantic content of the poem. It directly presents through formal features of the language what is described at a semantic level through the use of such words as "not," "few," "same," "bare," and "nothing."

The predominance of monosyllables is not deviant with respect to the rules of LANGUAGE, but it is deviant with respect to the alternatives available to the user of language. It is deviant because he imposes an unusual restriction upon himself, which is not imposed by the rules of LANGUAGE. He has imposed similar restrictions upon himself in constructing patterns of syntactic structures, repetitions of words, and sound resemblances. Deviance of any kind is an occasion for interpretation. What are the grounds for it? What aim—the conveying of what meanings— does it serve?

The deviance of "misery," both in its polysyllabicity and its meaning, is not deviance with respect to the rules of LANGUAGE, but only with respect to the characteristics of the linguistic context in which it is embedded or in other words the rules of the REALIZED LANGUAGE of the poem.

"Misery" is in every way such a deviant word in this language that I am especially struck by its sound. The initial "mi" sound has some little similarity to the initial sound of "mind" and therefore couples "misery" with "mind" on a sound as well as a semantic level. "Misery . . . wind" echoes sounds in "mind . . . winter."

"Wind" at the end of the line combines sounds from "mind" and "winter," as well as echoes a sound from "think" at the end of the previous line.

The "is" sound in "misery" contrasts with the "s" sound in "snow," but evokes the word "is" and its senses of existence and being which are represented and presented by various means throughout the poem. Over ten occurrences of "is" in the deep structure have been deleted by syntactic transformations.

The "z" sound sets up an anticipation which is satisfied when I hear the ending sound of "few leaves." And by the four occurrences of "is" in the last two stanzas of the poem (two occurring in the last climactic line of the poem).

Of the January sun; and not to think
Of any misery in the sound of the wind,
In the sound of a few leaves

Which is the sound of the land

The quasi-rhyme of "misery" and "January" also couples "misery . . . sound" with "January sun." The "sn" sound of "snow" in the first stanza was prolonged by the interpolation of a vowel in "sun" of the third stanza. Now in this central eighth line (in position and sense), the "sn" sound is prolonged to an even greater degree in "sound," adding to the intensity of this line, which seems to gather to itself all the preceding lines. And to bear the seeds of all the following lines.

"Sound" is repeated three times, once in the second and once in the third line of the third stanza, and again in the first line of the fourth stanza, in a context consisting of such words as "wind" and "land," which through similarities in sound reinforce it as it reinforces them and the connection of all three with "mind." The "wind," which at the semantic-syntactic level is the source of the "sound" belonging to the "land," and which combines sounds from both "mind" and "winter," is a pivot around which "mind," "winter," "sound," and "land" whirl in dynamic oppositions and are at the same time unified.

The repetition of "sound" heralds a transition to a new mode of perceiving reality, and prepares the way from the infinitives of "to regard," "to behold," and "to think," through "is blowing" in the fourth stanza to the active verb "listens" in the last stanza.

There are eleven syllables in the first line of this third stanza and four accents on the first syllable of "January," "sun," "not," and "think"; twelve syllables in the second line of the stanza, with its three accents; and seven syllables in the third line with three accents on "sound," "few," and "leaves." This arrangement just reverses the pattern in the preceding stanza where the first line is the shortest line followed by two longer ones.

The resemblance to the stepwise motion of a melody, rising to a climactic tone, is startling: the second stanza ends with two lines each of seven words, ten syllables; then, in the third stanza, there is a line of eight words, eleven syllables, then a line of nine words, twelve syllables, followed immediately by a sharp drop to a line of seven words, seven syllables.

> *Of any misery in the sound of the wind,*
> *In the sound of a few leaves*

The adjective "few" in the last line of the stanza has a negative in its sense which connects it with the emphatic "not" in the first line of this stanza.

The last line of the third stanza ("In the sound of a few

leaves"), which echoes and parallels the last two prepositional phrases of the line preceding it, supports the climactic emphasis on the preceding line through repetition of various phonological, syntactic, and semantic features of that line. At the same time through that same repetition this line suggests to me a recapitulation, a coda, a downward movement to the end—the beginning of the end.

Which is the sound of the land
Full of the same wind
That is blowing in the same bare place

For the listener,

This sequence of nested subordinate clauses:

which$_1$ is the sound of the land
[which$_2$ is] full of the same wind
that is blowing

is generated off of or modifies "sound" in the previous stanza, adding to the weight "sound" has already received from its repetitions in that stanza. "Which$_1$" is a pronominal for "the sound" of wind and leaves and, therefore, another repetition of "sound" at the level of deep structure. "Which$_2$" is a pronominal for "the land." "That" is a pronominal for "the wind." "Land" and "wind" are also repeated, therefore, at the level of deep structure. "Sound," "land," and "wind" are united by these repetitions, as well as by meaning relations and sound similarities.

Distance is described at the semantic level. The repetitions and concatenations of clauses embedded in other embedded clauses also present directly on evocation of trailing off into a distance. The distance is infinite, since I know language can generate recursively an endless sequence of such clauses ("the dog that chased the cat that ate the rat that ate the cheese . . ."). Since this recursive process is limited in performance, however, by extra-linguistic characteristics (memory, attention, fatigue, etc.—those having nothing to do with language as a system) of performer and audience, I know it must soon come to an end and, therefore, announces an impending end.

This fourth stanza has still another variation in the position of the shortest line, which here—as in the last stanza of the poem—is the middle line rather than the first (stanza two) or the third (stanza three) line of the stanza. In this stanza there occurs the greatest difference up to this point between the lengths of the shortest line and the longer lines that precede and follow it—7:5:8 words; or 7:5:9 syllables. The last stanza of the poem repeats this pattern, only the difference is even greater—8:4:10 words; or 11:7:12 syllables. The effect is to foreground the last, longest line in each stanza and especially the last line of the poem's last stanza.

The fourth stanza, which has two occurrences of the word "same" and one of "bare," is almost unrelievedly monosyllabic. It has only one bisyllabic word "blowing," which is also the first occurrence of a real verb (i.e., not a form of "to be" or "to have" and not an infinitive), here in the continuous present tense. "Blowing" is thereby foregrounded in this stanza as "misery" was in the previous stanza.

Sounds in "blowing" are reminiscent of "cold" ("blowing" reverses vowel and "l" sound), "behold" ("blowing" contracts the combination of "b" and "l" sounds as well as reverses vowel and "l" sound), and "long" ("blowing" prolongs the separation between "l" and "ng" sounds).

The initial sound of "blowing" is similar to that of "bare" and also to that of "place" ("pl" has many of the features of "bl"). "Blowing" thus anticipates the sequence "same bare place" which rings changes on the vowel sound. "Same" and "place" are additionally connected by the repeated "s" sound, so prominent in this language. Of course, "same," "bare," and "place" are also connected syntactically.

The repeated "l" sound in "land" and "full" (somewhat expanded from one to the other), and the combination of "l" and "n" sounds in "long" and "land," for example, have anticipated the prominence of "blowing."

This entire set and pattern of sounds anticipate the climactic "listener," who "listens" and "beholds" (active verbs in the present tense), in the poem's last stanza.

The repeated "same," whose meaning is presented directly by the frequent repetitions especially in the last two stanzas, results in my becoming disoriented. Same as what? An intricate syntax here directly presents the intricate relation of immersion and identification, on the one hand, and distinctness and separation, on the other, between man and nature that is the subject of the poem. The simple word "same" (with all comparative clauses—e.g., "same as . . ."—deleted) distinguishes by implication the winter scene of the first half of the poem, which is separate from any experience of it (no active verbs), from the winter scene in the last two stanzas, which is actively perceived by the listener who listens and beholds. The use of "same" in this way emphasizes that the scenes (which, "same" implies, are in some sense two separable scenes which can be described as "the same") are the same for this listener, just because he does have a "mind of winter."

> *For the listener, who listens in the snow,*
> *And, nothing himself, beholds*
> *Nothing that is not there and the nothing that is.*

"Boughs," "ice," "leaves," "place"—each a word at the end of a line in a different stanza (middle lines of stanzas one and two, last lines of stanzas three and four)—all (together with the central "misery") have led to the final "is." [57]

In this last stanza, the sounds of "listener," "listens," "snow"—for example, the relation of "l," "s," and "n" sounds—and of "nothing himself," "beholds nothing," "nothing that is not," "nothing that is" seem to pulsate in al-

57. Frankenberg (1949, p. 220) has described three chains of end-words all leading to "is": from the first line, "winter" leads to "glitter," "glitter" to "think," to "wind," "land," "wind," and "is"; from the second line, "bough" leads to "ice," "place," "is"; from the third line, "snow" leads to "snow," "beholds," "is." For another description than mine of the use of sounds in this poem, the reader would do well to consult Frankenberg's perceptive summary in the context of his reading of this poem (pp. 219–22).

ternations of contraction and prolongation: a presentation of heightened activity.

The pattern of the number of accents in the previous fourth stanza involves a rise from line to line (two in the first line, on "sound" and "land"; three in the second line, on "full," "same," and "wind"; four in the third line, on the first syllable of "blowing," "same," "bare," and "place"). The fifth stanza then starts with the normative beat of three, repeated twice, and ends in a long line with four beats (first line, on the first syllable of "listener," on the first syllable of "listens," and on "snow"; second line, on the first syllable of "nothing," on the second syllable of "himself," and on the second syllable of "beholds"; in the last line, on the first syllables of the two occurrences of "nothing," on "there," and on "is"). The last line of the final stanza is longer than the long last line of the previous stanza and has a greater number of accents than the second line of the third stanza, which is the only line that equals the poem's final line in syllable-length.

The sequence of nested subordinate clauses begun in the fourth stanza continues into the final stanza. The syntactic structure may be indicated as follows:

listener . . . who listens
listener . . . who beholds: nothing . . . that is not there
listener . . . who beholds: the nothing . . . that is.

The whole substructure of the final two stanzas, beginning with "which," modifies "sound." The whole *sub*-substructure following "listener" in the final stanza modifies "listener." This *sub*-substructure begins with "who," a human pronominal that substitutes for "listener" in the deep structure and therefore repeats it. "Listener" is extended not only by this *sub*-substructure but also by the appositional "nothing himself." "Listener" is repeated four times in the deep structure:

the listener listens
the listener is nothing
the listener is himself
the listener beholds

For the listener, who listens in the snow,
And, nothing himself, beholds

The first active verb "listens" is intransitive. The second active verb "beholds" is transitive—the only active transitive verb in the poem. I am reminded of the neutral "have" (with its early sense, to hold in hand) at the beginning of the poem and feel the contrast of the active "beholds" (to hold, so to speak, in the eye).

The second line of this fifth stanza is the poem's shortest in number of words and contrasts with the next shortest line in the poem (the second line of stanza four, which is five monosyllabic words long) by concentrating three bisyllabic words into its four words. This deviance (with respect to the norms established by the language of this poem) foregrounds "beholds."

And, nothing himself, beholds
Nothing that is not there and the nothing that is.

"Beholds" has two objects. One object of "beholds" is "nothing"; the other is "the $nothing_2$." "$Nothing_1$" is misery, the human feelings and motives, about which a mind of winter beholding winter does not think. "$Nothing_1$" is extended by the clause "that (repeating "$nothing_1$" at the level of deep structure) is not there." "The $nothing_2$" is winter or nature as it is, independent of human feelings or motives. "The $nothing_2$" is extended by the clause "that is" (repeating "the $nothing_2$" at the level of deep structure). The two active verbs associated with the human listener contrast with the two occurrences of "is" in the poem's final line.

Just as "mind of winter" and "same" were deviant in some way with respect to some rules of LANGUAGE (and, therefore, were occasions for interpretation), so "the nothing" is deviant.[58] "The" should not precede "nothing." That it does so

58. Personal communication from J. Hillis Miller.

suggests that "nothing" here is intended to convey, or does convey, the meaning "a thing almost tangible" that "is," rather than something that "is not."

"The listener is himself" and "the listener is nothing" occur at the level of deep structure and concisely present the opposition in the relation between man and nature. The listener with a mind of winter is himself, human and separate from nature, but in his perceptive identification with nonhuman reality he is also nothing.

The "nothing" in the very short second line of the final stanza is combined with two other bisyllabic words in that line. This relatively quiet introduction prepares for the dramatically foregrounded occurrences of "nothing" in the poem's final line, where the two occurrences of "nothing" are the only occurrences of bisyllabic words in a long concatenation of monosyllabic words.

The concentration of negatives in the last two lines decisively contrasts with and counteracts the "trailing off" evoked by the coda of embedded subordinate clauses and contributes to the sense of a definite conclusion. Similarly, the "and" structures:

> listens *and* beholds
> nothing *and* the nothing

recapitulate the syntax and therefore evoke the content of the major statement of the poem:

> one must have a mind of winter *and* have been cold a long time;
> to regard, to behold, *and* not to think of any misery.

The poem represents and presents a paradox. Its center is the emphatic "and not to think." Its conclusion is an assertion of the reality principle.

"One . . . is" combines the first and final words of the poem, emphasizing a state of apparent passive being—of identification with that which is—required of the mind of winter. But this human mind is active, engaged in an intense effort. For, after all, the act of true perception is not passive surrender and immersion, but the most accurate seeing and hearing. Such acts require discipline, the struggle to own up to and not to relinquish human qualities, not to attribute them to landscapes. Otherwise, acquiescence to the easy, the "romantic," the ultimately comforting transformation of alien, indifferent nature into an incarnation of human motives and feelings fatally interferes with any attempt to perceive the reality of things as they are.

12: The Sound of "The Snow Man": Meanings in the Music of Language

This chapter is a systematic consideration of sounds in language. It provides what I believe to be an especially useful conceptual framework for the psychoanalytic reader to use for analyzing language in his own studies. This conceptual framework includes categories—classes, subclasses, and families of sounds; operations, such as condensation, displacement, reversal, augmentation, diminution, and deletion (which Freud discussed in considering the dream-work proper as well as the vicissitudes of affects in dreams); and aims these operations may be used to serve, such as presentation, economy, allocation of value or emphasis, progression through implication, and resolution through realization of implications.

Language and the Presentation of Emotive Meaning

In reading "The Snow Man," I became aware of a complex affective state, which is somehow *presented* by the poem. What is stated in the poem must, of course, have something to do with this presentation, but the statement alone cannot account for the complexity of the affective state that is part of the conception symbolized by the poem. That part of the conception has to do with an evaluation of, attitude toward, or feeling about an idea, not simply the idea itself.

The complexity of the affective state presented by the poem may account for the variety of critical responses to the poem that I have previously noted. My own experience with the poem includes many paradoxes. I find myself in a world of sustained disciplined effort, yet also in a world somehow transient and evanescent. In this world, I hear persistently sounding in my mind's ear a dark, somber tone; yet at the same time a note that is elate, triumphant, not the triumph of a trumpet's blare, rather some light transparent song-like soar; and, with all this, also silence, which is more intense than any noise, yet still glides quietly downward uncertainly to a certain rest.

What is one to make of such a complex presentation? How is one to understand it? This is a problem with which the psychoanalyst grapples. He hears. He tacitly apprehends what is symbolized by what he hears. He must make sense of what he senses. He may suppose he is responding to the vicissitudes of an analysand's feelings, but what he is more likely to be doing is trying to interpret the analysand's conception of his own inner world at some moment in time, a psychic reality presented rather than described.

The possibility that sound is a material used by the analysand in constructing such a presentation is one I shall explore in this chapter. Let me state at once that I do not mean to imply that sounds are intrinsically symbolic or have fixed emotive or other meanings. What a sound (or syntax) may be used to present is of course likely to depend in part on, and to be constrained by, the cognitive sense of the sentence or utterance sound and syntax form. Nevertheless, there are many ways to say the same "thing." It is possible to select from among different sounds those that will present out of all possible attitudes or feelings particular feelings about or attitudes toward this "thing" that is said.

I have written in the previous chapter, "I have a feeling of listening to music, which seems to lie just below the surface of the language." As a psychoanalyst, I often become fleetingly aware in the course of a psychoanalytic session of this underground music. I have no words for it. This music belongs to that class of experiences which reside in an innominate realm; it lies too deep for words. So usually I remain unaware of it. I believe that this music continuously affects me, but I do not know how.

I do not mean by the music of language variations in such prosodic features as the pitch, loudness, and duration of sounds in the analysand's speech, or of alternations of sound and silence (silence is a kind of sound in music, not merely an absence of sound). These prosodic features are easily noticed. We have on the whole some kind of, and perhaps an almost adequate, vocabulary for the description of them. They do not affect the cognitive meaning of a message. They are expressive resources and available to convey other than cognitive meanings, such as emotive, conative, and phatic meanings. These features are obvious, and usually marked by the skilled psychoanalyst, who often interprets them as indices of the analysand's existent present emotions, intentions, wishes, or impulses—although, as I have indicated, it often may make more sense perhaps to interpret them as symbolic presentations of the analysand's conception of some past or present state of affairs or, more importantly, as symbolic presentations of aspects of the analysand's psychic reality.

The music that eludes me lies beneath variations in these prosodic features. To find the means to grasp and to capture this music in words is a difficult task.

I imagine I am listening to an orchestra. I hear the instruments of the orchestra one after another play the same pitch, with the same degree of loudness, and for the same duration. Although I do not hear a music of melody, of changes in pitch, yet I do not hear a sameness. I hear a music of colors, of qualities, a music that moves not from one pitch to another, but from one timbre to another. No matter what note is played, nor how loudly or long it is played, I recognize the instrument—the flute, the piano, the oboe—that plays it. No matter what melody is played, I hear beneath it the music that is the result of the passage of the melody or any part of it from one instrument to another.

In language, the music that is too deep for words is a music of timbres. Each distinctive phoneme or sound in a language is produced by changing the vocal tract in such a way that it becomes, in fact, for each sound a different instrument. Each phoneme is a distinctive bundle of the values of a limited set of variables or distinctive features, and this particular bundle of qualities differentiates it from all other sounds in the language. No matter how loudly, or with what duration, or at what pitch a particular sound of language is uttered, it is recognizable by the combination of qualities, which like the timbre of a musical instrument remains invariant through all changes of pitch, loudness and duration.[59]

I shall describe the way in which the sounds of language may be classified according to the values each one has with regard to ten or eleven distinctive features. Each such fea-

59. In the following discussion of distinctive features, I draw heavily upon the work of Jakobson, Fant, and Halle (1963), Jakobson and Halle (1956, 1968), Halle (1962, 1964), Chomsky and Halle (1968), and Schane (1973). In comments on the articulatory correlates of the distinctive features (the movements that shape the vocal tract), I have also drawn upon O'Connor (1973). In comments on the acoustical correlates of the distinctive features—a new and far from settled area of investigation—I have also drawn upon Fletcher (1953), Fant (1960, 1968), and Ladefoged (1962).

Throughout, in an effort to make this realm accessible to those who have little knowledge of it, I have used formulations that are loose or, given the state of the field, inadequately qualified and a terminology that is less abstract and less rigorous than that used by linguists.

It is enlightening, humbling, and exhilarating, especially for one who labors in a realm of subjective phenomena, to realize that also in significant "objective" endeavors, such as the investigation of the acoustical correlates of speech sound, we are at the beginning, and faced with enormous methodological and theoretical problems. Recordings of speech sounds are continuous. We hear these continuous sounds and they are processed by our brains as discontinuous quanta or segments; this discontinuity has no discernible representation in the physical record. We hear physical signals that are clearly different acoustically as the same speech sound, depending on the context in which they occur. Some characteristics of speech sounds, which we recognize and of which we make critical use, are not so far recordable.

For those familiar with linguistics or who wish to become so, I shall indicate where appropriate in the course of my discussion technical linguistic terms in parentheses.

ture has a distinctive articulatory correlate, a distinctive acoustical correlate, and endows the sound with a distinctive quality. Each feature has two values, one the inverse of the other.

To give the reader some idea of the magnitude of the task undertaken here, I shall point out the following. Combinations of two of the features (two values each) make possible a classification of the sounds of language into four major classes; these two features are concerned with the vocal tract as a noise-producing and a music-producing instrument. One of these major classes, involving the vocal tract primarily as a noise-producing instrument, may be further subdivided into four subclasses, depending on whether the noise is gradually or abruptly released and whether the noise—a high intensity, high frequency noise—is muted or not. The subclass of abruptly released muted noise may be further subdivided according to whether or not the noise is supplemented by music that is produced by a resonating chamber.

In addition, there are three-to-five features that may be used in distinguishing among members belonging to any of the significant groups already formed. These features concern the distribution of energy on the frequency-spectrum of overtones and the effort required to produce a particular sound. All speech sounds can be assigned, by combinations of these features, to different sound families, which intersect the classes and subclasses already described. (This account is a considerable simplification!)

It is conceivable, then, that in the attempt to make sense of sound, in the search for patterns of language sounds in any linguistic object, one might choose to follow the distribution, organization, or sequence of any one or number of these features, or any one or number of all the classes, subclasses, or families formed by combinations of these features. It is awesome that we are able to receive, process, construct, produce, and interpret linguistic objects consisting of patterns of relations from among such a vast set of relations. What must we assume about mind and brain to account for such processes and such a capacity?

To find a way of making explicit what we do unwittingly, a way to record and communicate it, much more to account for how and why we do it in the ways we do it on specific occasions and with respect to particular aims, is not an easy task. Nevertheless, I shall make a start. I shall endeavor to discover sound patterns in "The Snow Man." More generally, I shall try to discover what devices and operations in the realm of sound are used in the language of this linguistic object to present the complex affective state I have described. I do not know of any similar attempt, using the distinctive features as theoretical apparatus, to penetrate the secret of the music in a linguistic object such as a poem.

I shall remark upon phenomena that are examples of "deviance;" for example, a concentration of a sound or type of sound in a line which is deviant with respect to the concentration of that sound or type of sound in the poem as a whole. I shall describe processes in the realm of sound corresponding to condensation, displacement, and the reversal, inhibition, diminution, and augmentation of affect in dream-construction.

Throughout, questions shall persist. Are such patterns and processes in the realm of sound significant? Do they contribute to the interpretation of the linguistic object? Can we find a satisfactory warrant for a sound event in its status as a means to the end of conveying one or another kind of meaning? In the attempt to find such warrants, do we come to regard (mistakenly, I tend to believe) the qualities of language sounds, as determined by the values of distinctive features, to be intrinsically symbolic? Can we consider instead that sounds used in relation to syntax and cognitive sense are capable of presenting certain meanings and kinds of meanings because of some resemblance between the quality of a sound and some quality that is part of the meaning it serves to represent?

If a sound is appropriate by virtue of one or another of its qualities to the meaning presented, it is useful material to be chosen in constructing the presentation of the meaning. In the same sense Freud discusses how the characteristics, including the sounds, of language make it useful material in constructing dreams, jokes, and symptoms. Freud makes clear that in addition sounds, by their relations and deployment—their connections, resemblances, contrasts, and permutations—serve to suggest and to *make* relations among the meanings of the apparently unrelated words in which they appear.

Classes and Subclasses of Sounds

Let us begin the attempt to solve the problem of the paradoxical affective state presented by the language of "The Snow Man" by defining classes, subclasses, and families of sounds.

First, the two distinctive features MUSIC (vocalic-nonvocalic) and NOISE (consonantal-nonconsonantal), each with two values (present or plus, absent or minus), combine to form the four major classes: GLIDES; DUOPHONES (liquids); CHORDS (vowels); and NOISES (consonants).

MUSIC with a positive value signifies a periodic complex sound-wave, which is a combination of a number of simple sound-waves (pure tones). Each tone in music is always accompanied by overtones. The frequency of each simple sound-wave is a whole-number multiple or harmonic of the fundamental frequency (whatever it is) with which the complex sound-wave is itself regularly repeated. The fundamental frequency determines the pitch at which the sound is uttered; the overtones or harmonics determine the timbre or quality of the sound. The complex sound-wave is relatively stable in form and its amplitude changes relatively slowly. The distribution of energy among these simple sound-waves (which particular harmonics are involved and the amplitude of each simple sound-wave) is an invariant characteristic of, and differs for, each language sound or phoneme designated MUSIC. The vocal tract as an instrument produces MUSIC with vibrations of vocal chords transmitted through a relatively unobstructed channel.

NOISE with a positive value signifies an aperiodic complex sound-wave whose constituent sound-waves have no specifiable relation to the fundamental frequency of the sound. The form of the complex sound-wave tends to change with each repetition and its amplitude tends to diminish relatively rapidly. The vocal tract is shaped to dampen sound. The vocal tract produces NOISE through the creation of significant degrees of obstruction in the channel. Sound is produced primarily not by vocal chord vibration but by friction when air is forced through a narrowed channel, or by percussion when a complete closure, behind which air pressure has built up, suddenly opens.

Sounds that are designated MUSIC are high-energy sounds compared with sounds that are designated NOISE, which are low-energy sounds.

I. GLIDES (h, w, y) have a relative absence of MUSIC but also, because the vocal tract is relatively unobstructed, a relative absence of NOISE. These sounds glide smoothly into chords.

II. DUOPHONES (r, l) are the inverse (with respect to these feature values) of the glides. MUSIC and NOISE are both present. The power of the duophones is just below that of the chords. I use the term "duophones" to emphasize that the instrument producing these sounds is one capable of producing noise and music simultaneously.

III. CHORDS (the vowels) have MUSIC and not NOISE—vocal chord vibration and a relatively unobstructed vocal tract. These are the most powerful sounds and the apex of every syllable.

Other phonemes, singly or in combination, or "silence," may form the "attack" or ascent preceding the apical chord in a syllable, or (with the exception of the glides) the "release," "letting go," decay, or descent following the apical chord in a syllable. The psychoanalytic reader should note with interest how speech is thus organized into rhythmic pulses, so that speech like music may be a means to the symbolization or presentation of tumescence-discharge-detumescence or anticipation-climax-relaxation *through sound alone.* In the English language, an attack or ascent may consist of up to three phonemes; a release or descent up to four phonemes.

Two or more syllables may be connected usually by identity or similarity (but also possibly by contrast) in the *sound* of: (1) their attacks or ascents, for example, "man" and "mind"; (2) their apices, for example, "man" and "land"; (3) their releases or descents, for example, "sound" and "wind"; (4) their attacks or ascents *and* apices, for example, "wind" and "winter"; (5) their apices *and* releases or descents, for example, "cold" and "behold"; or (6) their attacks or ascents *and* releases or descents, for example, "one (wun)" and "win" (the first syllable of "winter").

In case such patterns are discoverable, the question that arises, of course, is: to what extend are they interpretable? What warrants them? For example, do sound patterns suggest or support relations among meanings?

IV. NOISES (p, b, f, v, m, t, d, th as in "there," th· as in "think," n, s, z, ch, j, sh, zh as in "azure," k, g, ng as in "long") are the inverse (with respect to these feature values) of the chords. NOISES have NOISE and no MUSIC. Vocal chord vibration, if present, is secondary and friction and percussion sounds are produced with various degrees of significant obstruction in the vocal tract.

The values of two additional features may be combined to form four major subclasses of NOISES. ABRUPT/GRADUAL (continuant/noncontinuant or interrupted) signifies a sudden or gradual change in power of sound. That is, sound begins abruptly or gradually; a build-up of pressure behind complete closure at the oral orifice is or is not present. AMPLIFIED/MUTED (strident/mellow) signifies the amplification of high-pitched high-frequency components, on the one hand, or the use of complex supplementary obstructions to mute these components, on the other.

A_1. PERCUSSIVES (plosives or stops b, d, g and p, t, k)

include as indicated two groups, those with and those without "voice"—supplementary vocal chord vibration resulting in low frequency sound waves or RUMBLING. PERCUSSIVES are ABRUPT and MUTED.

A_2. HUMS (nasals n, m, ng) are also ABRUPT and MUTED, but are the inverse of percussives with respect to the value of another feature NASAL. NASAL signifies vocal chord vibration and the deflection of air in the presence of closure at the oral orifice into the nasal chamber, which acts as a supplementary resonator, producing periodic complex soundwaves (lower-energy, subdued chords). Therefore, HUMS, while a subclass of NOISES and closely related to the PERCUSSIVES, are also part of the large family of SONORANTS (musical sounds), which includes the glides, duophones, and chords. These sonorants contrast with the NONSONORANTS (obstruents), consisting of the other subclasses of NOISES (the percussives and the hisses and buzzes).

B. HISSES and BUZZES (fricatives), which are the inverse of both percussives and hums with respect to the values of these two features, are GRADUAL and AMPLIFIED. Buzzes (v, z, zh) are distinguished from hisses (f, s, sh) by the presence of supplementary "voice" or RUMBLING.

C. MUTED HISS or BUZZ (th or th, respectively; these are also fricatives) are GRADUAL and MUTED.

D. ABRUPT HISS or BUZZ (the affricates ch and j respectively), which are combinations of an initial abrupt percussive followed by a gradual amplified hiss or buzz (ch is a combination of t and sh; j of d and zh), are ABRUPT and AMPLIFIED and are thus the inverse of subclass C with respect to the values of these two features.

Families of Sounds and the Presentation of Affective States

Any member of these major classes and subclasses may also be characterized by three additional features, and the CHORDS by two more features (five altogether).

The first such feature SUSTAINED/EPHEMERAL (tense/lax) signifies the effort required to produce a sound and the qualities of a sound produced by a maximum or minimum effort. In general, relatively SUSTAINED sounds involve a maximum effort: the more-or-less strenuous maintenance of the vocal tract in a maximally deviant state (with respect to a resting or neutral state); a build-up of high pressure prior to release of sound; and deliberate, controlled, relatively slow articulatory movements. Such sounds may not only be described as sustained but also as relatively forceful, decisive, distinct, active, assertive, tense, clear, precise, taut, or tight in quality. Relatively EPHEMERAL sounds involve a minimum effort: less tension in the muscles controlling the shape of the vocal tract; easy-to-create, less deviant states of the vocal tract; a build-up of less pressure prior to the release of sound; and casual, relatively rapid articulatory movements. Such sounds may not only be described as ephemeral but also as relatively weak, casual, blurred, passive, diffident, relaxed, amorphous, vague, slack, or loose in quality.

The choice of adjectives to describe the qualities designated by these and the following features is, of course, somewhat arbitrary, although suggested by the nature of their acoustical correlates, the language used to describe sounds in music, and various studies of "phonetic symbolism" cited in the literature.[60] In the discussion of each feature, I shall suggest alternative adjectives and also illustrate the contrast, as I am about to do in the discussion of SUSTAINED/EPHEMERAL, by pairs of sounds that exemplify it. A reader then may have the option of rejecting all offered adjectives and identifying a quality in his own thinking simply as that nameless quality which differentiates this or that pair of phonemes; the phonemes in each pair would be identical with respect to their values for all other features. So musicians may think of a sound as having that nameless quality which sounds produced by a flute, an oboe, a horn, or a

60. Examples may be found in Jakobson, Fant, and Halle (1963).

drum have, and perhaps, therefore, as flute-like or oboe-like or horn-like. At least from this present analysis, a reader shall always know, as he may not know when reading certain nontechnical literary or music criticism or when listening to different discussions on different occasions by the same psychoanalyst or to discussions by different psychoanalysts about emotional states, that when I use the same adjective or combination of adjectives to describe a sound or sounds I am indeed signifying in each use of an adjective the same quality.

So-called "long" vowels are sustained; "short" vowels ephemeral. Also: if t and d are compared, t is sustained and d ephemeral; p is sustained and b ephemeral; f is sustained and v ephemeral; s is sustained and z ephemeral; th is sustained and <u>th</u> ephemeral; k is sustained and g ephemeral; ch is sustained and j ephemeral; sh is sustained and zh ephemeral.

One may notice in articulating these sounds that "voice" or vocal chord vibration, which characterizes buzzes and such rumbling percussives as d, b, and g, is *not* possible when there is a high degree of tension (requiring maximum effort) in the muscles shaping the vocal tract. I have therefore assigned the feature EPHEMERAL not only to buzzes and these rumbling percussives but also to duophones and hums, which are characterized by vocal chord vibration requiring a relaxed vocal tract. In the case of duophones and hums, EPHEMERAL probably signifies primarily the extent of the effort involved in producing the sound rather than the duration of the sound; whereas in the case of the nonsonorants, EPHEMERAL probably signifies both relatively less effort and less duration.

Sounds then may be varied from syllable to syllable and from word to word with respect to this feature, to contrast sustained and ephemeral ascents, apices, and descents. There exists the possibility, therefore, that different emotive meanings on some occasions, although certainly not necessarily invariably, might be symbolized by using such variations in presentations of different durations of anticipation or tumescence, climax or discharge, detumescence or relaxation.

The four additional features concern the distribution of the energy of a complex sound-wave among its components on the frequency-spectrum and the qualities or timbres associated with such a distribution of energy among such a combination of components: LARGE/SMALL (compact/noncompact, applied only to vowels); SOFT/HARD (diffuse/nondiffuse); DARK/LUMINOUS (grave/acute); and OPAQUE/TRANSPARENT (flat/plain, applied only to vowels).

LARGE chords have a relative concentration of energy among components in the middle of the frequency-spectrum. A sound in that frequency range with a given intensity will be louder than a sound of the same intensity in a frequency range at either extreme of the frequency-spectrum. In producing large sounds, the vocal tract is relatively unobstructed or open. SMALL chords do not have such a relative concentration of energy in the middle of the frequency-spectrum. In producing small sounds, the vocal tract is relatively constricted.

LARGE sounds might also be described as voluminous, spacious, expansive, full, capacious, or cavernous; and SMALL sounds as contracted, constricted, circumscribed, empty, cramped, or pinched. So: $\overline{\text{aw}}$ in "frost" is large and $\overline{\text{o}}$ in "snow" is small; a in "man" is large and e in "self" is small. Each of these pairs is alike in all other features.

SOFT sounds have a relative concentration of energy among components in the extremes of the frequency-spectrum; HARD sounds do not have such a concentration. SOFT sounds are produced with a narrowing in the front of the vocal tract and therefore a relatively small or absent resonant chamber in the vocal tract in front of this narrowing. HARD sounds are produced with a narrowing in the back of the vocal tract and therefore a relatively large resonant chamber in the vocal tract in front of this narrowing.

SOFT sounds might also be described as thin or weak; HARD

sounds as dense, strong, or potent. So: e in "self" is hard and i in "wind" is soft; o in "not" is hard and oo in "full" is soft; ō in "snow" is hard and o͞o in "who" is soft; ā in "same" is hard and ē in "trees" is soft. Also: r is hard and l soft; zh is hard and z soft; n̲g̲ is hard and m soft; g is hard and b soft; sh is hard and s̄ soft; k is hard and p soft. Each of these pairs is alike in all other features.

DARK sounds involve predominance of the low end of the frequency-spectrum; LUMINOUS sounds involve predominance of the high end of the frequency-spectrum. I have not called these "high" and "low" sounds, because that terminology might suggest the fundamental frequency or pitch at which a sound is uttered, whereas this feature involves the invariant combination of particular frequencies or overtones, the timbre of a sound, no matter at what pitch it is uttered.

DARK sounds might also be described as falling, somber, or absorbent; LUMINOUS sounds as rising, bright, or reflecting. So: u in "crust" is dark and e in "self" is luminous; ew in "few" is dark and ē in "trees" is luminous. Also: b is dark and d luminous; v is dark and z luminous; m is dark and n luminous; p is dark and t luminous; f is dark and s luminous. Each of these pairs is alike in all other features.

OPAQUE sounds involve the use of rounded lips as a low pass filter which screens out high frequency components; TRANSPARENT sounds do not involve such a filter. The use of the filter selects overtones closer to the fundamental frequency and produces, therefore, a more pure and less rich sound. The filter filters out some frequencies and therefore some energy; a sound uttered without the lips rounded will seem to recede, therefore, if it is uttered with the lips rounded but without altering pitch or loudness.

OPAQUE sounds might also be described as deep, profound, distant, receding, heavy, rough, dull, saturated, or monochromatic; TRANSPARENT sounds as superficial, high, shallow, near, motionless, light, smooth, sharp, iridescent, or polychromatic. So: o in "not" is opaque and u in "crust" transparent; $\overline{\text{aw}}$ in "frost" is opaque and ah in "regard" transparent; $\overline{\text{oo}}$ in "who" is opaque and ew in "few" transparent. Each of these pairs is alike in all other features.

Again, it is possible that on some occasions, although certainly not necessarily invariably, emotive meanings might be symbolized by using variations in HARD and SOFT to present different degrees of intensity of, and variations in DARK and LUMINOUS to present different values (somber or elate) associated with: anticipation or tumescence, climax or discharge, detumescence or relaxation.

The following families of language sounds, which intersect the major classes and subclasses, are now possible to define. The reader will notice that with respect to the values of SOFT/HARD and DARK/LUMINOUS, families 1 and 4 are inversions of each other; as are families 2 and 3.

1. SOFT and LUMINOUS

EPHEMERAL

glide: y
duophone: l
hum: n
percussive: d
buzz: z
muted buzz: t̲h̲
chord: i, in "winter," is SMALL and SOFT, LUMINOUS and TRANSPARENT

SUSTAINED

percussive: t
hiss: s
muted hiss: th
chord: ē, in "trees," is SMALL and SOFT, LUMINOUS and TRANSPARENT

2. HARD and LUMINOUS

EPHEMERAL

duophone: r
buzz: zh
abrupt buzz: j
chords: a, in "man," is LARGE and HARD, LUMINOUS and TRANSPARENT
e, in "self," is SMALL and HARD, LUMINOUS and TRANSPARENT
ə "schwa" (the unstressed vowel sound), is SMALL and HARD, LUMINOUS and TRANSPARENT (This sound is extremely ephemeral and all its qualities extremely attenuated or inconspicuous, because it only appears in unstressed syllables—e.g., the second and third syllables of "junipers.")

SUSTAINED

hiss: sh
abrupt hiss: ch
chord: ā, in "same," is SMALL and HARD, LUMINOUS and TRANSPARENT

3. SOFT and DARK

EPHEMERAL

glide: w, which is DARK and OPAQUE
hum: m
percussive: b
buzz: v
chord: oo, in "full," is SMALL and SOFT, DARK and OPAQUE

SUSTAINED

percussive: p
hiss: f
chords: $\overline{\text{oo}}$, in "who," is SMALL and SOFT, DARK and OPAQUE
ew, in "few," is SMALL and SOFT, DARK and TRANSPARENT

4. HARD and DARK

EPHEMERAL

hum: ng
percussive: g
chords: aw, in "for," is LARGE and HARD, DARK and OPAQUE
o, in "not," is SMALL and HARD, DARK and OPAQUE
u, in "must," is SMALL and HARD, DARK and TRANSPARENT

SUSTAINED

glide: h
percussive: k
chords: a̅w̅, in "frost," is LARGE and HARD, DARK and OPAQUE
ō, in "snow," is SMALL and HARD, DARK and OPAQUE
ah, in "regard" and as the sound that begins the diphthong ī (ah plus i), as in "mind," and the diphthong ou (ah plus oo), as in "sound," is LARGE and HARD, DARK and TRANSPARENT

It is possible that on some occasions, although certainly not necessarily invariably, emotive meanings might be symbolized by using one or another family of sounds or combinations of sounds from a particular family to present affective states that might be characterized as: (1) ephemeral, mild, elate; (2) sustained, mild, elate; (3) ephemeral, intense, elate; (4) sustained, intense, elate; (5) ephemeral, mild, somber; (6) sustained, mild, somber; (7) ephemeral, intense, somber; (8) sustained, intense, somber. Similarly, ambivalence might be presented by using combinations of sounds from families of opposite qualities.

Sounds and the Dream-Work

Freud discussed in *The Interpretation of Dreams* how words may allude to one another because they share the *same* sounds, as do "man" and "misery;" "snow" and "cold;" "wind" and "sound;" "wind" and "winter;" "cold" and "behold," and so on. This partial sameness in sound, which links one word to another, is a useful means in constructing the manifest dream, a rebus-like presentation in images of words or syllables. The words or syllables ultimately chosen have the kind of "representability" that makes such presentation possible. In addition, they are condensations. That is, they are related by a complex network of similarities and oppositions in meaning as well as sound to a maximum number of the words that represent latent thoughts. These condensations are unraveled—such a network is reconstructed—by the procedure of "free association" in the work of psychoanalysis. The use of intermediate words to form links between the verbal representations of latent thoughts and the concrete words that may be translated into images results in displacements of salience, value, interest, or importance from those words representing the latent thoughts to the quite different words resulting from the process of dream construction which are eventually presented in the images of the manifest dream.

Now, we see from our grouping of sounds according to their distinctive features that words are able to allude to, and substitute for, one another, and each word is therefore potentially a condensation of an entire set of words and their meanings, because they share sound qualities of which we are not ordinarily focally aware. It is not at all obvious, then, what sounds, and therefore what words, may evoke each other. Sounds seem to be alike and opposite in ways that we do not ordinarily consciously recognize, but of which we may have tacit knowledge.

For example, in "The Snow Man," "bouz (boughs)," which satisfies considerations of representability, is able not only to allude to, but also to link, both "man" and "miz (misery)," through sound. The sounds b and m are both abrupt, muted noises; and both soft and dark. The sounds n and z are both soft, luminous noises. Even the diphthong ou includes ah, which is hard (like the sound a), and oo, which is soft (like the sound i). We know that poets use these similarities, just as they use processes of displacement and condensation. In his poem "Metamorphosis" (1954, pp. 265–66), Stevens uses explicit processes of displacement and condensation to present a conception of "metamorphosis," for example, in the sequence formed by the last line of the first stanza, the last line of the second stanza, and the last two lines of the fourth stanza: "Sep - tem - ber. . . . / Oto - otu - bre. / To and to and fro/Fro Niz - nil - imbo." The last two words of the poem are a condensation—what Freud would have termed a condensation by composition—of "November," "frozen," "nil," and "limbo." Is there any reason to suppose that psychoanalysts and analysands, who certainly have knowledge of displacement and condensation, do not possess a similar linguistic knowledge or competence with regard to sound qualities, even if this knowledge is tacit or used outside awareness?

"The Snow Man" is constructed so that its sounds are organized in relation to each other to form discoverable patterns. These sound patterns appear to be related in a complex way to patterns of syntax and meaning. The poet, because of his aims (which include the representation and presentation of many kinds of meaning, including emotive meaning), has imposed unusual and, in this sense, deviant constraints upon the syntactic and lexical selections he has permitted himself to make in constructing this linguistic object. The constraints make the extraordinary degree of organization possible.

Such a degree of organization is, of course, not likely to be found in the speech utterances of the psychoanalytic session. However, that should not automatically bar us from considering the possibility that some lesser degree of organization—involving similar kinds of constraints upon lexical and syntactic selections, and similar kinds of patterns, to those found in "The Snow Man"—might occur (even if only occasionally, but nevertheless in order to achieve similar aims) in psychoanalytic sessions. Suppose a psychoanalyst should hear an extraordinary concentration of words in two or three sentences that *all* begin with the soft, luminous, ephemeral, rumbling percussive noise d. Is it to be supposed that such a phenomenon even if unnoticed by the psychoanalyst has no effect upon him? Is such a phenomenon, unlike no other in psychoanalysis, to be considered *not* determined—meaningless? If it is meaningful, how shall it be interpreted? Perhaps, indeed, the psychoanalyst—who above all is, like the snow man, a "listener, who listens . . . and beholds"—might be expected to come to his work with a special interest and investment in, and a special sensitivity to, "sounds" as meaningful events sensuously and not only cognitively apprehended.

The notion that such selectional constraints affect the construction of symbolic entities is not new in psychoanalysis. According to Freud's account in *The Interpretation of Dreams,* similar constraints (although not as stringent from the point of view of achieving the aim of communication) are imposed upon the dreamer. He must in his choice of words submit to considerations of representability (in visual imagery) as well as to the condition that each word finally chosen for presentation in the manifest dream should be connected by a network of other intermediate words, related by sound and sense, similarity and contrast, to a *maximum* number of those words representing the latent thoughts. So, the poet submits to the constraint that his choice of words must maximize the relation of sound, syntax, and sense.

Condensation and Displacement

In a linguistic object such as a poem, one may discover at the level of sound operations that correspond to the operations of the dream-work (condensation and displacement). Freud used the term "identification" to describe one kind of condensation. In the realm of sound, this kind of condensation may also occur. Any member of a class, subclass, or family of sounds may evoke all the other members of that class, subclass, or family of sounds. Any representative of a class, subclass, or family of sounds may evoke one or more of the features shared by the members of that class, subclass, or family of sounds. For example, the sound s may evoke the whole class of noises, the whole subclass of hisses and buzzes, or the whole family of sustained, soft, luminous sounds, and therefore signify, stand for, or mean "noise," "hiss or buzz," or "sustained, soft, and luminous."

Another kind of condensation in the realm of sound corresponds to Freud's condensation through the selection of different features of different people, for example, to form a composite image, which signifies or alludes to what the different people have in common. So, a word or syllable, which is a composite image of different sounds and different kinds of sounds, may evoke what all its sounds have in common. For example, "lawng (long)" which is a combination of a duophone, a chord, and a hum, is made up of different sounds all of which are sonorous; also "wun (one)" and "man" are made up of sounds all of which are sonorous. The different sounds in "wind," "fool (full)," and "lēvz (leaves)" are all soft. The different sounds in "wind," "man," "wun (one)," and "land" are all ephemeral. The different sounds in "that," "thār (there)," "land," and "trēz (trees)" are all luminous.

Displacements also occur and are important in conveying or presenting certain kinds of meanings in the realm of sound. Suppose that emphasis, focus, value, or intensity could be shown to be related to particular sounds in contrast to other sounds, for example, sonorant sounds in contrast to nonsonorant sounds (hums in contrast to percussives); sustained sounds in contrast to ephemeral sounds; large chords in contrast to small chords; hard sounds in contrast to soft sounds; or amplified hisses or buzzes in contrast to muted hisses or buzzes. Then, a change in the position of one such sound might be considered a displacement of intensity from one position to another. If the sound s, for example, is found first as an ascent to a high-energy chord, as in "sun," and then as a descent from a high-energy chord, as in "plās (place)," one might under certain circumstances want to say that the intensity attached to an ascent has been displaced to a descent. Similarly, the sonorant duophone l may be found inside a pattern ABA, i.e., in the B position—for example, in the sequence **K L T** in the ascending sounds of the words in the fourth line of "The Snow Man:" Ⓚ**ōld** . . . Ⓛ**awng** Ⓣ**īm.** Subsequently, this sonorant duophone may be found at the boundaries of such a pattern, i.e., in the A position(s) —for example, in the sequence **R DG L** in the ascending sounds of the stressed syllables in the sixth line: Ⓡ**uf** (rough) . . . Ⓓ**is**-(tant) . . . ⒼⓁ**it**-(ter). One might want to say, then, under certain circumstances, that the intensity attached to the center of a pattern has been displaced to the boundaries of the pattern.

Similarly, emphasis, focus, value, or intensity may be related to location itself, as in the difference in salience and power associated with words and syllables given different degrees of stress or accent, or in the difference of duration and power of the same sound depending on its location in the ascent to an apical chord or the descent from an apical chord. Then, for example, if the sounds m and w are found in the ascents to apical chords of stressed syllables in a line and in the next line the sounds g and r are found in similar locations, one may want to say under certain circumstances that intensity has been displaced from the sounds m and w to the sounds g and r.

Reversal, Augmentation, Diminution, and Deletion

One may also discover at the level of sound operations that correspond to the "transformations" Freud postulated to account for the vicissitudes of affects in dream-construction: (1) the reversal of an affect (actually achieved not by changing the affect itself but by recruiting from some other available source its opposite to substitute for it, that is, recruiting another *signifier* evoking an opposite affect); (2) complete inhibition or elimination of an affect (deletion); (3) diminution of the intensity of an affect; and (4) augmentation of the intensity of an affect (achieved by recruiting additional sources of or, in other words, other *signifiers* evoking the same affect).

A sound quality may be said to be augmented or diminished if: (1) the frequency of the sound quality is increased or decreased from one segment of a sequence to another; (2) the frequency of the sound quality is increased or decreased with respect to some normative frequency; (3) if the frequency of the sound quality in a pattern is increased or decreased from one occurrence of the pattern to another; or (4) if a pattern in which the sound quality appears increases or decreases in frequency over some span.

A sound quality may be said to be eliminated if the sound quality no longer appears in subsequent occurrences of a pattern; if the pattern in which the sound quality appears ceases to recur; or if the sound quality itself disappears from a sequence of sounds.

Examples of reversal, augmentation, diminution, and deletion in "The Snow Man" may be found by studying Tables 1 through 6.

Table 1. The Snow Man

1)	One	must	have	a	mind	of	winter
	W	m	H		**M**		**W** t
	U	u	A		**AH+I**		**I** ə
	N	s	V		**N**		**N** r
		t			**D**		

2)	To	regard	the	frost	and	the	boughs
				F			
	t	r **G**		**R**			**B**
	o͞o	ē **AH**		**A͞W**	a		**AH+OO**
		R		**S**	n		**Z**
		D		**T**	d		

3)	Of	the	pine-	trees	crusted	with	snow;
				t	**K**		**S**
			P	r	**R**	w	**N**
	u		**AH+I**	ē	**U** ə	i	**Ō**
	v		**N**	z	**S** d	th	
					T		

4)	And	have	been	cold	a	long	time
		H	b	**K**		**L**	**T**
	a	A	i	**Ō**		**A͞W**	**AH+I**
	n	V	n	**L**		**NG**	**M**
	d			**D**			

5)	To	behold	the	junipers	shagged	with	ice,
	T	b **H**		**J** n p	**SH**	w	
	o͞o	ē **Ō**		**O͞O** ə ə	**A**	i	**AH+I**
		L		r	**G**	th	**S**
		D		z	**D**		

6)	The	spruces	rough	in	the	distant	glitter
		S					
		P					**G**
		R	**R**			**D** t	**L**
		O͞O ə	**U**	i		**I** ə	**I** ə
		S z	**F**	n		**S** n	**T** r
						t	

7)	Of	the	January	sun;	and	not	to	think
			J y	**S**		**N**	t	**TH**
	U		A o͞o E ē	**U**	a	**O**	o͞o	**I**
	V		N R	**N**	n	**T**		**NG**
					d			**K**

8)	Of	any	misery	in	the	sound	of	the	wind
			M			**S**			**W**
	u	E ē	**I** ə Ē	i		**AH+OO**	u		**I**
	v	N	**Z** r	n		**N**	v		**N**
						D			**D**

9) In the sound of a few leaves,

In	the	sound	of	a	few	leaves,
		S			F	L
i		AH+OO	u		EW	Ē
n		N	v			V
		D				Z

10) Which is the sound of the land

Which	is	the	sound	of	the	land
W			S			L
I	i		AH+OO	u		A
CH	z		N	v		N
			D			D

11) Full of the same wind

Full	of	the	same	wind
F			S	W
OO	u		Ā	I
L	v		M	N
				D

12) That is blowing in the same bare place

That	is	blowing	in	the	same	bare	place
		B					P
TH		L			S	B	L
A	i	Ō i	I		Ā	Ā	Ā
T	z	ng	N		M	R	S

13) For the listener, who listens in the snow,

For	the	listener,	who	listens	in	the	snow,
							S
f		L	h	L			N
aw		I e E	o͞o	I ə	i		Ō
r		S n R		S n	n		
				z			

14) And, nothing himself, beholds

And,	nothing	himself,	beholds
	N	h S	b H
a	U i	i E	ē Ō
n	TH ng	m L	L
d		F	D
			Z

15) Nothing that is not there and the nothing that is.

Nothing	that	is	not	there	and	the	nothing	that	is.
N	TH		N	TH		th	N	th	
U i	A	i	O	Ā	a	ē	U i	a	I
TH ng	T	z	T	R	n		TH ng	t	Z
					d				

Table 2. Hisses-Buzzes and Hums

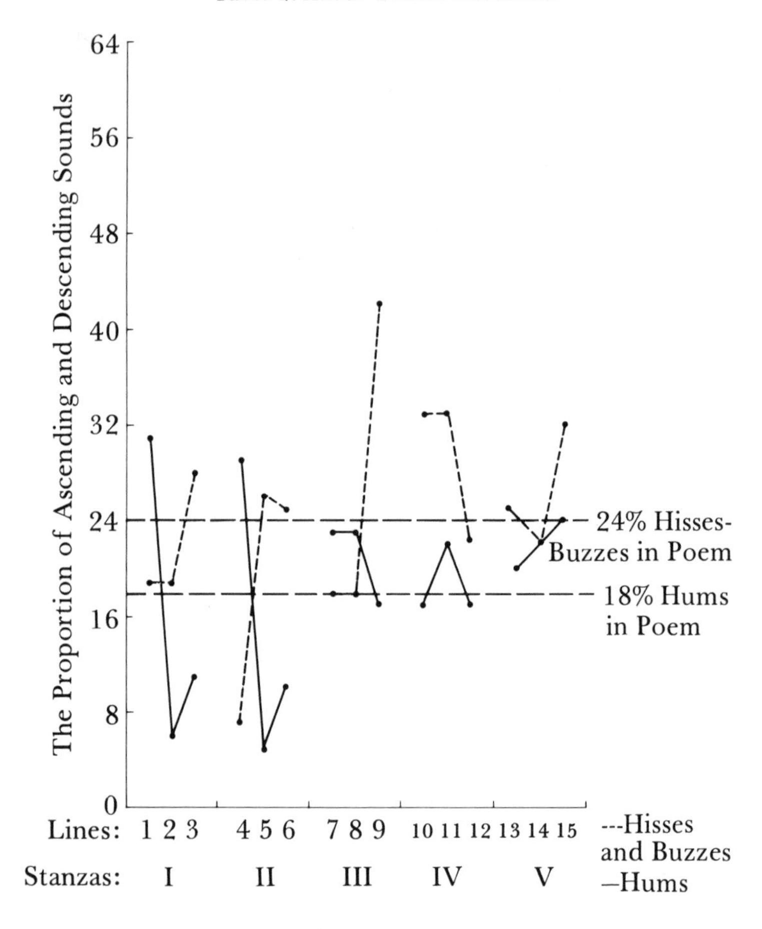

Table 3. Glides and Hums

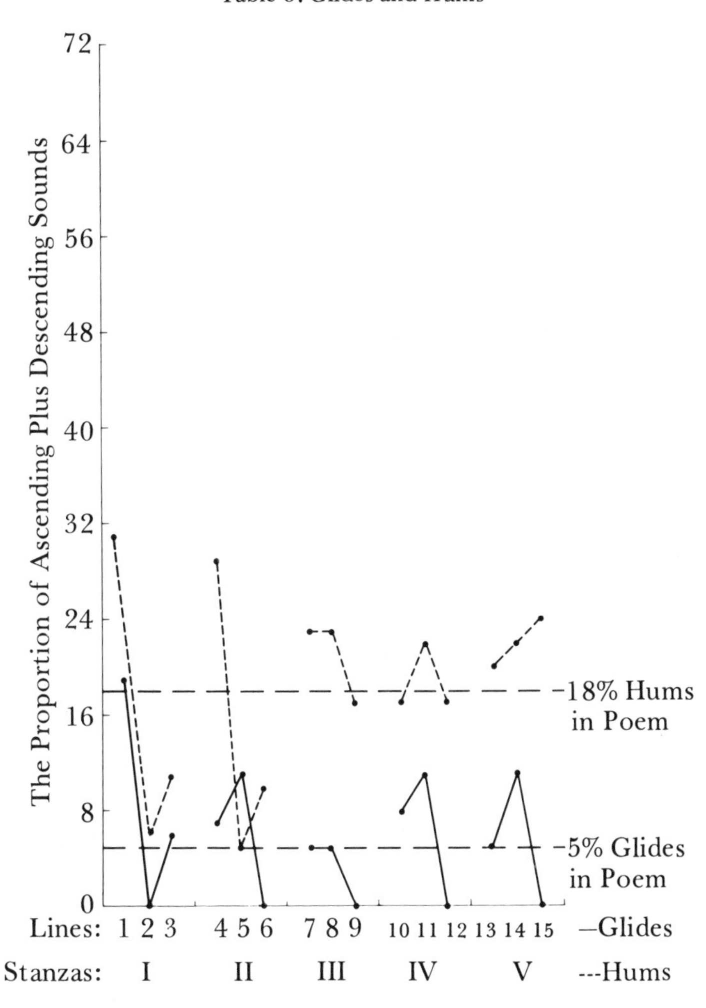

Table 4. Percussives and Duophones

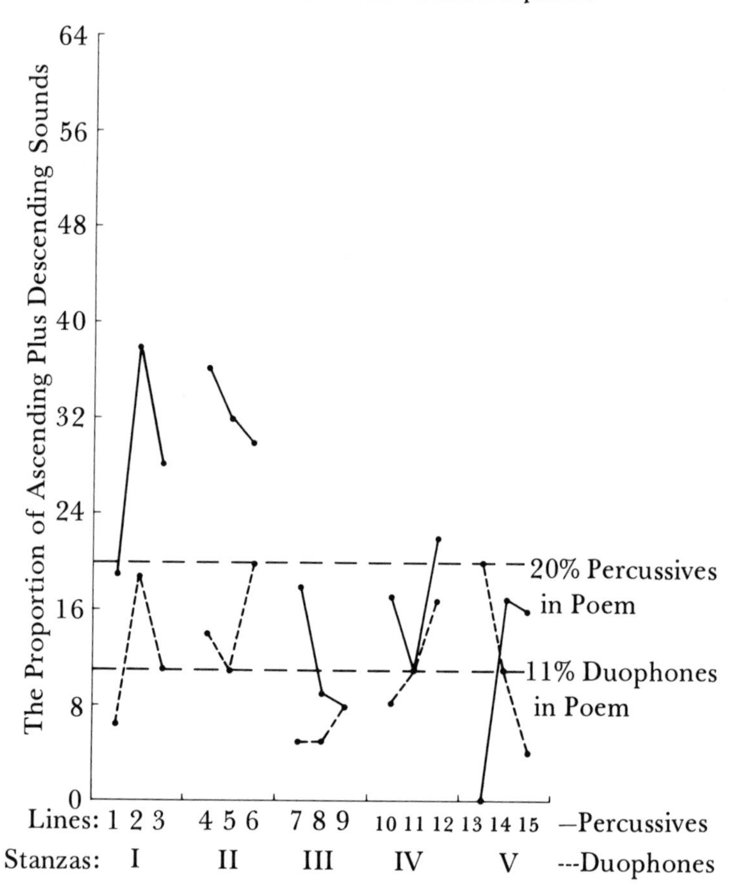

Table 5. Hisses-Buzzes and Duophones

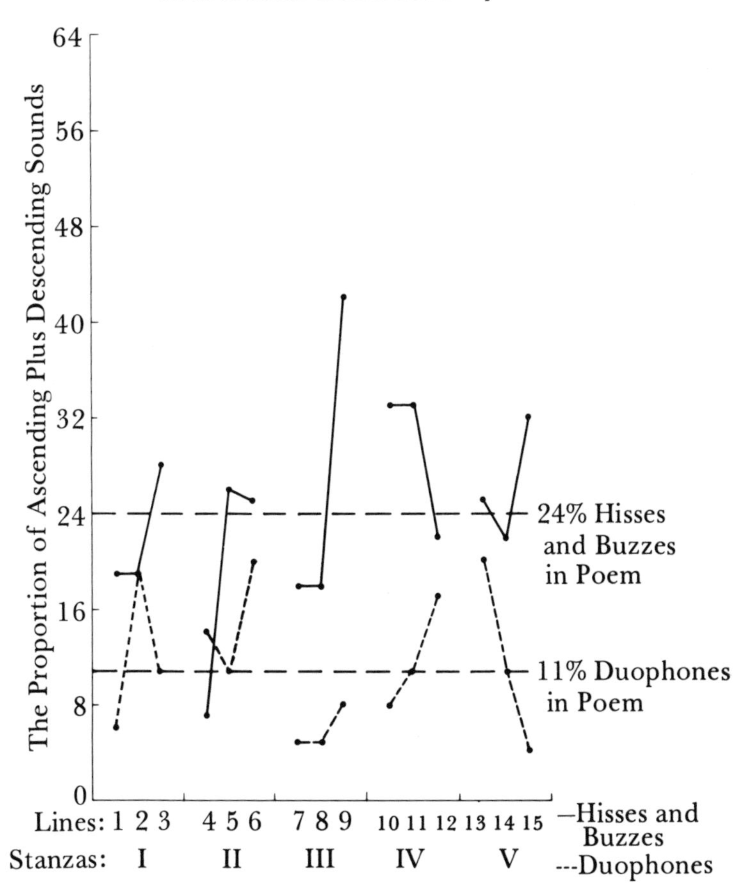

Table 6. Sonorants, Nonsonorants, and Silence

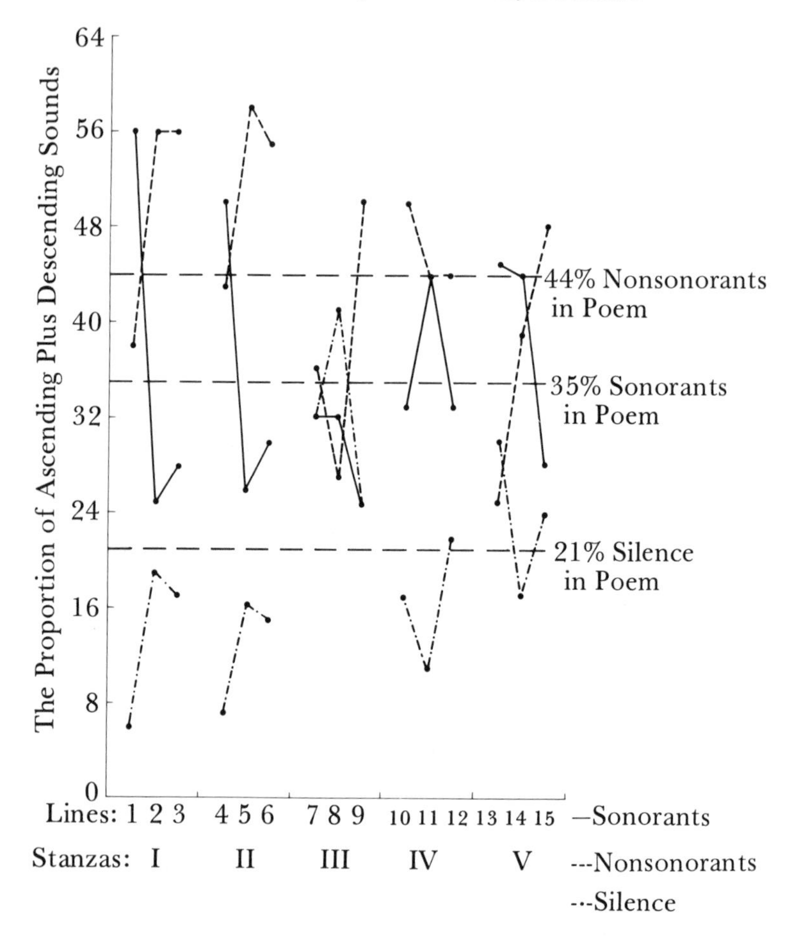

Table 1 is a restatement of the poem, with phonemes substituted for letters, ascents printed above chords and descents below chords, and syllables with no stress in small letters, syllables with secondary stress in capital letters, and syllables with primary stress in bold capital letters. In this discussion I shall follow Winters' metrical analysis (see footnote 56, above).

Tables 2 through 5 represent such vicissitudes as augmentation, diminution, and deletion of classes or subclasses of sounds. A "melodic curve" appears for each class or subclass of sounds in each stanza, based on the proportion of ascending plus descending sounds in each line that are members of that class or subclass. The curves therefore show the pattern of augmentation, diminution, or deletion of a class or subclass of sounds in each stanza. The extent of the selectional deviance in any line (the concentration of a sound in that line compared to its concentration in the poem as a whole) may be noted by referring to the line across each table for a class or subclass of sounds that indicates its percentage of all ascending and descending sounds (including silence, which can be an ascent to or descent from an apical chord) in the whole poem.

Table 6 summarizes the selectional constraints resulting in augmentations and diminutions of sonorants, nonsonorants, and silence. The augmentation of sonorants in the first line of the first and also of the second stanza, followed by a diminution in the last two lines of each of these stanzas, supports the syntactic structure of these two stanzas. The diminution in sonorants from the first to the second line in each of the first two stanzas is repeated from the second to the final line in each of the last three stanzas.

The first line is foregrounded by its unusual augmentation of sonorousness. The lower-energy sonorants, glides and hums, are especially characteristic of the first line. In contrast, the higher-energy sonorants, duophones, are especially characteristic of the sonorous thirteenth line. The first line begins the poem; the thirteenth line begins the final stanza of the poem. The substitution of duophones for glides and hums changes the emotive meaning. It is as if someone's speech had changed, but oh so subtly, from a subdued murmur to a powerful roar, but also to a sound that *presents* "synthesis" (because it *is* a synthesis of noise and music) in approaching a climactic resolution of the meanings represented and presented by the poem.

Aims: Presentation, Economy, Emphasis, Implication, Resolution

The poet (and other users of language, to a lesser degree) will use unusually stringent or deviant selectional constraints, condensation, displacement, reversal, diminution, augmentation, and deletion (and other means as well) to achieve a number of aims.

One aim is the presentation of a conception, not only the conventional representation of an idea but the symbolic presentation in sound of a conception of an attitude or affective orientation to that idea. Presentation makes possible the signification of other kinds of meanings than those conveyed by the cognitive sense of words, such as emotive or conative meanings. Presentation makes possible the signification of conceptions of innominate realms of experience, for which there may be no adequate names, like certain inner states.

Another aim is economy. Economy implies the presentation (and representation) of a maximum density of meanings and different kinds of meanings, with the minimal resources "that will suffice."

Still another aim is the distribution of value, emphasis, interest, or intensity to make clear, or to obscure, a conception of desirable, or undesirable, states or relationships, or a hierarchy of values.

A fourth aim is to achieve a forward, goal-oriented impetus, a progression through implication.

As every psychoanalyst knows, metaphor is implicative. A metaphor (spoken or unspoken) involving a comparison of an event in one realm and, for example, the act of defecation—"he is always shitting on me"—may transform the psychoanalyst's interpretation of words in a discourse (perhaps about an experience in a classroom) having nothing to do with defecation: I EXAMINED his paper; it was MESSY; he should be EXPELLED; I told him to GET his THINGS and GO; he WENT but refused to GIVE UP THINGS which BELONG to the school; he LET GO a lot of FILTHY words at me as he WENT OUT the door.

Whatever the multiple potential meanings of such words, as given in the dictionary, they are not in this discourse ambiguous. They are disambiguated by the context of the discourse. Nevertheless, as one of my students [61] recently demonstrated in a report to a seminar on psychotherapy and language, a metaphor may govern the way (the "level" at which) such unambiguous words are heard by psychotherapist or psychoanalyst.

The implications a metaphor evokes in the mind of a listening psychoanalyst may be realized possibly as a result of an act of interpretation in subsequent utterances: accounts of phantasies; reports of the emergence of memories; or descriptions of hitherto concealed preoccupations now revealed.

If a metaphor may have implications, why not a similar "generative event" (Meyer's term in his book *Explaining Music*) in the realm of sound?

Deviant selectional constraints may make it possible to signify conceptions of innominate realms of experience by creating patterns of similarity, contrast, or sequence, at levels of both sound and syntax. These patterns may imply relationships, not at all immediately apparent, between words and their meanings. Such generative events require interpretation—a search for the warrants, grounds, or reasons for the pattern that will suffice.

A fifth aim, achievable through the use of the means we

61. John Bartlett.

have been describing, is resolution, through confirmation or realization of implications.

The Presentation of Affect in "The Snow Man"

I shall be handicapped, as I attempt to demonstrate the achievement of such aims through the use of such means in the realm of sound in "The Snow Man," because I do not have, and I do not share with my reader, a concise language of form, which is equally applicable to perceived and abstract, hierarchical and nonhierarchical structures, to details and the vaulting arch, to simultaneous configurations and sequential processes, to language and music. I shall necessarily make do here with a poor substitute for such a language, hoping that what vocabulary I have pressed and do press into service shall not stand too much in the way of an appreciative apprehension of the very events the vocabulary is intended to capture and reveal.

In many cases the perceptive reader may see an event long before I have finished describing it. A sorrier case might be provided by the reader who is tenaciously caught up in a painstaking account of detailed sound phenomena. That reader's very persistence and focused preoccupied effort may come between him and a sudden, what has often been for me a breathtaking, revelation of the more or less abstract, orderly, and relatively simple structures hiding in the confusion of a thousand entangled instances and possibilities.

Of course, I have had to impose limitations upon which classes and subclasses, which patterns, and which characteristics of the sounds in these patterns to consider. There are almost countless possibilities involving the invariance of some and the concomitant variation of other characteristics; and countless possibilities also in the variation of the duration or span over which any particular characteristic or combination of characteristics is varied or held invariant in relation to another characteristic or combination of characteristics.

I do not know whether to be more awed by the great variety of patterns—some relatively blatant, some conspicuous, and some mere nuance—which the poet has generated and transformed in this brief poem; or by the consummate skill that has enabled him to know exactly which relatively few of the almost countless possibilities to select in order to construct within these constraints a poem that achieves its aims. In any event, I have focused my comments on phenomena that seem to me to bear upon solving the riddle of the complex, paradoxical emotive meaning presented by the poem—at least in my mind's hearing of it.

The title of the poem is a kind of tonic or home chord; or it is a musical key or a set of norms; or it is a statement of a complex of meanings and different kinds of meaning in a highly condensed form. In this latter respect, it is similar to a manifest dream, and perhaps its full meanings might similarly be unfolded by tracing the links of its phoneme constituents to other elements and expanded contexts in the poem.

The hum n, which appears so prominently in both title and poem, is likely to appear, of course, with high frequency in any sample of the English language. It is the particular distribution of this phoneme in this organized linguistic object, resulting in deviant concentrations of this phoneme in particular lines with respect to its frequency in the poem as a whole, that requires interpretation.

In the title, the relations between hiss (s) and hum (n, m), and between luminous (s, n, a) and dark (m, ō) sounds, especially, are generative events. They are implicative for the poem that follows, a poem that begins with "W U N (one)" and ends with "**I Z** (is)."

The most powerful melody of timbres in the poem is, of course, that of the chords. This melody moves continuously, with a number of variations, from dark (possibly a presentation of "somber") to luminous (possibly a presentation of "elate"). It moves also from hard and dark ("intense, somber") ultimately to soft and luminous ("mild, elate").

Following is a detailed hypothesis concerning the way in which the most salient chords in the poem might be used to present affective meanings. (Refer throughout to Table 1.)

In the title, the initial sustained intense somber **Ō** (in "snow") moves to the ephemeral intense elate **A** (in "man").

mUst hAv mAH+Ind wIn-tər

In the first line, displaced to positions of less stress or salience, a now ephemeral but still intense somber chord, **U** (in "one"), moves again to the ephemeral intense elate **A** (in "have"). Then the "ambivalent" combination of sustained intense somber **AH** and ephemeral mild elate **I** (**Ī,** in "mind") resolves to the ephemeral mild elate **I** (in "winter") at the end of the first line.

rē-gAHrd frA͞Wst bOUz
pAH+In krUst-əd snŌ

In the second and third lines, the sustained intense somber **AH** (in "regard") is followed by: (1) the sustained intense somber **A͞W** (in "frost"); (2) the combination diminishing an initial sustained intense somber **AH** to a final ephemeral mild somber **OO** (in "boughs"); and (3) the ambivalent combination of sustained intense somber **AH** and ephemeral mild elate **I** (in "pine"). The sequence ends this time with the cadential movement from the *ephemeral* intense somber **U** (in "crusted"), now in a more salient position, back to the poem's initial chord, the *sustained* intense somber **Ō** (in "snow").

These sustained sounds, which imply intense effort, are appropriate to, and possibly a presentation of, the act of disciplined perception of things as they are, which is part of the meaning the second line has begun to represent. The opacity of **A͞W** may contribute to a presentation of the remoteness and distance in the perceived reality of winter-as-it-is. It will escape no reader's notice that in this world-as-seen, the chord **AH** plus **OO** (in "boughs") anticipates the later augmentation of the same chord in the repetitions of the word "sound" as the poem moves into the world-as-heard.

k**Ō**ld l**A̅W̅**ng t**AH**+**I**m
bē-h**Ō**ld j**O̅O̅**-nə-pərz sh**A**gd **AH**+**I**s

In the fourth and fifth lines, the initial sustained intense somber **Ō** (in "cold" in the fourth line and "behold" in the fifth) moves through a sustained *intense* somber **A̅W̅** (in "long" in the fourth line) and then a sustained *mild* somber **O̅O̅** (in "junipers" in the fifth line) and an ephemeral intense elate **A** (in "shagged" in the fifth line) to end both times upon the ambivalent **AH** plus **I** (in "time" and "ice").

r**U**f d**I**s-tənt gl**I**t-ər s**U**n

In lines six and seven, the symmetrical cadential movement from an initial ephemeral intense somber **U** (in "rough") to a final **U** (in "sun") is interrupted by an augmented ephemeral mild elate **I** (twice repeated, in "distant" and "glitter"). The sequence **U** to **I** repeats that in the first line: WUN to **WIN-.**

n**O**t th**I**ngk m**I**z-ər-ē
s**AH**+**OO**nd w**I**nd
s**AH**+**OO**nd f**EW** l**Ē**vz
s**AH**+**OO**nd l**A**nd
f**OO**l s**Ā**m w**I**nd

This semi-cadence is followed immediately by five movements from somber to elate. The first, in lines seven and eight, a more ephemeral intense somber **O** (in "not")—instead of **Ō**—culminates in an again augmented ephemeral mild elate **I** (twice repeated in "think" and "misery"). Then the second, third, and fourth: the combination diminishing an initial sustained intense somber **AH** to a final ephemeral mild somber **OO** (in "sound") ends, *first* (line eight) on (once again) the *ephemeral* mild elate **I** (in "wind"); *second* (line nine), following a sustained mild somber **EW** (in "few"), on the *sustained* mild elate **Ē** (in "leaves"); and *finally* (line ten) on the ephemeral but intense elate **A** (in "land"). Finally, the fifth such movement, in line eleven, the ephemeral mild somber **OO** (in "full"), followed by the *sustained intense* elate **Ā** (in "same"), ends, once again, on the *ephemeral mild* elate **I** (in "wind").

bl**Ō**-ing s**Ā**m pl**Ā**s l**I**s-ən-ər l**I**s-ənz sn**Ō**

In lines twelve and thirteen, as in lines six and seven, the symmetrical cadential movement from an initial, this time *sustained* (rather than the *ephemeral* **U**) but still intense somber **Ō** (in "blowing") to a final **Ō** (in "snow") is again interrupted. This time the just-heard-sequence of **Ā I** occurs between the two chords **Ō,** with first the sustained intense elate **Ā** augmented (repeated twice, in "same" and "place") and then the ephemeral mild elate **I** augmented (repeated twice, in "listener" and "listens").

n**U**th-ing him-s**E**lf be-h**Ō**ldz
n**U**th-ing th**Ā**r n**U**th-ing **I**z

In the fourteenth and fifteenth lines, the ephemeral intense somber **U** (line fourteen, in "nothing") moves first, following the *ephemeral* intense elate **E** (in "self"), to a semicadential sustained intense somber **Ō** (in "beholds"). Then **U** (line fifteen, in "nothing") moves to the *sustained* intense elate **Ā** (in "there"). Finally—in a repetition of the movement from the chord **U** in the first secondarily stressed syllable "one" to the chord **I** in the penultimate primarily stressed syllable in "winter" in the first line, but now with both these chords in primarily stressed syllables and no longer separated by the span of a line—**U** (line fifteen, in "nothing") moves to end the poem on the final ephemeral mild elate **I** (in "is").

Implication in "The Snow Man"

In conclusion, I shall look at the way implications are generated and resolved in patterns throughout the poem. With respect to the problem of the affective state presented by the poem, the implications and resolutions generated and confirmed in patterns involving the title's combination of hiss (and by implication buzz) and hum are critical. (Refer throughout to Table 1.)

Before turning to the hiss and hum combination, let us take a brief look at some of the other significant patterns in the poem. In the first line, $\begin{smallmatrix}\mathrm{W}\\\mathrm{U}\\\mathrm{N}\end{smallmatrix}$ and $\begin{smallmatrix}\mathbf{W}\\\mathbf{I}\\\mathbf{N}\end{smallmatrix}$ emphasize the importance of the first line by standing like two pillars at its beginning and end. From one syllable to the other, the apical chord has undergone transformation while ascent and descent have remained invariant.

The first line is also distinguished by the unusual degree of its musicality, although its music is somewhat subdued.

A melody of timbres, an expansion of the "mind of winter" motive, is formed by the ascending sounds in the first line:

Ⓦ	ⓜ	Ⓗ	**Ⓜ**	**Ⓦ**	t
u	u	a	ī	i	ə
n	s	v	n	n	r
	t		d		

The proximal descending sounds in the first line form a rather inconspicuous anticipation of what will become an expansion of the "snow" motive:

w	m	h	m	w
u	u	a	ī	i
Ⓝ	ⓢ	Ⓥ	**Ⓝ**	**Ⓝ**
	t		d	

Separating these two sequences—although the following sequence

W N m s H V **M N W N**

is the one actually heard—has its analogue in music analysis.

This rather dull melody, consisting of the following notes of the scale of C Major c g b f c e b d c, although a linear sequence, may be analyzed as a "compound melody," consisting of one melodic sequence c b c b c and a second melodic sequence g f e d c, which, in contrast to the ascending movement in each of the first four measures, descends over the five measures. Similarly, a linear melodic sequence c e g may be understood as an arpeggiated triadic chord and heard, as it were, as a "simultaneously" sounded combination of tones. To check this, listen, for example, to Bach's works for violin solo.

In the first melody of the poem, all the sounds are dark. In the second melody, all the hums are luminous; the buzz, however, is dark. The two melodies thus present the major oppositions in the poem and are a beginning realization of the implications in the title.

Is it possible that a psychoanalyst ever senses the degree of cathexis, value, or importance, of the meaning(s) being conveyed by the analysand—the key to what particular symbolic world is inhabited, what world of idea and mood is represented and presented, at some moment in time by the analysand—and what is yet to come, from an unwitting perception of such sound events as these?

The psychoanalyst cannot in his work become focally aware of sound events; but he might, later studying a transcript, supposing that one were available, discover that his interventions were related outside of his awareness to such events. The analysand does not organize his speech consciously or consistently to the degree the poet organizes sound in a poem. But, as I have suggested, it is possible that he does so unwittingly, perhaps quite transiently, in an occasional but what also might be a critical psychoanalytic session. It is surely no more fantastic that we attribute such competence to the analysand than that we attribute to him, as Chomsky does, the competence to generate an infinite set of sentences according to rules he cannot make explicit and of which he is not aware. I am reminded of Freud's laconic comment in *The Interpretation of Dreams:* "Ganglion cells can be fantastic too" (p. 87).

The little figure at the end of the first line t ə r with its unstressed apical "schwa," is very different from the rest of the line. This inconspicuous detail is like a tiny inconspicuous detail in a manifest dream, whose implications in associations turn out to be critical. The warrant for this deviance would appear to be its function, immediately apparent *upon hearing the next line:* to imply the sound pattern of the line following it.

This example illustrates the way in which interpretation is retrospective. One must first discover the place to which one has come before one can interpret the meaning of events now understood as steps on the way to this place.

In another implication, the t of t ə r may link with W I N to form W I N t and herald the sound of "wind." Do the prominent glides in the first line (like the y oo in "January," which is echoed in "few" and "who" and in the many ou chords) also imply the meaning of "wind" through a presentation of it?

This figure at the end of the first line is immediately augmented in the first two syllables of the second line: t oo r e

We may say that a displacement has increased the intensity of the little figure in the first line t ə r to become an expansion of the "regard the frost and boughs" motive in the second line:

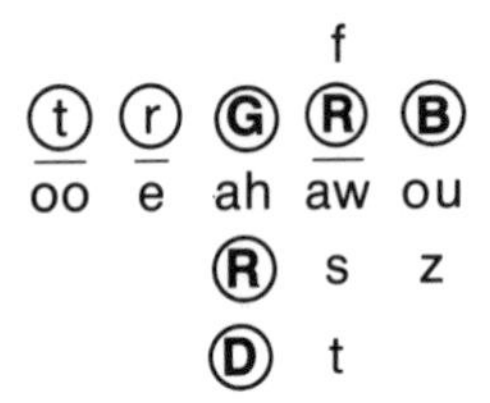

This melody (like the "mind of winter" melody in the first line) has essentially the pattern ABABA. The percussives, substituting for the hums, occupy the A positions in this pattern filled previously by glides; the duophones, substituting for the glides, now occupy the B position in this pattern filled previously by hums. A complicated but elegant and highly organized set of displacements and substitutions! The shift from hums to percussives and to the descending sounds **R D** is a decrease in intensity. The change from glides and hums to duophones and percussives is as dramatic and evocative as if the meaning(s) presented by images of soft breezes and murmurs were suddenly changed to roars, muted abrupt rumbling, taps, and snaps.

Do these changes suggest a movement into another "scene," another world of meanings, related to but different from the meanings of the first line in similarly complex ways? The poem progresses from "mind of winter" to an act involving visual perception of the reality of winter.

The percussive plus duophone melody in line two undergoes hypothetical changes to become

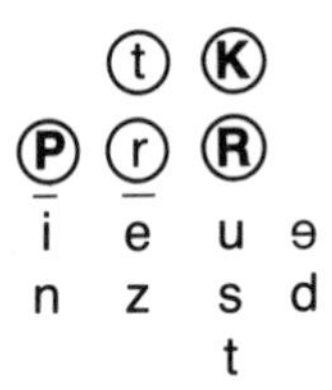

in line three. **P** and **K** are the sustained counterparts of **B** and **G.**

B t r **G R D R**	1. **B** is displaced to beginning of sequence (hypothetical).
B t r **G R**	2. **D** and **R** are deleted (hypothetical).
P t r **K R**	3. Sequence in line 3 of poem.

In lines four and five, Ⓗ ⓑ Ⓚ and Ⓣ ⓑ Ⓗ are

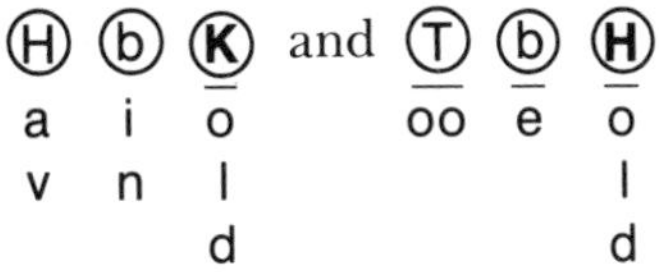

a i ō   ōō ē ō
v n l   l
d   d

mirror images. The pattern H/**K L D L T**/**H** is a condensation of the "mind of winter" and the "regard frost and boughs" motives.

In lines five and six, p r z and S P R are almost mirror images. The pattern p r z S P R is a condensation of the "snow" and the "regard frost and boughs" motives.

In line six, the "regard frost and boughs" melody continues as

R D G L T r or Ⓡ Ⓓ Ⓖ/Ⓛ

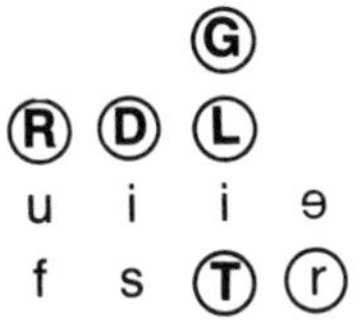

u i i ə
f s Ⓣ ⓡ

and in line twelve as

B L B R **P L** or Ⓑ/Ⓛ Ⓑ Ⓟ/Ⓛ

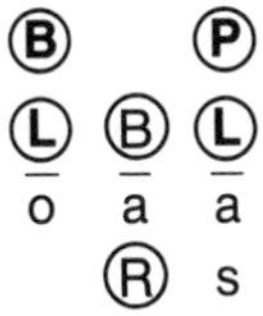

ō ā ā
Ⓡ s

(a combination of luminous duophones and dark percussives, ending with a coupling of a sustained mild somber and a mild luminous sound). The sequence **B L** was implied by the sequence b **K L** (fourth line) and b **H L** (fifth line) and implies h **L** in line thirteen and b **H L** in line fourteen.

I leave it to the reader to think through other condensations, displacements, reversals, augmentations, diminutions, and deletions in these transformations.

Resolution in "The Snow Man"

What is the ultimate fate of the t ə r figure from "winter" at the end of line one? We see it augmented in line two (t/oo r/e) to become a melody of percussives and duophones in the first two stanzas. The sounds t and r are joined to the sound z in t r/e z in line three. At the end of the sixth line, the figure **Tr** appears (in "glitter") among the descending sounds. In line twelve, just preceding the last stanza, not only does the percussive and duophone melody reappear, primarily among the ascending sounds, but the sounds T and z appear once more with the sound R, as in t r/e z, less conspicuously among the descending sounds. This combination reappears finally in the last line as part of the climactic resolution (which includes, as we shall see, also the final resolution of the "snow" melody):

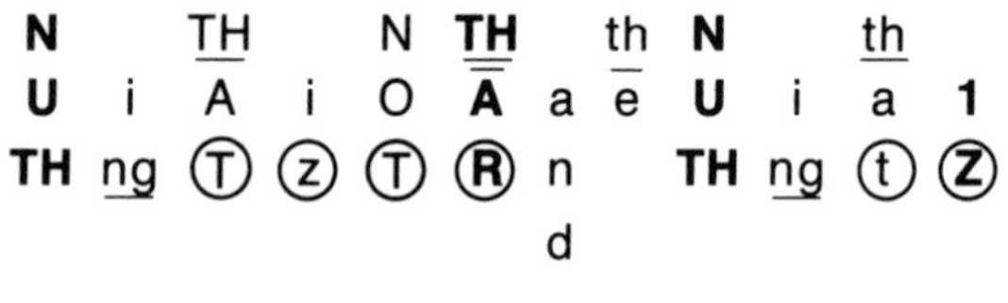

N		TH		N	**TH**		th	**N**		th	
U	i	A	i	O	**Ā**	a	ē	**U**	i	a	**1**
TH	ng	Ⓣ	ⓩ	Ⓣ	**Ⓡ**	n		**TH**	ng	ⓣ	**Ⓩ**
						d					

Here we have (standing like the two pillars W U N and **W I N** in the first line): Tz **TR tZ.** The **R,** a sound of both music and noise, the great sound of synthesis and resolution, of two-in-one, appears saliently in the center of a sequence in the final line bounded by the cadential: Tz→**tZ.**

The vicissitudes of the hiss and hum melody generated by "snow" are ideal for studying the way in which condensation, displacement, reversal, augmentation, diminution, and deletion are used to imply and to resolve. It is in this melody in the poem that the various devices of resolution, of semi-cadence and full cadence, are most dramatically exemplified.

The moments of semi-cadence and full cadence are:

SNOW		SNOW
	SUN	
ICE		IS

This cadential series is a beautiful presentation of a kind of change the psychoanalyst knows from his work. A change to an opposite (e.g., "snow" to "sun") may be very dramatic, but, as "in the unconscious," opposites are closely linked, such a change may not be much of a change at all—merely "the other side of the same coin." At the same time, a dramatic change like this may involve a stirring, a premonition, an implication of change to come. And, then, the quiet change ("ice" to "is") does come. The analysand is the *same person* at the end as at the beginning—with a "slight difference," perhaps recognizable only by himself and felt within. But what a difference that slight difference is. **Ī S** to **I Z.**

Let us follow then the patterns of hiss-and-buzz and hum through the poem.

Line 1

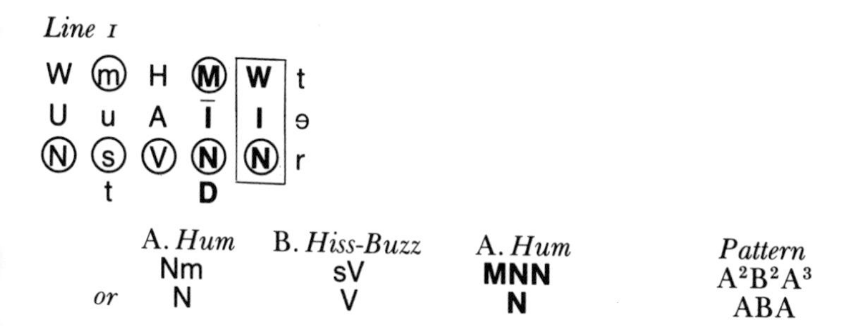

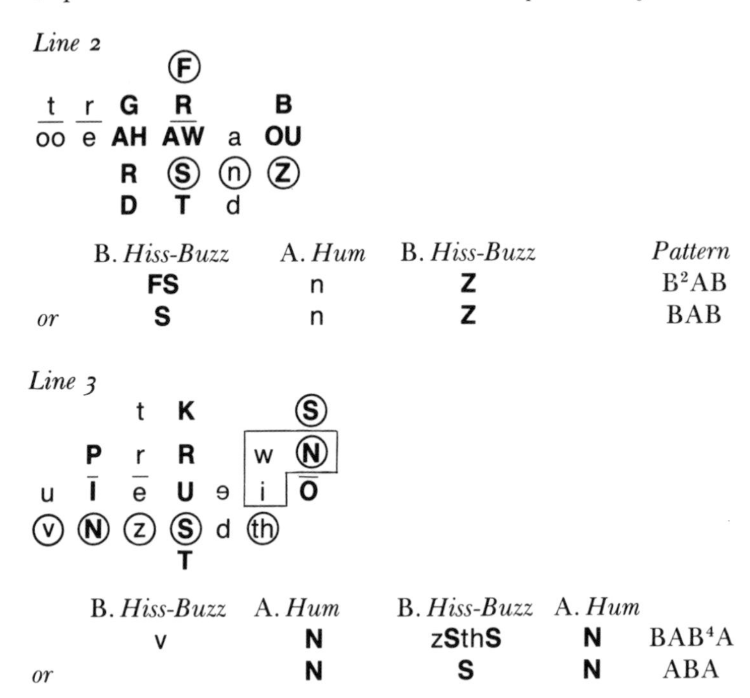

What devices contribute to the semi-cadence at "snow?" The melody becomes increasingly luminous, as the dark buzz v decreases in salience and the dark hum m in line one and the ascending dark hiss f in line two are deleted. The hum n decreases in salience and is displaced to the center of the pattern in line two. In the third line, the pattern is turned inside out to return to the pattern of the first line with the hum now more salient and ascending as well as descending. The third line ends with a sequence of glide w, chord i, and hum n, which alludes to the sequence in "winter" at the end of the first line. Finally, in the last syllable, the hiss s and hum n ascend to the chord ō; here, this hiss and hum are together again, unseparated by other sounds, untransposed, in a repetition of "snow" from the title.

Do such events in sound have their justification or warrant in the careful preparation for, and achievement of, an arrival "home," which will become at the same moment the place from which we shall again depart? Where to?

Is it possible that a psychoanalyst ever senses from an unwitting perception of such phenomena as these that the analysand has achieved some degree of resolution in the world of complex, often conflicting meanings and kinds of meaning represented and presented in one hour or a long sequence of hours? Does the psychoanalyst just as certainly sense that the analysand is about to set off again? Does the psychoanalyst find himself just then asking, in his own mind, without knowing why, where the analysand is going? Where to?

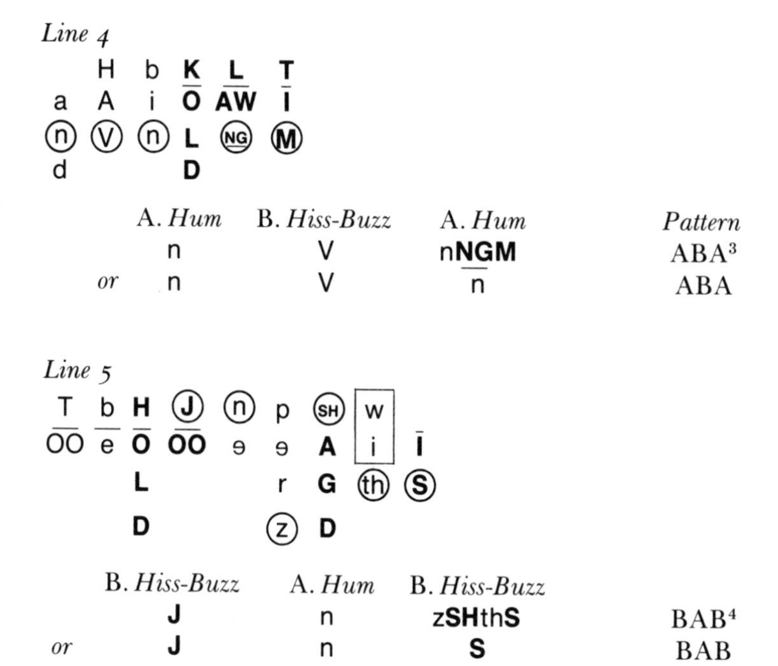

Similarly, we may examine what devices contribute to the semi-cadence at "ice?" Line four begins with an allusion in the arrangement of the sounds n and v to a pattern in line one. Both patterns (lines one and four) end with a three-fold augmentation of the hum. In line five as in line two, the hum is displaced to the center.

In line five, for the first time, powerful, ascending, and hard nonsonorants predominate. The powerful ascending hard abrupt buzz j begins the pattern, which ends with a descending muted soft hiss th and soft hiss s; the soft hisses are preceded and augmented by the powerful, ascending, hard hiss sh. In both the third and fifth lines, the semi-cadential hiss s is augmented four-fold.

The sequence glide w and chord i from lines one and three reappears just before the semi-cadence at the end of line five. Here, the hum is deleted and the final hiss descends rather than ascends.

The word "ice" implies the final word of the poem "is." The change from one to the other involves only a change from the ambivalent chord ah plus i to the ephemeral i and from the sustained hiss to the ephemeral buzz that is its counterpart.

Line 6

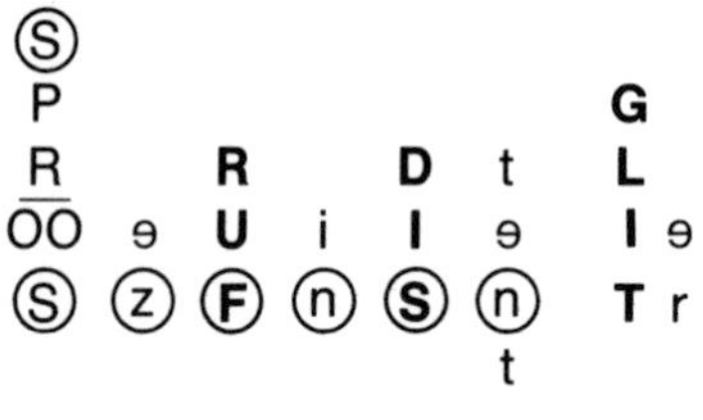

Ⓢ
P G
R **R** **D** t **L**
O͞O ə **U** i **I** ə **I** ə
Ⓢ ⓩ Ⓕ ⓝ Ⓢ ⓝ **T** r
t

	B. *Hiss-Buzz*	A. *Hum*	B. *Hiss-Buzz*	A. *Hum*	*Pattern*
	SSz**F**	n	**S**	n	B⁴ABA
or		n	**S**	n	ABA

Line 7

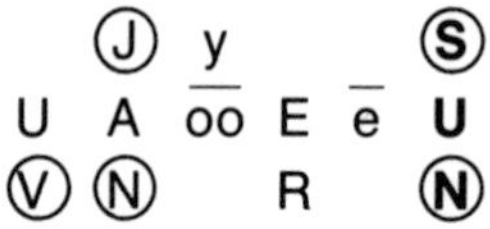

Ⓙ y Ⓢ
U A o͞o E ē **U**
Ⓥ Ⓝ R Ⓝ

	VJ	N	**S**	**N**	B²ABA
or		N	**S**	**N**	ABA

In moving to the semi-cadence at "sun," the pattern ABA is repeated. At the second occurrence, both outside hums have increased in salience. The semi-cadence at "sun" involves an ascending hiss **s** (rather than descending, as in "ice") and a descending hum **n** (rather than ascending, as in "snow").

The sequence Ee̅ / R anticipates the central "misery" in the next line. The semi-cadence at "sun" precedes the central line of the poem and the critical idea in the seventh and eighth lines, following which the poem moves into the reality-of-winter-as-heard.

Line 7

(N) t (TH)
a O o̅o̅ I
(n) T (N̲G̲)
d K

	A. *Hum*	B. *Hiss-Buzz*	A. *Hum*	*Pattern*
	nN	TH	NG	A^2BA
or	N	TH	N̅G̲	ABA

The hum followed by a muted hiss is implicative for the full cadence in the last two lines of the poem.

Line 8

(M) (S) W
u E e̅ I ə E̅ i OU u I
(v) (N) (Z)r (n) (N) (v) (N)
D D

	B.	A.	B.	A.	B.	A.	B.	A.	*Pattern*
	v	NM	Z	n	S	N	v	N	BA^2B ABABA
or		M			S	N			ABA

M / I / Z ("misery") is another anticipation of the final I / Z ("is") in the poem. The opposition of dark and luminous from the title is also found in this central word "misery," which as we have previously observed is markedly deviant in the language of this poem, in its meaning (signifying human feeling) and its polysyllabicity, and therefore is foregrounded.

The sequence may be picked up again in line 13.

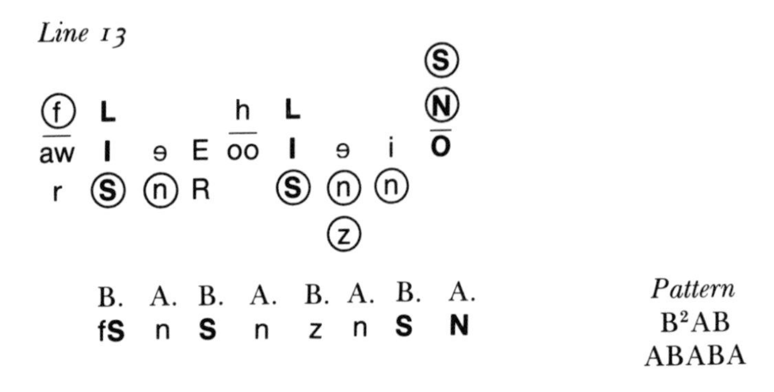

or **S** n **S** n z n **S** **N** BAB ABA BA

Pattern BAB is followed by ABA and then by a second semi-cadence at "snow."

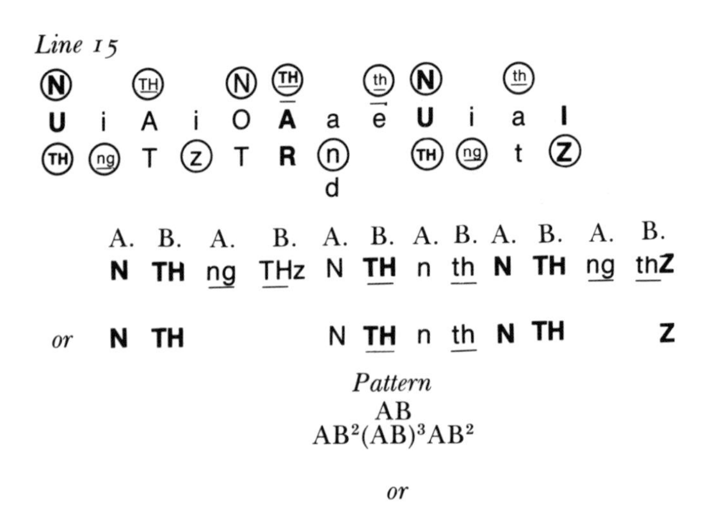

$(AB)^4B$

In the final line the ascending hum alternates with ascending muted buzzes and descending muted hisses, all soft, all luminous. The muted sounds are subdued attenuated allusions to the initial hiss in the title and its counterpart, the amplified final buzz in this line.

Because the muted hiss and muted buzz come before and after the hum in the linear sequence of the last line, there is an ambiguity about whether or not the order of hiss and hum is the same as that in "snow" or a transposition of it (an "ambiguous undulation?"). The drop to the final ephemeral **Z** resolves the ambiguity.

These phenomena are warranted by the meanings of the last line and the movement "downward on extended wings" to a full closure. This ending recalls that reached in the famous last lines of one of Stevens' most beautiful poems—"Sunday Morning."

> And, in the isolation of the sky,
> At evening, casual flocks of pigeons make
> Ambiguous undulations as they sink,
> Downward to darkness, on extended wings.

Bibliography

AUSTIN, J. L. (1962), *How to Do Things with Words.* New York: Oxford University Press, 1965.

BALKANYI, C. (1964), On Verbalization. *Int. J. Psycho-Anal.,* 45 : 64–74.

——— (1968), Verbalization and the Superego: Some Thoughts on the Development of the Sense of Rules. *Int. J. Psycho-Anal.,* 49 : 712–18.

BENAMOU, M. (1972), *Wallace Stevens and the Symbolist Imagination.* Princeton, N.J.: Princeton University Press.

BLACK, M. (1962), *Models and Metaphors.* Ithaca: Cornell University Press.

BLACKMUR, R. P. (1952), *Form and Value in Modern Poetry.* New York: Doubleday Anchor Books, 1957.

BLESSING, R. (1970), *Wallace Stevens' "Whole Harmonium."* Syracuse: Syracuse University Press.

BLOOM, H. (1973), *The Anxiety of Influence.* New York: Oxford University Press.

BORGER, R. & CIOFFI, F., eds. (1970), *Explanation in the Behavioural Sciences.* Cambridge: Cambridge University Press.

BORROFF, M., ed. (1963), *Wallace Stevens.* Englewood Cliffs, N.J.: Prentice-Hall.

BROOKS, C. (1947), *The Well Wrought Urn.* New York: Harvest Book.

BROWN, A. & HALLER, R. (1962), *The Achievement of Wallace Stevens.* Philadelphia: J. B. Lippincott.

BROWN, M. (1970), *Wallace Stevens: The Poem as Act.* Detroit: Wayne State University Press.

BRUSH, S. (1974), Should the History of Science Be Rated X? *Science,* Vol. 183, No. 4130 (22 March), pp. 1164–72.

BUCHANAN, S. (1929), *Poetry and Mathematics.* Philadelphia: J. B. Lippincott, 1962.

BURNEY, W. (1968), *Wallace Stevens.* New York: Twayne Publishers.

CASSIRER, E. (1944), *An Essay on Man.* New Haven: Yale University Press.

CHATMAN, S., ed. (1971), *Literary Style: A Symposium.* London: Oxford University Press.

——— & LEVIN, S., eds. (1967), *Essays on the Language of Literature.* Boston: Houghton Mifflin.

CHOMSKY, N. (1957), *Syntactic Structures.* The Hague: Mouton.

——— (1961), *Degrees of Grammaticalness.* In: Fodor & Katz (1964), pp. 384–89.

——— (1965), *Aspects of the Theory of Syntax.* Cambridge, Mass.: M.I.T. Press.

——— (1966), *Cartesian Linguistics.* New York: Harper & Row.

——— (1971), Deep Structure, Surface Structure, and Semantic Interpretation. In: *Semantics,* eds. D. Steinberg & L. Jakobovits. Cambridge: Cambridge University Press, pp. 183–216.

——— (1972), *Language and Mind.* Enlarged Edition. New York: Harcourt Brace Jovanovich.

——— & HALLE, M. (1968), *The Sound Pattern of English.* New York: Harper & Row.

COOPER, G. & MEYER, L. (1960), *The Rhythmic Structure of Music.* Chicago: University of Chicago Press.

DEUTSCH, B. (1952), *Poetry in Our Time.* New York: Doubleday Anchor Book, 1963.

DOGGETT, F. (1958), Wallace Stevens' Later Poetry. *ELH,* 25 (June): 137–54.

——— (1966), *Stevens' Poetry of Thought.* Baltimore: Johns Hopkins Press.

EDELSON, M. (1971a), *The Idea of a Mental Illness.* New Haven: Yale University Press.

——— (1971b), Toward a Study of Interpretation in Psychoanalysis: An Essay on Symbolic Process in Psychoanalysis and the Theory of Action. In: *Explorations in General Theory in the Social Sciences,* eds. J. Loubser, R. Baum, A. Effrat, & V. Lidz. New York: The Free Press, 1975 (in press).

——— (1972), Language and Dreams: The Interpretation of Dreams Revisited. *The Psychoanalytic Study of the Child.* New York: Quadrangle Books, 27 : 203–82.

EHRMANN, J. (1966), *Structuralism.* New York: Anchor Books, 1970.

EMPSON, W. (1930), *Seven Types of Ambiguity.* New York: New Directions.

——— (1967), *The Structure of Complex Words.* Ann Arbor: University of Michigan Press.

ERIKSON, E. (1958), The Nature of Clinical Evidence. *Insight and Responsibility*. New York: Norton and Company, 1964, pp. 49–80.

FANT, G. (1960), *Acoustic Theory of Speech Production*. The Hague: Mouton.

——— (1968), Analysis and Synthesis of Speech Processes. In: *Manual of Phonetics,* ed. B. Malmberg. Amsterdam: North Holland Publishing Co., pp. 173–277.

FLETCHER, H. (1953), *Speech and Hearing in Communication*. New York: D. van Nostrand.

FODOR, J. & KATZ, J., eds. (1964), *The Structure of Language*. Englewood Cliffs, N.J.: Prentice-Hall.

FORTE, A. (1962), *Tonal Harmony in Concept and Practice*. New York: Holt, Rinehart and Winston.

——— (1973), *The Structure of Atonal Music*. New Haven: Yale University Press.

FRANKENBERG, L. (1949), *Pleasure Dome*. New York: Doubleday Dolphin Book.

FREEMAN, D. (1970), *Linguistics and Literary Style*. New York: Holt, Rinehart and Winston.

FREUD, S. (1900), The Interpretation of Dreams. *Standard Edition,* 4 & 5. London: Hogarth Press, 1953.

——— (1901), The Psychopathology of Everyday Life. *Standard Edition,* 6. London: Hogarth Press, 1960.

——— (1905), Jokes and Their Relation to the Unconscious. *Standard Edition,* 8. London: Hogarth Press, 1960.

——— (1911–15), Papers on Technique. *Standard Edition,* 12 : 89–171. London: Hogarth Press, 1958.

——— (1915), The Unconscious. *Standard Edition,* 14 : 159–215. London: Hogarth Press, 1957.

——— (1916–17), Introductory Lectures on Psycho-analysis. *Standard Edition,* 16 : 243–463. London: Hogarth Press, 1963.

——— (1937), Constructions in Analysis. *Standard Edition,* 23 : 257–69.

FRYE, N. (1973), Wallace Stevens and the Variation Form. In: *Literary Theory and Structure,* eds. F. Brady, et al. New Haven: Yale University Press, pp. 395–414.

GREENBERG, J., ed. (1966), *Universals of Language*. Cambridge, Mass.: M.I.T. Press.

HALLE, M. (1962), Phonology in Generative Grammar. In: *Phono-*

logical Theory, ed. V. Makkai. New York: Holt, Rinehart & Winston, pp. 380–92.

——— (1964), On the Bases of Phonology. In: *Phonological Theory,* ed. V. Makkai. New York: Holt, Rinehart & Winston, pp. 393–400.

HAMMER, E., ed. (1968), *Use of Interpretation in Treatment.* New York: Grune & Stratton.

HARTMANN, H. (1958), Comments on the Scientific Aspects of Psychoanalysis. *Essays on Ego Psychology.* New York: International Universities Press, 1964, pp. 297–317.

——— (1959), Psychoanalysis as a Scientific Theory. *Essays on Ego Psychology.* New York: International Universities Press, 1964, pp. 318–50.

———, KRIS, E., & LOEWENSTEIN, R. M. (1953), The Function of Theory in Psychoanalysis. *Papers on Psychoanalytic Psychology,* Psychological Issues, Vol. IV, No. 2, Monograph 14. New York: International Universities Press, 1964, pp. 117–43.

HOLLAND, N. (1966), *Psychoanalysis and Shakespeare.* New York: McGraw-Hill.

——— (1968a), *The Dynamics of Literary Response.* New York: Oxford University Press.

——— (1968b), Prose and Minds: A Psychoanalytic Approach to Non-Fiction. In: *Victorian Prose as Art,* eds. G. Levine & W. Madden. New York: Oxford University Press, pp. 314–37.

JACOBS, R. (1973), *Studies in Language.* Lexington, Mass.: Xerox College Publishing.

——— & ROSENBAUM, P. (1968), *English Transformational Grammar.* Waltham, Mass.: Xerox College Publishing.

———, eds. (1970), *Readings in English Transformational Grammar.* Waltham, Mass.: Ginn.

——— (1971), *Transformations, Style, and Meaning.* Waltham, Mass.: Xerox College Publishing.

JAKOBSON, R. (1955), Aphasia as a Linguistic Problem. In: *On Expressive Language,* ed. H. Werner. Worcester, Mass.: Clark University Press, pp. 69–81.

——— (1960), Linguistics and Poetics. In: Sebeok (1960), pp. 350–77.

———, FANT, G., & HALLE, M. (1963), *Preliminaries to Speech Analysis.* Cambridge: M.I.T. Press.

——— & HALLE, M. (1956), *Fundamentals of Language.* The Hague: Mouton.
——— (1968), Phonology in Relation to Phonetics. In: *Manual of Phonetics,* ed. B. Malmberg. Amsterdam: North Holland Publishing Co., pp. 411–49.
JARRELL, R. (1955), *Poetry and the Age.* New York: Vintage Books.
——— (1962), Robert Frost's "Home Burial." *The Third Book of Criticism.* New York: Farrar, Straus & Giroux Noonday Press, 1971.
JONES, E. (1913), Anal-Erotic Character Traits. *Papers on Psycho-Analysis.* Baltimore: Williams & Wilkins, 1948, pp. 413–37.
——— (1916), The Theory of Symbolism. *Papers on Psycho-Analysis,* pp. 87–144.
JUMPER, W. (1961), The Language of Wallace Stevens. *Iowa English Yearbook,* 6(Fall): 23–24.
KATZ, J. J. (1964), Semi-sentences. In: Fodor & Katz (1964), pp. 400–16.
——— (1971), *The Underlying Reality of Language and Its Philosophical Import.* New York: Harper Torchbooks.
——— (1972), *Semantic Theory.* New York: Harper & Row.
——— & POSTAL, P. (1964), *An Integrated Theory of Linguistic Descriptions.* Cambridge, Mass.: M.I.T. Press.
KERMODE, F. (1960), *Wallace Stevens.* New York: Grove Press.
KLEIN, G. (1973), Two Theories or One? *Bull. Menninger Clin.,* 37 : 99–132.
KRIS, E. (1952), *Psychoanalytic Explorations in Art.* New York: Schocken Books, 1964.
——— (1956a), On Some Vicissitudes of Insight in Psycho-Analysis. *Int. J. Psycho-Anal.,* 37 : 445–55.
——— (1956b), The Recovery of Childhood Memories in Psychoanalysis. *The Psychoanalytic Study of the Child.* New York: International Universities Press, 11 : 54–88.
LACAN, J. (1956), Seminar on "The Purloined Letter." In: *French Freud: Structural Studies in Psychoanalysis.* New Haven: *Yale French Studies,* No. 48, pp. 39–72.
——— (1957), The Insistence of the Letter in the Unconscious. In: Ehrmann (1966), pp. 101–37.
——— (1968), *The Language of the Self: The Function of Language in Psychoanalysis.* Tr. by A. Wilden. Baltimore: Johns Hopkins Press.
——— (1970), Of Structure as an Inmixing of an Otherness

Prerequisite to Any Subject Whatever. In: Macksey & Donato (1970), pp. 186–200.

LADEFOGED, P. (1962), *Elements of Acoustic Phonetics*. Chicago: University of Chicago Press.

LANGER, S. (1942), *Philosophy in a New Key*. New York: Penguin Books, 1948.

——— (1953), *Feeling and Form*. New York: Scribner's.

——— (1962), *Philosophical Sketches*. New York: Mentor Book, 1964.

LEAVY, S. (1970), John Keats's Psychology of Creative Imagination. *Psychoanal. Quart.*, 39 : 173–97.

——— (1973), Psychoanalytic Interpretation. *The Psychoanalytic Study of the Child*. New Haven: Yale University Press, 28 : 305–30.

LEECH, G. N. (1969), *A Linguistic Guide to English Poetry*. London: Longman.

LEVIN, S. (1967), Poetry and Grammaticalness. In: Chatman & Levin (1967), pp. 224–30.

LEVI-STRAUSS, C. (1958), *Structural Anthropology*. New York: Anchor Books, 1967.

——— (1962), *The Savage Mind*. Chicago: University of Chicago Press, 1966.

——— (1964), *The Raw and the Cooked*. New York: Harper Torchbook, 1970.

LIDZ, T. (1963), *The Family and Human Adaptation*. New York: International Universities Press.

LOEWALD, H. (1970), Psychoanalytic Theory and the Psychoanalytic Process. *The Psychoanalytic Study of the Child*. New York: International Universities Press, 25 : 45–68.

——— (1971), On Motivation and Instinct Theory. *The Psychoanalytic Study of the Child*. New York: International Universities Press, 26 : 91–128.

LOEWENSTEIN, R. M. (1956), Some Remarks on the Role of Speech in Psycho-Analytic Technique. *Int. J. Psycho-Anal.*, 37 : 460–68.

LOUCH, A. R. (1966), *Explanation and Human Action*. Berkeley: University of California Press.

LUSTMAN, S. (1972), A Perspective on the Study of Man. *The Psychoanalytic Study of the Child*. New York: Quadrangle Books, 27 : 18–54.

LYONS, J. (1970), *Noam Chomsky*. New York: Viking Press.

MACKSEY, R. (1965), The Climates of Wallace Stevens. In: Pearce & Miller (1965), pp. 185–223.

——— & Donato, E., eds. (1970), *The Structuralist Controversy: The Languages of Criticism and the Sciences of Man.* Baltimore: Johns Hopkins Press Paperback, 1972.

Martz, L. (1958), Wallace Stevens: The World As Meditation. In: Borroff (1963), pp. 133–50.

——— (1966), *The Poem of the Mind.* New York: Oxford University Press.

Mehlman, J. (1972), French Freud. . . . ; The "floating signifier": from Levi-Strauss to Lacan. *French Freud: Structural Studies in Psychoanalysis.* New Haven: *Yale French Studies,* No. 48, pp. 5–37.

Merton, R. K. (1965), *On the Shoulders of Giants.* New York: Harcourt, Brace & World, Inc.

——— (1973), *The Sociology of Science.* Chicago: University of Chicago Press.

Meyer, L. (1956), *Emotion and Meaning in Music.* Chicago: University of Chicago Press.

——— (1967), *Music, the Arts, and Ideas.* Chicago: University of Chicago Press.

——— (1973), *Explaining Music.* Berkeley: University of California Press.

Miel, J. (1966), Jacques Lacan and the Structure of the Unconscious. In: Ehrmann (1966), pp. 94–101.

Morse, S. (1970), *Wallace Stevens: Poetry as Life.* New York: Pegasus.

O'Connor, J. D. (1973), *Phonetics.* Baltimore: Penguin Books.

Ohmann, R. (1964), Generative Grammars and the Concept of Literary Style. In: Freeman (1970), pp. 258–78.

——— (1966), Literature as Sentences. In: Chatman & Levin (1967), pp. 231–38.

Parsons, T. (1937), *The Structure of Social Action.* New York: The Free Press of Glencoe, 1949.

Paul, L., ed. (1963), *Psychoanalytic Clinical Interpretation.* New York: Free Press of Glencoe.

Pearce, R. & Miller, J., eds. (1965), *The Act of the Mind.* Baltimore: Johns Hopkins Press.

Peirce, C. S. (1893–1910), Logic as Semiotic: The Theory of Signs. *Philosophical Writings of Peirce,* ed. J. Buchler. New York: Dover, 1955, pp. 98–119.

Piaget, J. (1945), *Play, Dreams and Imitation in Childhood.* New York: Norton, 1962.

——— (1970), *Structuralism.* New York: Basic Books.

——— & INHELDER, B. (1966), *The Psychology of the Child.* New York: Basic Books, 1969.

PINKERTON, J. (1971), Wallace Stevens in the Tropics. *Yale Rev.,* 60 : 215–27.

PIOUS, W. (1961), A Hypothesis About the Nature of Schizophrenic Behavior. In: *Psychotherapy of the Psychoses,* ed. A. Burton. New York: Basic Books, 1961, pp. 43–68.

POLANYI, M. (1958), *Personal Knowledge.* New York: Harper Torchbook, 1964.

——— (1959), *The Study of Man.* Chicago: University of Chicago Press.

——— (1966), *The Tacit Dimension.* New York: Doubleday Anchor Books, 1967.

PUMPIAN-MINDLIN, E., ed. (1952), *Psychoanalysis as Science.* Stanford, Calif.: Stanford University Press.

RAPAPORT, D. (1951), The Autonomy of the Ego. *The Collected Papers of David Rapaport,* ed. M. Gill. New York: Basic Books, 1967, pp. 357–67.

——— (1957), The Theory of Ego Autonomy. *The Collected Papers of David Rapaport,* pp. 722–44.

——— (1959), The Points of View and Assumptions of Metapsychology. *The Collected Papers of David Rapaport,* pp. 795–811.

——— (1960), On the Psychoanalytic Theory of Motivation. *The Collected Papers of David Rapaport,* pp. 853–915.

RICHARDS, I. A. (1925), *Principles of Literary Criticism.* New York: Harvest Book.

——— (1929), *Practical Criticism.* New York: Harvest Book.

——— (1936), *The Philosophy of Rhetoric.* New York: Oxford University Press, 1965.

——— (1955), *Speculative Instruments.* New York: Harvest Book.

RIDDELL, J. (1965), *The Clairvoyant Eye.* Baton Rouge: Louisiana State University Press.

ROSEN, V. H. (1961), On Style. *Int. J. Psycho-Anal.,* 42 : 446–57.

——— (1966), Disturbances of Representation and Reference in Ego Deviations. In: *Psychoanalysis—A General Psychology,* ed. R. M. Loewenstein, et al. New York: International Universities Press, pp. 634–54.

——— (1967), Disorders of Communication in Psychoanalysis. *J. Amer. Psychoanal. Assn.,* 15 : 467–90.

——— (1968), A Re-examination of Some Aspects of Freud's

Theory of Schizophrenic Language Disturbance. *J. Hillside Hosp.*, 17 : 242–58.

——— (1969a), Introduction to Panel on Language and Psychoanalysis. *Int. J. Psycho-Anal.*, 50 : 113–16.

——— (1969b), Sign Phenomena and Their Relationship to Unconscious Meaning. *Int. J. Psycho-Anal.*, 50 : 197–207.

Rubinstein, B. (1972), On Metaphor and Related Phenomena. In: *Psychoanalysis and Contemporary Science*, eds. R. Holt & E. Peterfreund. New York: Macmillan.

Salzer, F. (1962), *Structural Hearing*. 2 Vols. New York: Dover.

Schafer, R. (1973), Action: Its Place in Psychoanalytic Interpretation and Theory. *The Annual of Psychoanalysis*, Volume One. New York: Quadrangle Books, pp. 159–96.

Schane, S. (1973), *Generative Phonology*. Englewood Cliffs, N.J.: Prentice-Hall.

Scott, N., ed. (1965), *Four Ways of Modern Poetry*. Richmond, Va.: John Knox Press.

Sebeok, T., ed. (1960), *Style in Language*. Cambridge, Mass.: M.I.T. Press.

Shapiro, D. (1965), *Neurotic Styles*. New York: Basic Books.

Sharpe, E. F. (1940), Psycho-Physical Problems Revealed in Language: An Examination of Metaphor. *Int. J. Psycho-Anal.*, 21 : 201–13.

Stevens, H., ed. (1966), *Letters of Wallace Stevens*. New York: Alfred A. Knopf.

——— (1971), *The Palm at the End of the Mind*. New York: Vintage Books, 1972.

Stevens, W. (1951), *The Necessary Angel*. New York: Vintage Books.

——— (1954), *The Collected Poems of Wallace Stevens*. New York: Alfred A. Knopf.

——— (1957), *Opus Posthumous*. New York: Alfred A. Knopf.

Sukenick, R. (1967), *Wallace Stevens: Musing the Obscure*. New York: New York University Press.

Taylor, L. W. (1943), *Fundamental Physics*. Boston: Houghton Mifflin.

Thorne, J. (1965), Stylistics and Generative Grammars. In: Freeman (1970), pp. 182–96.

Vendler, H. (1965), The Qualified Assertions of Wallace Stevens. In: Pearce & Miller (1965), pp. 163–78.

——— (1969), *On Extended Wings*. Cambridge, Mass.: Harvard University Press.

Voth, H. (1970), The Analysis of Metaphor. *J. Amer. Psychoanal. Assn.,* 18 : 599–621.

Wellek, R. & Warren, A. (1962), *Theory of Literature.* New York: Harcourt, Brace, & World, Inc.

Werner, H. (1955), A Psychological Analysis of Expressive Language. In: *On Expressive Language,* ed. H. Werner. Worcester, Mass.: Clark University Press, pp. 11–18.

Wilden, A. G. (1966), Jacques Lacan: A Partial Bibliography. In: Ehrmann (1966), pp. 253–60.

Wimsatt, W. (1968), How to Compose Chess Problems, and Why. In: *Game, Play, Literature,* ed. J. Ehrmann. Boston: Beacon Press, 1971.

Winch, P. (1958), *The Idea of a Social Science.* New York: Humanities Press.

Winters, Y. (1937), Primitivism and Decadence. *In Defense of Reason.* Chicago: The Swallow Press, 1947.

——— (1943), *On Modern Poets.* New York: Meridian Books, 1959.

Index